Improvisational Leaders

Improvisational Leaders

Integrating Business, Mindfulness, and Improvisation

Bill Prinzivalli and Gerard Farias

A Foreword by Chris Laszlo

Strategic Book Publishing and Rights Co.

Strategic Book Publishing and Rights Co., LLC
USA | Singapore
www.sbpra.net

For information about special discounts for bulk purchases, please contact Strategic Book Publishing and Rights Co. Special Sales at bookorder@sbpra.net.

ISBN: 978-1-68235-588-6

Cover Image – Courtesy of ESA/Hubble, "A Deep Look At Two Merging Galaxies". Hubble captured a spectacular pair of galaxies engaged in a celestial dance… the pair will eventually merge into a single giant galaxy.
Cover Design – Masha Goltsova-Lanoue
Authors' Note – this beautiful image was selected to represent the dance between Duality and Integration.

Dedication

To the Ancient Ones who guide us on our paths …
…. and to family, friends, and colleagues who inspire us to
continue.

Acknowledgements

From Bill Prinzivalli:

There are many people that I wish to acknowledge who have assisted me in one way or another that culminated in the writing of this book.

There are those dedicated friends who read certain sections of the book as I was writing it to give me specific feedback regarding accuracy of areas related to their expertise and/or feedback as a general reality check. These include Gerd Winkler, Dick Nodell, Jeanne Prinzivalli, Tamar Stone, Chris Griggs, Rosalie Prinzivalli, Rob Jokel, Marina Maurino, Joseph Maurino, Raji Thron, Rose Fitzgerald, Rich Leitman, and Debbie Broadman. Also, there are those supporters who were willing to read the final manuscript to provide feedback and commentary. Many thanks to all for sharing your valuable reading time with me.

Special thanks go to my sister Rosalie who has supported me in more ways than I can number throughout this and other phases of my life. Similar support came from my brother Joe, my sister-in-law Fran, my daughter Jeanne, my son Chris, my 100 year-young Aunt Lee, and of course my Mom and Dad who love and support me from another dimension. Much love to all.

A special thanks goes to my dear friend Rob Jokel with whom I made a pact on one New Year's Day a couple of years back to support him in the final creation of an important film he was making while he supported me in writing this book. We would meet biweekly to support each other through the various challenges and cycles that we encountered during our respective processes.

Special thanks go to my close circle of friends, namely Gerd Winkler who lived with me for two years during his life transition, his partner Rita Gendelman who lived with me for three months during her life transition, Marina Maurino with whom I shared many fun, rich, and deep conversations as we rode to and from weekly improv classes for seven years, and Joseph Maurino with whom I share the Mankind Project experience, and with whom I became very dear friends.

Special gratitude goes to my mentor, friend, and soul brother Dick Nodell, whose love and support have carried me for many years across more obstacles than I know.

I wish to acknowledge my many improv teachers, the first of whom was Erin Flowers from The Open Door Acting Company whose open heart beautifully invited me into the improv arena; her mentor Carl Stillitano who encouraged me to perform on a New York stage after a single weekend workshop; and their mentor Jerry Brody (protege of Lee Strasberg) who founded the company; to all my instructors at The Pit; to my many Covid Zoom improv coaches (notably Kimberly Alu, Chris Griggs, and Adam Wade); and to the variety of coaches at many wonderful improv theaters including The Pit, Magnet, Squirrel, Viola Spolin, UCB, Pack Theater, WGIS, Impro Theatre, and others who have taught me since the writing of this book. Equally important are all my improv friends who I play with, including the teams with whom I currently perform as well as all my classmates in the various improv classes. What a ride!

Much gratitude and thanks go to Jodi Shems Prinzivalli, my former wife of twenty years, who always encouraged me to reach higher; and to Jyldyz Wood who inspired me to visualize a future Ted talk.

I also wish to thank a group of elite, conscious, and wise souls who taught and guided me in the ways of metaphysics, spirituality, and consciousness. They include Don Yott, Jean Munzer, Harriet Wagniere Kupka, Ginny Stern, Victoria Christgau, Dee Weldon, Sherry Burger, Alberto Villoldo, and many others unnamed, in addition to institutions, large and small, that promoted a plethora of such teachings including the Metaphysical Center of New Jersey, Omega Institute, and Kripalu Center for Yoga and Health.

A special thanks go to Hal and Sidra Stone, and to Hal's daughter Tamar, for personally teaching me their pioneering work of Voice Dialogue.

I also wish to thank my many brothers in the Mankind Project who share a strong desire and action to be responsible, conscious, and loving men in our society today, and who are dedicated to teaching other men on their journey.

I wish to thank my longest friend, Mike Pilo, who I've known since I was five, and two other college fraternity brothers, Rich Bova and Cliff Stehle. We have maintained close contact all these years and they keep me humble and real, as they would see through any facade I may try to assume.

Much gratitude and thanks go to my many friends at the Brookside Racquet and Swim Club with whom I spar regularly on the tennis courts in a cooperatively competitive manner allowing each of us to improve our skills. Playing tennis in a Covid-distant manner in 2020 was a saving-grace gift during a socially-distant pandemic.

Special thanks go to members of my peer advisory groups, TAB and Collaberex, who continually support me to move forward with this book and with the messaging of my deepest passion to bring consciousness to the business world.

A universal thanks go to the many friends and acquaintances who I have encountered in my lifetime, for each has provided me with joy and support as well as challenges and obstacles—I have learned from each one (sometimes reluctantly).

From Gerard Farias:

It has been a pleasure working with Bill on his independent studies, which evolved into a partnership as we explored ideas and life experiences. It has been fun! This is mostly Bill's work—I wrote just a small part of it.

There are so many people to thank for all the knowledge and ideas I have been exposed to over the years. A special thanks goes to my family, Christine, Divya and Jeevan who are a constant inspiration.

Testimonials

We can never have too many books that combine the practices of leadership, mindfulness, and improvisation. *Improvisational Leaders* will provide both theoretical and practical tools to integrate these dimensions for more successful relationships and productivity. We are all improvisers. Now we get to learn how to be more conscious ones. Share these practices with your friends and colleagues. Our worlds will be better for it.

> — Barbara Tint, PhD, Global Facilitator, Professor, Trainer, Psychologist, Improviser, Storyteller, Consultant, Mediator

Improvisational Leaders lays out a groundbreaking work that finally puts all the pieces together and provides a roadmap for more effective business leadership and self-awareness. Read this book with an open mind, let your right brain in for a more complete understanding, and add improv training to the mix to foster optimal team cooperation, effectiveness, creativity, and innovation.

> — Jonathan Rosen, Founder and CEO of Collaberex

Improvisational Leaders is at the forefront of an emerging leadership philosophy that incorporates aspects of spirituality, Applied Improv, mindfulness, and values exploration. The result of Bill's years of self-exploration, business experience, and natural curiosity, *Improvisational Leaders* is an enjoyable and useful handbook for leading within the "New Normal."

> — Izzy Gesell, M.ED, CSP (Certified Speaking Professional), Organization Alchemist, Humorologist, Facilitator, Keynoter, Author of *Playing Along (1997)*

In this innovative approach, *Improvisational Leaders* contains important principles and ideas about respecting, exploring, and expressing the uniqueness of the individual. Including a comprehensive compilation of meditation styles, these concepts are profoundly aligned with my work in helping people heal by becoming more uniquely themselves. I support and recommend this book.

> — Larry LeShan, Researcher, Psychologist, Author of *How to Meditate: A Guide to Self-Discovery (1974)*

Improvisational Leaders provides the reader with a clear and practical path towards leadership that transcends the limiting patriarchal model of growth and profit at any cost, to benevolent leadership where a holistic perspective is embraced.

This book will challenge the leaders of the future to embrace the interconnectedness of all things and all people on the planet. *Improvisational Leaders* will impact many leaders and potentially a new generation of conscious leadership where all people and the planet are valued.

> — Vincenzo Falone, Certified Co-Leader Mankind Project

Improvisational Leaders is a well-written and easy to understand book that discusses the relationship dynamic between management and their employees, including the meaning of success. For example, the days of telling employees that the financial bottom line is all that matters, and that the end justifies the means mentality, are old paradigms that are no longer effective.

This is a must read for any CEO or top level manager who wants to inspire and motivate their work force by implementing innovative techniques, ranging from meditation and mindfulness to improvisational practices. These techniques will uplift and elevate their awareness and importance of integrity in both their professional and personal life alike.

Bill draws upon his many years of direct experience as both a business consultant and owner of his own companies. As a former director of a multi-disciplined Mind-Body Wellness Educational center, I found this book highly informative, practical, and valuable.

> — Dr. Kenneth Harris, Founder of the Waldwick Wellness Center, Director of the Mind-Body Education Center, Author of *Synchronicity (2019)*

Read *Improvisational Leaders*:

- If you want to discover how to have FUN learning what DEEP LISTENING is about and its profound positive effects both in the business world and personally. (I taught listening skills for many years to health professionals and I wish I had had this book!)
- If you want to define what SUCCESS is for you as a unique one of a kind individual—and the personal power and freedom this brings.
- If you want to create greater connection with your emotions and thus greater connection with others.
- If you want to develop strategies to better manage uncertainty which again allows us more freedom to take risks and to live truer to ourselves and with more passion!

Bill writes with amazing clarity and makes a great case for the integration of spiritual principles (such as being kind, respectful, and in integrity) with business and how this benefits us all. Bill puts the SOUL back in business!

It is my hope that this book becomes a landmark text for all those studying business.

> — Robert Jokel, Producer and Director of the documentary film *Immune to Cancer, Bring the Full Strength of Your Immune System to the Aid of Your Medical Program*

The key to the success of *Improvisational Leaders* is that the authors provide practical, concrete techniques to prosper in business as well as in life. The tools described in meditation, mindfulness practices, and psychological modalities give readers a wide range of activities to choose from as they explore all parts of the book. The skillful combination of personal stories with a wealth of research and references helps the reader to achieve an integrated state of conscious wholeness in the workplace and in everyday life.

Bill's understanding of the metaphysical principle of polarity marries the dualities so that, rather than choosing an either/or approach, he shows how a more conscious person will operate from a both/and perspective bringing about the alignment of oneness.

> — Peggy Neligan, PhD, President of the Metaphysical Center of New Jersey

Bill is very passionate about how improv can help all of us be better in business and in life. *Improvisational Leaders* is a great deep dive into how the art form can help you be your highest self, particularly in Chapter 9 where he emphasizes key improv principles and values, and then shows the direct relationship to one's place of work. The exercises are also very pragmatic, easy to follow, and helpful to build your overall improv proficiency. It's a great combination of best business practices academically with an understanding of the human spirit as well.

> — Chris Griggs, Former Ad Executive; now Standup Comedian, Actor, and Improviser; Faculty Member teaching improvisation at The People's Improv Theater and AMDA Conservatory (NYC)
> chrisgriggscomedy.com

Improvisational Leaders is engaging and enlightening—a must read for everyone. The tools in this book guide you into self-mastery in all areas of your life, so you live life in confidence and not fear. Although detailed and very exploratory, it's easy to read and so well explained that it leaves me with no questions which is rare in a book.

A conscious encyclopedia for all social gatherings, events, and businesses, *Improvisational Leaders* is a total A to Z of self-management to be the best we can be without judgement—a treasure chest of guidance that will benefit every reader personally, ethically, and in business. This book is a ◈ .

Examples of everyday tasks and real people's experiences make this book relatable to everyone not just businesspeople, and Bill's experiences on his journey adds the depth of genuine understanding vs. only a mental familiarity.

I now understand that improv is not living to an agenda but trusting yourself to live a quality life that is not one way, but multifaceted with infinite choices. It's trusting that you have enough experience to adapt to all situations.

> — Dee Weldon, Author of *This Is All There Is (2021),
> I SENSE: This is all there is… (2021), Where There
> is Love, There is No Gender: Understanding Love,
> Sex, & Relationships (2020), From Both Sides of the
> Fence: The Gifts in U (2019), Soul Disclosure: 100%
> Access (2019), The Map of the Universe: A Traveler's
> Guide (2019), Connecting to Life's Compass: You're
> not lost – you just think you are (2019)*

In our cold logic, dollars-and-sense, "show-me-the-money" world, *Improvisational Leaders* illuminates the potential of spontaneity and intuition in effective business leadership. This fresh outlook and insightful writing encourage us all to "look inside" and find the human magic that, when integrated with objective evidence, can help us make better decisions, build stronger relationships, grow, and succeed. I strongly recommend *Improvisational Leaders.*

— Al Cini, Managing Partner, Brand and Culture Alignment Toolkit®

In *Improvisational Leaders*, Bill Prinzivalli uses a lifetime of entrepreneurship, personal and professional experiences, and a good intuitive sense to propose a new, exciting, and fun way to approach challenges in the business world. With well-articulated reasoning and skillfully designed exercises, Prinzivalli demonstrates the importance of moving from fear to truthfulness in the workplace.

It is a refreshing approach to a time-worn system based on constriction and the bottom line. He presents a compelling scenario of a management down vision of an open and expansive work environment that benefits all. Prinzivalli clearly explains how valuing openness and authenticity leads to more creative thinking, a happier environment, and overall success.

— Marina and Joseph Maurino, Psychotherapists for individuals and couples

It was 2015 when Bill invited me to an improv class in New York City. By then I had a successful career in the field of Autism and to my astonishment, many of the improv classes encouraged me to look deeper, and be more authentic and connected to my co-actors.

Daring to be more spontaneous, listening more, and bringing out the full potential of each individual child, improv helped me improve my skill with the children. *Improvisational Leaders* is a constant reminder for me to strive for closer connections, deeper understanding, and loving honesty towards self and fellow human beings.

Bill has become a powerful leader in masterfully weaving improv into the fabric of personal relationships, business, and general engagement in life. *Improvisational Leaders* brings together the body, mind, and soul in a delightful, joyous way that only a man with intimate experience can write.

> — Gerd Winkler, Director of Global Autism Solutions
> www.globalautismsolutions.com

This book *(Improvisational Leaders)* around business leadership is so refreshing to read in today's work environment. A combination of mindfulness and improvisation will build a stronger team environment that leads to extraordinary results. A must-read for any business leader.

> — Christopher Salem, CEO, Business Executive Coach, Award-Winning Author of *Master Your Inner Critic (2016)* and *Mastering the Art of Success (2017)*

Brilliantly insightful, nuanced, and transformational, *Improvisational Leaders* is a breakthrough in creativity resulting in a new and enlightened business model for the future—and the future is now. Using the paradigm of the latest neuroscientific knowledge of the brain, Prinzivalli has skillfully married both right (intuition) and left (rational) brain function through the bridge (corpus callosum) between them by ingeniously devising a practical connection with techniques and exercises from mindfulness and improvisation—integrating a whole brain approach. This vision is not only novel and dynamic, but also concrete, practical, and surprisingly fun. It is a system destined to become a textbook for a new and inspired, successful business pattern of operation.

> — Harriet Wagniere, BS, MA, Director Emeritus of the Metaphysical Center of New Jersey

Improvisational Leaders is one of the biggest contributions I believe Bill can make in the world of business, because he himself has been a businessman who took a risk and shared himself so deeply with the support of the improv community. He is by far one of the most qualified businessmen to speak on the subject of improv and business. Bill's experience allows him to speak about these seemingly unrelated subjects from a place of deep knowing because he has experienced it in his own skin. This book is truly a labor of love that gives voice to a myriad of tools for any businessperson who desires to make a deeper contribution to humanity.

> — Rita Gendelman, Integrative Occupational Therapist specializing with children on the Autism Spectrum

Improvisational Leaders makes a compelling case for the value of practicing various mindfulness modalities, including meditation and yoga, to bring creativity into an unpredictable modern business environment. The authors point the reader towards a paradigm that goes beyond conventional business models.

— Raji Thron, Founder, Co-director Yoga Synthesis

Table of Contents

PART TWO
MINDFULNESS/AWARENESS—Tools and Suggestions

PART THREE
IMPROVISATION—The Freedom to Experiment

Foreword
by Chris Laszlo

This book weaves together several strands trending in the popular business imagination: leadership based on inner wisdom, entrepreneurial creativity, mindfulness practices, quantum science, and improv. The latter brings a delightful lightness of touch to the serious business of leading with integrity and authenticity.

Prinzivalli and Farias find myriads of ways to make wholeness a daily practice. They go beyond resolving the duality of achievement versus wellbeing, left versus right brain, being versus doing. Business success is recast to embrace health, relationships, and wellness of spirit. Leadership practices are extended to caring for the whole person. The authors show that, somewhat paradoxically, their approach can lead to even greater professional attainment than a narrow focus on winning.

Their message is critical for a workforce that is burned out from the pandemic, from online meetings, isolation, anger, and divisiveness in our communities. For years surveys have shown that over half the American workforce self-identifies as disengaged at work. Covid-19 only poured more fuel on the fire. The cost of employee disengagement, in human terms as well as in reduced productivity and diminished creativity, has been enormous.

There is a sense in the public sphere that we are at a tipping point: reaffirming democracy or destroying it, business as a force for good or evil, regenerating nature or trashing it. Readers should take the core messages of this book to heart. *Improvisational*

Leaders makes an important contribution to understanding what it will take, individually and collectively, for today's leaders to tip our systems back to a sustainable path forward.

Drawing on their extensive personal experience, as well as wide-ranging sources in both the popular and academic press, the authors engage the reader in bit-size narrative chunks. Part I introduces the key concepts for greater consciousness and authenticity in business. Part II offers excellent mindfulness tools and direct-intuitive practices that help transform who leaders are being. Each tool or practice is followed by documented wellness benefits and insights from neuroscience, followed by the deeper framing of quantum reality as whole and interconnected. Part III takes the reader on a deep dive into the world of improv, based on the lead author's first-hand experience, to reveal it as a rich source of entrepreneurial creativity and listening for the emergent future. The book concludes with practical applications in business. Benefits range from greater self-awareness, resilience, and relational skills to highly specific proficiencies such as enhanced public speaking.

In today's complex and turbulent business environment, *Improvisational Leaders* provides a refreshingly simple but powerful set of concepts, tools, and practices. Anyone who wants to flourish at work and in life will benefit from its wisdom.

Chris Laszlo, PhD Professor of Organizational Behavior Weatherhead School of Management, Case Western Reserve University

Books published by Stanford University Press
Quantum Leadership (2019), *Flourishing Enterprise* (2014),
Embedded Sustainability (2011), and *Sustainable Value* (2008)

Foreword
by R. S. Nodell

Readers of *Improvisational Leaders* will find themselves lucky to have discovered this pragmatic guide to leading oneself, even as they attempt to lead others. Most leadership books pass over this critical dimension of leadership and dive directly into the necessary protocols and processes for leading others. The more sophisticated of these leadership books will go so far as articulating an effective use of language or laying out the particulars of strategic thinking. Some even go to the physics of nonlinear dynamical systems to understand the complexity of organizational systems. Very few tackle the most difficult terrain: preparing *oneself* to lead.

In an entrepreneurial career spanning decades, Bill Prinzivalli, has led several successful startup ventures followed more recently by an equally successful practice as executive coach and organizational consultant. In these pages, Bill articulates a variety of self-disciplines and practices that have contributed to his own effectiveness. These practices are culled from a wide variety of disciplines ranging from the esoteric to the dramatic. He draws upon what is often called "the eternal wisdom" discovered in his own developmental journey and he shares that journey with his readers.

This book is not for everybody. It is certainly not for the passive reader who looks for answers and directions from experts. This book is for the leader who recognizes the inherent need to engage in continuous self-development in order to lead well.

The work demands an active and experimental engagement with studying the impact of leading on the leader. Real learning can only happen in the doing. An active reader will find many riches, not in answers the book provides but in employment of the many exercises and approaches to thinking the book articulates.

These exercises and experiments open new internal resources for leaders. As an organizational consultant myself, I believe that our intuition and unconscious resources are a good deal smarter than our intellectual capacities. Our business education and critical thinking skills are not enough to meet the demands of leading in our crisis ridden twenty-first century. The authors direct us to find greater wisdom not merely in thought but in our bodies and imagination, in our attentiveness and our whimsy.

I have known and worked with Bill for over twenty years and know him to be true to these practices. I have walked with him through the inevitable ups and downs of business cycles, the many successes, and the occasional failures. Through it all, Bill has shown himself to be what the Danish philosopher, Soren Kierkegaard called a "Knight of Faith." He has followed the path his intelligence, working in tandem with his pragmatic experimentalism, has projected for him. In this book he is not merely cataloguing a series of concepts and ideas he has thought and read about. Bill has lived this journey and gives his readers a field guide from his lifetime of discovery. If you are courageous enough to try this alternative path, you will be richly rewarded with purpose, meaning, and probable success.

R. S. Nodell
Co-Founder of GAMT & Triadic Consulting
Co-Author of *Managerial Magic: A Medicine Man's Guide to Organizational Life*

Preface

Three time's a charm!

The first time I attempted to write this book, or an incarnation thereof, was in the early 1990s when I developed and taught an adult education class entitled, "Business Success through Inner Wisdom" for the Metaphysical Center of New Jersey. The focus of that class was on awareness and the development of our intuitive, creative, and mindful selves. It was intended to be an adjunct to the traditional, linear information learned in academia and in the workplace.

The class was approximately ten weeks long and each class session reviewed a different nonlinear concept aimed to induce and integrate our intuitive mind with our logical mind to produce a more comprehensive approach to our particular work. The subjects included meditation, mindfulness, the meaning of success, right brain experience, executive ESP, Tao of Leadership, goal setting, and more. Wisdom from notables such as Albert Einstein and Thomas Edison was introduced as well as examples from the business world where intuition played an important part in their success stories. The essence of the course message was, "Why use only our left brain when we can use our entire brain?"

I referenced the work of many others and thought these concepts were groundbreaking enough for the business world to explore this approach. However, the circle of interested leaders remained small as did the size of my classes. The book was to be a documentation of the class material I was presenting but I did not manage to write it at that time.

I revisited the book in approximately 2015. Friends and family advised me that the original book design would be dry and boring without personal stories and strongly suggested I incorporate personal stories into the text. With that suggestion, I spent time writing many of my personal stories that had some relation to the book with the goal of integrating them into the material to produce a new design of my book. I now had two sets of ideas—the original material plus my personal stories—and struggled to devise an integration of the two to create a book with an updated design. Once again, no book was completed.

Separately, I took my first improvisation class in February of 2012 intending it to be a single evening of entertainment and fun. That single evening turned into an immediate weekend workshop followed by an immediate performance on a New York stage—a single evening of fun turned into an exhilarating and terrifying evening, performing improv for the first time in my life. Since that first day in 2012, I have been regularly practicing the art form of improvisation. I was initially surprised at my continued interest but quickly saw that it was compelling, challenged me in many ways, facilitated self-growth, was sometimes therapeutic, and was based on principles of caring, giving, and consciousness. Hence, I am still practicing.

Again, separately, in late 2018, I got the urge to complete an MBA that I had mostly completed many years prior, as it always annoyed me that I needed an asterisk next to the MBA initials signifying that I had not completed the required thesis. To that end, I met with the Dean at Fairleigh Dickinson University to review the courses I had taken and what might be required to complete the degree. (I was secretly hoping that he would say

I had enough business experience that could be applied to earn the degree, but I guess that was more hope than reality). In our conversation, I told him about a book I had always wanted to write and asked if there were any classes that related business and consciousness. He recommended I speak to Professor Gerard Farias who specializes in management and sustainability in their graduate program.

In my conversation with Dr. Farias, he appreciated and was very aligned with my passion to integrate business and consciousness and suggested that, instead of taking classes, I do independent studies with him that related to conscious and sustainable organizations. We began that study, which included the examination of various conscious organizations. Toward the end of that study, he discovered through our conversations that I do improv in New York City and relayed to me that they study improvisation in the management curriculum. I was unaware of this intersection of improvisation and management and we decided to next do a study on the feasibility of applying improvisation into the business world.

That study encouraged me to revisit writing the book I always wanted to write – but this time adding improvisation as an important component of the nonlinear practices helpful to access the creative and intuitive mind.

Part One of this book provides the overall concepts of the book's basic message. Part Two focuses on awareness and has been in my head for years as I have been a practitioner of these traditions for many years. Part Three of this book focuses on improvisation, including principles, benefits, and exercises. I am honored that Dr. Farias has agreed to write Chapter 11 of this book, which discusses improvisation and values driven leadership.

I often use the phrase, "follow the energy," which has generally been a very accurate guide for me. This book would not have been written had I not followed the energy in several, seemingly disparate, directions—my original passion to integrate consciousness and business, my willingness to try improv, my desire to complete my MBA, and my good fortune to have met Dr. Farias, who I am now happy to call my friend.

The universe then conspired to time these events to coincide with the Covid 19 pandemic that absolutely impacted my consulting practice thereby affording me the entire year of 2020 and much of 2021 to design, research, and write this book. These different, unrelated energy streams converged in an amazing and auspicious manner, allowing me to write this book.

Introduction

At its core, this book is aimed to increase the level of consciousness and integrity in the business world. Its general technique is to promote mindfulness, self-awareness, acceptance, authenticity, creativity, and a cooperative nature to individuals at all levels of the organization, thereby facilitating greater leadership and enhanced organizational performance.

In recent decades, various books and articles have been written demonstrating the improved effectiveness and productivity of organizations that foster these qualities and embrace a caring attitude toward their employees.

Personally, I saw the need for greater consciousness and authenticity as I progressed through my own career. My first profession out of college was that of a mathematician, followed by several years in computer programming. In those professions, facts were king, and consciousness and authenticity were not much of an issue. When I moved into sales of computer software, I quickly saw the lack of consciousness and ethics. Some of my colleagues secured their sales through deception, lies, and coercion. Moreover, their managers applauded them for their results, never questioning the quality of the sale. It was then that I realized that the profession of sales was a breeding ground for the attitude of "the end justifies the means." I also observed that this was frequently true in the legal profession, and that these two professions were among those inherently ripe for such unethical behavior.

It has since been my goal to help integrate consciousness and authenticity into the business world. Although it should have been sufficient to promote integrity and values, my approach was to suggest that utilizing these positive attributes would actually produce better overall results—results that would include individual wholeness and fulfillment, greater creativity, a better client relationship, and a more successful long-term strategy. As there was only moderate interest when I taught classes on the subject in the 1990s, I have since looked for ways to introduce this into the world, but was frustratingly limited to utilizing it in my own companies and in my consulting work. But then the opportunity presented itself to connect improvisation to the business world via my independent studies with Dr Farias and the writing of this book.

Generally unknown, improv principles include connecting to your partner, deep listening, being honestly self-aware, speaking authentically, giving to your partner, inclusivity, patience, and more. These are clearly qualities of consciousness (being aware of yourself and your surroundings) and authenticity (being in alignment with your true beliefs).

I now see an opportunity to offer the business community strategies and techniques that integrate mindfulness practices with traditional business strategies. To that end, I will present several tools and practices to assist the development of self-awareness, including meditation techniques, mindfulness activities, and psychological modalities. Next, I will review the art form of improvisation, including its structural environment, its guiding principles, and its many benefits. I will also provide examples and exercises that can be explored with the goal of improving skills applicable to both your personal and workplace environment.

Rather than simply lecture on these processes, this book presents a variety of tools, practices, and exercises to experience and develop these qualities in each individual. The practices span from some that are ancient and proven, to others that are more modern, and finally to the art form of improvisation that is both fun and experiential. Many of the practices can be performed on your own while some of the more advanced improv exercises may be better experienced with a facilitator.

I recommend that the leaders of our corporations exercise and adopt these qualities within themselves and their organization, and I also encourage each individual to independently develop these practices. Once a critical mass is reached, the entire organization may be able to operate in a state of flow and creativity, perhaps even reaching the "zone." Some would call this a conscious organization.

What's in this Book

Part One of this book presents the basis of this book's message. It discusses my observation of the business world and describes my belief that integrating nonlinear practices with the predominant linear practices will improve both personal and business success. The subsequent parts and chapters delve more deeply into the subjects of awareness and improvisation, providing theory, applications, and exercises.

The highlights of each chapter are presented at the beginning of that chapter. These highlights are intended to provide you with a synopsis or outline of its content, allowing you to decide if you wish to dive more deeply into that subject or to move to the next chapter.

Part Two presents wide-ranging topics of awareness (including self-understanding, meditation, mindfulness, psychology) and the application of these practices into daily life.

Part Three delves into the art form of improvisation discussing its principles, benefits, and applications, and includes exercises for both personal and business use.

PART ONE

HOW TO SUCCEED IN BUSINESS –
A Deeper View

Chapter 1

Today's Business Climate

"A leader is best when people barely know he exists, when his work is done, his aim fulfilled, they will say: we did it ourselves." Lao Tzu

"I believe fundamental honesty is the keystone of business." Harvey S. Firestone

"Before I can tell my life what I want to do with it, I must listen to my life telling me who I am." Parker Palmer

---

Chapter Highlights

1. Business is complex and leaders are always searching for the best means to succeed.
2. Most business leaders use only half their brain. Einstein knew better.
3. Corporations are now incorporating nonlinear activities to enhance their success.

Every business is looking for the best means to succeed, whether it be hiring expert staff, automating certain systems, creating efficient internal processes, HR training, regular progress reviews, improving product/services, enhancing marketing and messaging, offering competitive pricing, maximizing client satisfaction, analyzing market research, developing important client relationships, staying abreast of economic conditions, monitoring the competition, polling prospects, optimizing the financial basis, heightening the reputation, performing research for future products, and developing a vision for the future.

As you can see, managing a business is a complex task. Defining its mission, producing products/services, operating efficiently, maintaining client satisfaction, inspiring employees, developing efficient internal procedures, and producing an acceptable profit can be overwhelming. Adding to this list is the entire set of uncontrollable factors including the economic, competitive, and political environments. It is no wonder that new businesses fail at an alarming rate and existing businesses frequently find themselves in a stressful or even chaotic condition.

To determine how to best advance a business may require a crystal ball, and furthermore, to help revive a failing business can be a Herculean task. It is no surprise when we see business leaders operate in a seemingly haphazard manner, for there are so many parameters to examine to determine the greatest cause of the issues and the best approach to solve their problems. It seems like an impossible task for any one brain, and yet most leaders are regularly tasked with such a dilemma.

Although these leaders may consult with peers to expand the power of their single brain, many of their decisions are made individually. I also observe that many leaders further handicap themselves by using only half of their brain/mind, i.e., their linear, logical, and analytical brains versus integrating it with their nonlinear, intuitive, and creative minds.

I see this not as a fault of their own but instead as a fault of education. For example, an engineer will initially learn their subject matter in academia and will continue learning their craft through their employer and/or continuing education. This education is generally focused on the linear mind and capabilities and does not include any nonlinear processing to complement and integrate—a technique that uses only half of your abilities. And when we consider the complexity of business success, it makes little sense to limit yourself in this manner. I understand that part of the problem is that many believe there is no room for nonlinear processing in their particular area of work. In fact, some would denounce it as frivolous or even detrimental. With all the scientific knowledge we now have about our nonlinear capabilities, it is most unfortunate to denounce half of our capabilities.

America's preeminent scientist, Albert Einstein, has frequently discussed the importance of the nonlinear function of intuition:

> *The intuitive mind is a sacred gift and the rational mind is a faithful servant. We have created a society that honors the servant and has forgotten the gift.*

> *I believe in intuition and inspiration. Imagination is more important than knowledge. For knowledge is limited, whereas imagination embraces the entire world, stimulating progress, giving birth to evolution. It is, strictly speaking, a real factor in scientific research.*

> *The intellect has little to do on the road to discovery. There comes a leap in consciousness, call it Intuition or what you will, the solution comes to you and you don't know how or why.*

> *One who scorns the power of intuition will never rise above the ranks of journeyman calculator.*

Another of America's great inventors, Thomas Edison famously took naps on a regular basis to access his intuition. In this napping state, the linear mind quiets and the nonlinear, intuitive mind operates. Many solutions have come from this state of mind.

Joyce Brothers, American psychologist, advice columnist, and writer described that nonlinearity and intuition are not based on nothing but instead exhibit a connection to the linear mind, stating, "Trust your hunches. Hunches are usually based on facts filed away just below the conscious level." In this statement, Brothers demonstrates the interconnectedness of the linear and nonlinear mind.

Clarissa Pinkola Estés, a first-generation American writer, a Jungian psychoanalyst, and author of *Women Who Run with the Wolves*, contends that intuition is a power given at birth saying, "Practice listening to your intuition, your inner voice; ask questions; be curious; see what you see; hear what you hear; and then act upon what you know to be true. These intuitive powers were given to your soul at birth."

Another link between the linear and nonlinear was artfully described by French author Delphine de Girardin when she said, "Instinct is the nose of the mind," and American clinical psychologist and author Anne Wilson Schae gave us clear warning to not ignore our intuition when she stated, "Trusting your intuition often saves us from disaster."

In the business world, former CEO Maggie Wilderotter makes a direct link between intuition and business by simply stating, "Intuition is a powerful business tool. Use it." In a nutshell, this is one of the main messages of this book. Thank you Maggie.

The time seems to be ripe to introduce and integrate these nonlinear practices within most all organizations. Some are now following the research and embracing activities that help balance the mental, linear aspects of the job. We see corporate offerings of yoga classes, meditation classes, exercise rooms, quiet areas, and we see greater caring of employees with child facilities, enhanced HR, maternal/paternal leave, and more. There seems to be a recognition that a more balanced or integrative approach to our humanity is better for the corporation as well as for the individual employee.

Hence, I wish to bring greater awareness to the duality of linear and nonlinear processing. I will highlight many nonlinear principles, including many techniques and practices that I have used in my personal life and business career. In general, they have helped me to remain centered and focused, to assist with important business decisions, to help me remain calm (mostly) amidst the chaos, to keep things in perspective, and to feel a sense of wholeness. To be clear, the success rate of these activities is fluid, i.e., not always successful, and hence they are called practices. And just as with most practices, there are good days and not so good days but the general trend line over time produces more and more success with these principles and practices.

The practice of these techniques will expand creativity and intuition, thereby enhancing the contribution to the success of the organization. That, in itself, would convince business leaders to incorporate such techniques. However, there is a greater good that will be generated. These techniques will also foster selflessness, sensitivity, a bigger-picture view, and heart-centered understandings—all elements that will positively affect all stakeholders, including employees, clients, vendors, shareholders, and all who have contact with your organization. Ultimately, these practices will help bring greater consciousness to the entire business community.

A Farmer's Story

This is a story about a farmer who followed in the footsteps of several generations of farmers before him.

The family farm was comprised of a comfortable home with two significant patches of farmland, both east and west of their homestead. Each patch of farmland had somewhat different characteristics, including the angle and times of direct sunlight, the moisture level, the wind effect, the surrounding environment, the texture of the soil, and the type of crops that would be supported.

Although both patches of land were fertile and likely productive in the past, somewhere in the generational lineage it was deemed more superior to develop the west patch of land. That patch of land was more straightforward to develop, more easily understood, and generally fruitful. As this process continued, the understanding of the east patch of land became more mysterious and therefore more ignored. All development, improvements, and attention were placed on the west patch.

Although the east patch of land naturally produced some crops—on its own and without special attention from the farmer—the farmers never quite understood how to best use those crops and of course how to develop them further. If any family member were to suggest developing the east patch, they were generally criticized as being naïve and uninformed, as it was considered nontraditional, mysterious, and unrecognized by the family. It would be counter to the family teachings and considered immature or irresponsible to expect results from that part of the farm.

Basically, no one truly understood the nature of the east patch, and all the focus and attention were on the west patch. In fact, even when the west patch was fully developed and fully producing, any additional attempts to increase the yield was still focused on the west side. Over time, there were less and less improvements available as the farmers continually sought improvements from the west side via the use of additional labor, newer technology, and new ideas. The improvements were therefore incremental at best.

There were a few sages who would occasionally come through town and discuss their successes with land similar to the east patch. However, they were met with skepticism and confusion, and were generally not taken seriously as the farmers were unable to fully grasp their means of success. Hence, they carried on developing only the west patch. Further reinforcement of the west patch preference was confirmed as neighboring farmers concluded the same.

In fact, many farmers totally disregarded the natural production of crops from the east side even when those crops were brought to market. They either minimized their value or totally denounced it crediting the west side for its production.

Even the most advanced farmers, i.e., the "Einsteins" of farmers who developed both east and west type land, would be ignored with the sentiment of "I don't understand them; they're different and odd; and I cannot duplicate what they do."

During these years, there were a few farmers who harvested with only east type patches of land. They clearly knew that they were in the minority and frequently criticized. Like most farmers, they were sometimes successful and sometimes not, but it always remained unclear as to their exact process as well as their exact success. With little clarity or understanding, few farmers followed their path. In fact, these east type farmers may not have been certain themselves if their techniques were superior to others, but they did know that this east type farming resonated with them and was the only way they knew how to operate, hence leaving them with only this option.

It may have seemed logical for each of these farmer types to collaborate and teach the other their techniques and their success, but there was such a lack of understanding and skepticism of the other that few seemed willing to embark on that path. Therefore, the situation continued whereby each farmer type respected only their form of farming, denounced the other as inferior, and continued in their myopic manner.

If this sounds familiar, it is, for it is highly analogous to left and right brained people. (The next chapter will discuss the history and accuracy of these terms.) The left, linear brained people can tell you exactly how they operate and generally feel strongly that it is the correct way, especially since it can be clearly explained. The right, nonlinear brained people know and trust how they operate but cannot always explain it, especially in a logical fashion. Of course they cannot—it's not a logical process!!

So, the two sides are different and cannot always communicate clearly. But they are both useful, important, fruitful, and complement each other. Each side alone can be competent but working together ... they will be superior, outstanding, and always greater than either one part alone. It is therefore a very wise move to cultivate and harvest both the east and west patches of our brain!!

Chapter 2

Duality

"The direction of life is from duality to unity." Deepak Chopra

"Transcendence means going beyond duality. Attachment means remaining within duality." Rajneesh

"The divorce of our so-called spiritual life from our daily activities is a fatal dualism." Mary Parker Follett

---

Chapter Highlights

1. Duality is pervasive in life; examples are everywhere—male/female, light/dark, hot/cold, inner/outer, linear/nonlinear.
2. In the 1960s, science identified separate functionalities of each hemisphere of our brain—the left hemisphere was responsible for linear and analytical functions and controlling the right side of our body, while the right hemisphere being responsible for creative and intuitive functions and controlling the left side of our body.
3. Today's science has determined that the discoveries of the 1960s were gross oversimplifications and

---

that both hemispheres of the brain are involved in most all functions.

4. Regardless of today's science, the vernacular of left brain and right brain still persist to identify linear and nonlinear functionality.

5. Most teachings in our educational system, as well as our business environment focus on content and linear functionality. There is little taught relating to nonlinear functionality.

6. Elite athletes incorporate nonlinear functionality to achieve their highest results. They practice meditation, visualization, and centering to maximum their performance—and get into "the zone." Businesses should follow their lead to maximize their success.

Duality is pervasive in life; examples are everywhere. We see male/female, earth/sky, left/right, light/dark, clockwise/counterclockwise, hot/cold, up/down, inner/outer, linear/nonlinear, sympathetic/parasympathetic, soul/personality, separate/together, catabolic/anabolic, being/doing, and so many more. Although we can view duality as being comprised of opposites, differences, or separation, we can also view them as polar ends of the same organism, e.g., hot/cold are both descriptions of temperature, but just different ends of the temperature spectrum. Regardless, defining these apparent opposites can help us to distinguish, describe, analyze, and understand them.

History

This principle of duality has been acknowledged and is discussed in many arenas. For example, *The Kybalion* (1912), a philosophical study of ancient Egypt and Greece defines The Principle Of Polarity as, "Everything is dual; everything has poles; everything has its pair of opposites; like and unlike are the same; opposites are identical in nature, but different in degree; extremes meet; all truths are but half-truths; all paradoxes may be reconciled." (Additional principles from *The Kybalion* can be found in Appendix A.)

This duality or polarity principle has also been the subject of scientific research. For example, in the study of human performance in the late twentieth century, scientists studied the human brain dissecting it into the left hemisphere and right hemisphere. These studies seem to emanate from research in the 1960s when patients had experienced the severing of the corpus callosum (the connecting tissues between the hemispheres) and subsequently experienced different responses to various stimuli. Their early findings hypothesized a different functionality for each hemisphere, with the left hemisphere (labeled left-brain) being responsible for linear type functionality, and the right hemisphere (labeled right-brain) being responsible for nonlinear activity. There were many books and articles written as this was a popular hypothesis and discussion.

In one such book entitled, *The Right-Brain Experience* (1983), Marilee Zdenek reviews the functionality of each hemisphere of the brain, emphasizes the creativity available from the right brain, and notates various success stories emanating from the right brain. Although she discusses the integration of each hemisphere, she emphasizes the clear differences that were thought to be more distinct at that time. She noted, "Researchers discovered that each side of the brain has its own area of specialization and processes information in its own way. Subsequent tests have shown that in a normally functioning brain, the corpus callosum enables both hemispheres to work together for almost every activity, although one hemisphere or the other will predominate for a specific task."

She defines specialization or dominance of the left brain for the following tasks: verbal, analytical, literal, linear, mathematical, and controls movement on the opposite side of the body. Specialization for the right brain includes the following types of activity: non-verbal, holistic, nonlinear, spatial, musical, metaphoric, imaginative, artistic, emotional, sexual, spiritual, dream maker, and controls movement on the opposite side of the body.

The chart below displays the left/right brain attributes of the hypotheses at that time:

Left Brain and Right Brain Attributes	
Left	**Right**
Linear	Nonlinear
Mind	Heart
Mental	Intuitive
Science	Arts
Rational	Emotional
Intellectual	Instinctive
Analytical	Creative
Logical	Free-thinking
Detail/fact-oriented	Able to see the big picture
Numerical	Visual
Sequential	Holistic
Objective	Subjective
Systematic	Musical
Factual	Imagination
Verbal	Non-verbal
Words	Images

Black and white	Color
Outer	Inner
Calculated	Sensitive

Neuroscience

The neuroscientists of today note that this description of the left/right brain was at least a mass oversimplification, and at most inaccurate. For example, their findings determined that linearity is not exclusively the property of the left hemisphere of the brain but that both hemispheres are involved in most brain activity.

In one example, physicist Ransom Stephens, PhD and author of *The Left Brain Speaks, The Right Brain Laughs*, looks at the neuroscience of innovation and creativity in art, science, and life. In his book, he notes that, "While the left and right brains look quite similar, they assume distinct roles in sensory and language processing. The obvious generalization is that the left and right lobes play different roles and perform separate tasks. The legend of your left brain as the inner accountant and your right brain as the inner artist emerged in 1960 and turned out to be a gross oversimplification."

Stephens continues, "The right brain does play a big role in creativity, but so does the left brain. The left brain breaks things down into little, understandable pieces, but the right brain makes sure that those pieces still fit a greater whole." And finally he makes light of his own book title stating, "The title of this book … is a glaring example of a mythic oversimplification."

In another example, an August 2, 2019, article by Carl Sherman and Kayt Sukel of the Dana Foundation, shares a similar sentiment stating, "In recent years, the two sides of the brain have come to symbolize two sides of human nature; the left brain hailed (or disparaged) as logical, analytical, and intellectual, and the intuitive right brain as the avatar of emotion and creativity." The article continues stating, "a host of popular books, educational strategies, and even therapeutic interventions have ensued ... The reality is not so simple—and a good deal more interesting. And like so much in neuroscience, far from fully understood."

Regarding creativity, the article notes, "Perhaps the most seductive and tenacious belief about brain lateralization is that the right hemisphere is the creative side .... But creativity remains an elusive phenomenon that resists simple explanations .... It may be that rather than reflecting the dominance of one hemisphere over the other, creativity in essence represents a glowing demonstration of their ability to work together."

Quantum Physics

Duality is also prominent in the study of quantum physics, as it is based on the duality of particles and waves. While the science still evolves, most discussions of quantum physics describe this wave/particle duality as its foundation.

Wikipedia describes the wave/particle duality as such:

In physics and chemistry, wave/particle duality holds that light and matter exhibit properties of both waves and of particles.

A central concept of quantum mechanics, duality addresses the inadequacy of conventional concepts like "particle" and "wave" to meaningfully describe the behavior of quantum objects.

The idea of duality is rooted in a debate over the nature of light and matter dating back to the 1600s when competing theories of light were proposed by Christiaan Huygens and Isaac Newton.

Through the work of Albert Einstein, Lewis de Broglie, and many others, it is now established that all objects have both wave and particle nature and that a suitable interpretation of quantum mechanics provides the over-arching theory resolving this ostensible paradox.

Another example of this duality is discussed in the TED-Ed lessons by Chad Orzel. He is a professor in the Department of Physics and Astronomy at Union College and author of *How to Teach Quantum Physics to Your Dog*, and defines the basic nature of the universe as dual. He notes that, although we see waves in water and particles in rocks, everything in the universe behaves as both a particle and a wave at the same time. This is the essential mystery and study of quantum physics. He credits Albert Einstein's conclusion in 1905 of the dual nature of light, work that Einstein picked up from Max Planck.

Another description of this duality is presented in an August 19, 2020, *Forbes* article entitled, "In Quantum Physics, Even Humans Act as Waves," where Senior Contributor Ethan Siegel opens the article with the question: "Is it a wave or is it a particle?" Although the response is quite lengthy, his essential message is, "Under appropriate conditions, we can measure either wave-like or particle-like behavior for photons—the fundamental quantum of light—confirming the dual, and very weird, nature of reality. This dual nature of reality isn't just restricted to light, but has been observed to apply to all quantum particles."

In other arenas, there are comparisons of the particle/wave duality to the left/right brain duality, specifically hypothesizing that the nature of the particle is comparable to the left brain functionality while the nature of the wave is comparable to the right brain functionality. In these theories, the particle/

left brain attributes relate to linearity, problem-solving, and separation, while the wave/right brain attributes relate to the creative, energetic, and sensory qualities. Contrary to the hypotheses of the 1960s, those who make these comparisons are in harmony with current neuroscience discoveries noting that, although there may be a predominance, the brain processes in a dual manner using both the left/particle and right/wave functionality.

In *Quantum Leadership*, Tsao and Laszlo relate the linear and nonlinear mind to connectedness and the quantum field. They state, "Our analytic, task-oriented, problem-solving state of mind tends to suppress our emotional self-awareness, social cognition, and ethical decision-making capabilities. The existence of the quantum field adds a possible explanatory factor. By slowing the analytic cognition of the brain, the practices of connectedness allow us to be more present in the interconnecting and coherence-producing effects of the quantum field, which can guide us on our evolutionary paths in life, if we let it."

Finally, there are those who connect quantum physics to spirituality and esoteric concepts. Although complex, their comparison of the wave/particle duality relates to the interactions of matter and energy. Their essential conclusions are that everything is energy, that we are all connected, that matter does not separate us because we are not matter but particles of energy, and that the power of perception can be used to create our own reality. We have all seen books, dating back to the 1970s, embracing the concepts that we can create our own reality, that telepathic communications occur even at a distance (as various governments have studied), that we are "all one," and that energy healing is a reality. Perhaps quantum physics is the scientific explanation of these seemingly esoteric concepts.

Language

Although neuroscience and quantum physics have shown that the left/right brain identification has been well-publicized as a myth, or at least an oversimplification, the terms left brain and right brain are still prevalent in our culture today in describing linear and nonlinear processing. And although science shows that both hemispheres are involved in all processing, there appears to be those of us who process predominantly in a linear fashion versus those of us who process in a nonlinear manner. Whether accurate or not, this predominance (or illusion) identifies our strengths and/or tendencies, and the terms left brain and right brain seem to be the favored choice of words for these tendencies.

As such, the terms left and right brain remain prevalent in literature and in the media, whether because of ignorance of the science, or because of familiarity, or because they've become accepted as grandfathered terminology. (As I racked by brain—both left and right side—for better terminology, the best alternative I could find for the overarching terms are linear and nonlinear; and hence I will use left/right or linear/nonlinear within this book).

The Battle of the Better Side

There is frequently criticism by linear personality types toward nonlinear types and vice versa, each likely not fully understanding the other and each believing that their tendency is the better one. How often have we heard linear types criticize nonlinear types as flighty, ungrounded, or dreamers, with the underlying sentiment being irresponsible? And conversely, how often have we heard nonlinear types criticize linear types as boring, anal, narrow-minded, with the underlying sentiment being small-minded?

19

It has always been my view that the best approach to any situation is to access and integrate both aspects of our being in order to make the best decision. Why would we only wish to use half of our resources to make important decisions? Why would we not wish to consult with the other half of ourselves prior to making potentially life-changing choices? This never made sense to me and hence I have always been a strong proponent of the use and integration of both linear and nonlinear processing.

Science now shows us that we can and do use both, even if there is a predominance or preference of one or the other. It is my goal to activate and integrate both aspects of our being. And since my observation is that education and business focus on linearity, and that subsequently many of us are predominantly linear, it is my intention to help activate and employ our nonlinear aspects. Therefore, the subsequent chapters in this book present many nonlinear concepts and practices to help activate and integrate those aspects to provide an enhanced and more holistic approach to our life and workplace situations.

Olympians and the "Zone"

There are many examples of the acknowledgment and importance of each side of this duality when we look at the performance of humans, especially at the highest level.

Olympic athletes are at a pinnacle level of human dexterity and performance. In these activities, we are looking at what many consider super-human achievements. And when we consider that we are talking about only a handful of athletes out of the seven billion people on this planet, we are truly speaking of the super elite.

We have all watched the Olympics and understand that to reach this point of competition, the athletes have already gone through the most rigorous and elite training for their particular sport. Although we don't see it, we can imagine the hours and hours of hard work, coaching, sacrifice, and total dedication required to get to this level of excellence. When we watch the athlete performing, we can see the brilliance of their performance that has resulted from that hard work. Moreover, we see something else prior to their performance that is not exactly related to the physical aspects of their particular sport. We see them centering themselves, visualizing, relaxing, listening to music, focusing, and the like—trying to get into "the zone." Beyond their physical training, we see elite athletes with a pregame routine that may include meditation, visualization, accessing a quiet inner space, etc. Intuitively, we know this is an activity that will likely be helpful to their performance. I maintain that this is more than a minor assistance but instead a very necessary ingredient to maximize their performance.

We, in fact, see that all professional athletes have their pregame routine. We also see that this is not limited to physically enduring activities as similar preperformance routines exist for chess players, card players, etc. Therefore, we see that to perform at our highest levels we need both the highest level of practice/preparation of our particular skill as well as the highest level of practice/preparation of our mind, emotions, and attitude. These nonlinear elements are clearly the complementary component to the linear aspects of their performance.

The next obvious question is this: are these practices useful in the business world? I maintain that, if we wish to excel at business to the highest levels, we need to incorporate both the nonlinear as well as the linear attributes of our being.

Business Performance and Nonlinearity

Our preparation for the business world includes our studies at universities, on-site corporate trainings, on-the-job training, and mentoring from our managers. All these approaches generally consist of content-oriented information and material necessary to understand our particular craft—all linear activities. There is little to no mentoring of nonlinear information or practices. It is debatable whether this occurs because of ignorance of the benefits of nonlinear practices, or the conscious decision that the linear practices are far more important, or belief that nonlinear practices are not useful, or the incapability of employers to offer these nonlinear practices.

Recent research has shown that certain nonlinear practices are helpful to the employees and to their performance, and therefore to the benefit of the corporation. To that end, we see corporations embracing and offering yoga classes, exercise rooms, meditation spaces, nature walks, and the like. They are moving in the direction from viewing their employees as robotic producers to caring more humanely for them and their needs. They are realizing that if their employees are feeling more whole about themselves, more balanced as individuals, and generally less stressful, they will not only execute their tasks more consistently but will also have a greater capacity to be more creative allowing for greater participation in issues and solutions. In general, they will be greater contributors to the organization.

A greater impact for organizations will occur when the leadership embodies these nonlinear attributes. As our business leaders embody the "being" qualities of caring, flourishing, authenticity, connectedness, oneness, awareness, as well as the "doing" qualities of producing profits, they will model these attributes in all their interactions—whether consciously or unconsciously—resulting in a positive impact of greater consciousness.

In their book, *Quantum Leadership*, Tsao and Laszlo state, "Quantum leadership focuses on adaptive skills that change who the leader is *being* rather than only on what the leader is *doing*." Relating business success to this leadership shift, they state, "It is important always to emphasize that the new consciousness makes good practical business sense. A quantum leadership approach offers you a better chance of financial success because it improves your entrepreneurial skills. You become less restricted in your thinking. You can see better and more clearly, and you feel more courageous and adventurous. In short, it makes you a better entrepreneur or corporate leader. Conflict between the short-term goal of keeping your company alive and financially healthy and the longer-term challenge of elevating consciousness and awareness are a matter of balance."

Financial Success and Nonlinearity

Skeptics may wish to quantitatively measure this greater contribution or better performance (from nonlinearity) to ensure it results in greater financial success. In one sense, it sounds like an unnecessary or shortsighted request—a request perhaps made because of their hesitation of this nonlinear approach. For example, would you deny that improvements in a company's product or services is a good thing? Or would you have to quantitatively prove that these improvements bring greater financial rewards? Although there are exceptions, (e.g., a vast over improvement of an already successful product), a better product or service would generally yield greater customer satisfaction, increased referrals, greater repeat business, fewer complaints, less maintenance issues, a greater reputation, an esteemed position in the marketplace, and more. It makes little business sense to deny that these are positive attributes whether or not they produce immediate financial gains, for it is easily understood that the long-term sustainability of the products and the financial success of the organization would be enhanced with these improvements. There are therefore certain qualities that do not need quantitative proof, for we know, perhaps with our nonlinear mind, that they are beneficial to the organization.

These beneficial attributes will also be extended beyond the organization, i.e., to all stakeholders—to the employees, customers, vendors, and society at large. In fact, many consider benefits to all stakeholders, in addition to shareholders, to be the true purpose of a business. In this vein, business success is not limited to profitability but to the achievement of benefits to shareholders and stakeholders alike.

Chapter 3

Success

"Success is the ability to go from one failure to another with no loss of enthusiasm." Winston Churchill

"Success comes from knowing that you did your best to become the best that you are capable of becoming." John Wooden

"Try not to become a man of success, but rather try to become a man of value." Albert Einstein

---

Chapter Highlights

1. Success has many varied definitions.
2. Personal success seems to be more heart-based and business success more material-based.
3. It is difficult to define success by an arbitrary outer measurement, such as a sales goal, versus one's personal best performance.
4. Develop awareness and find YOUR success!
5. Awareness success can emanate from personal sessions or improv experiential workshops.
6. Is it easy to determine success or failure? Maybe. (Includes a personal story).

The Meaning of Success

The traditional definitions of success are basically explained as achieving one's goals or the accomplishment of one's objectives. Some discuss the emotional aspect stating success is a feeling of excitement about what you do while others posture that success is multidimensional and personal. The action oriented definitions include doing your best, setting important goals, and accomplishing tasks important to you. Some discuss that it is both a journey and a destination; many conclude its meaning is personal to each of us; and some offer their views in poetic language, as seen below.

Somewhere in my travels, I came across this beautiful poem by Linda Lee Elrod:

> *Success*
> *is many things to many people,*
> *but if you have the courage to be true to yourself,*
> *to live up to your potential,*
> *to be fair with others,*
> *and always look for the good in any situation …*
> *then you will have been the best you can be,*
> *and there is no greater success than that.*

Ralph Waldo Emerson also writes beautifully about success:

> *Success*
> *To know that even one life has breathed easier*
> *Because you have lived*
> *This is to have succeeded.*

Paramahansa Yogananda has presented us with these pearls of wisdom in his booklet, "*The Law of Success.*" Although his teachings are generally esoteric in nature, these words are quite practical.

Your success in life ... also depends on your determination to grasp opportunities that are presented to you.

The season of failure is the best time for sowing the seeds of success.

Success is hastened or delayed by one's habits.

Success should therefore be measured by the yardstick of happiness; by your ability to remain in peaceful harmony with cosmic laws. Success is not rightly measured by the worldly standards of wealth, prestige, and power. None of these bestow happiness unless they are rightly used.

The *Tao of Leadership* discusses success in terms of praise, reputation, and fame, stating:

If you measure success in terms of praise and criticism, your anxiety will be endless. If the group applauds one thing you do, and then you feel good, you will worry if they do not applaud as loudly the next time. If they are critical, if they argue or complain, you will feel hurt. Either way, you are anxious and dependent.

Regarding reputation, they state:

Having a good reputation or becoming well-known for your work can be a hindrance to your further development. A good reputation naturally arises from doing good work. But if you try to cherish your reputation, if you try to preserve it, you lose the freedom and honesty necessary for further development.

27

And regarding fame, they state:

> *Fame is as burdensome as caring for yourself properly. In order to do good work, you must take good care of yourself. You must value yourself and allow others to value you also. But if you make too much of yourself, you will become egocentric, which injures both yourself and your work.*

They conclude by stating:

> *If you can live with the fruits of success and care for yourself properly, you will be able to foster success in other people.*

Although most professions are subjected to praise, fame, and reputation, the performing arts are prime candidates for these trappings. American singer-songwriter, Anita Baker wisely said, "Applause felt like approval and it became a drug that soothed the pain, but only temporarily."

Personal Success Versus Business Success

The definition of success seems to be different whether it refers to personal success or business success. When we speak of personal success, we frequently include health, family, loving relationships, financial security, social activities, and personal achievement. When we speak of business success, we frequently discuss money, status, power, and fame.

In this model, there seem to be certain aspects of personal success that are not included in our concept of business success, e.g., our health, loving relationships, or anything having to do with the heart. This follows an old concept that business is heartless or that there is no room for the heart in business. And this attitude has spawned the phrase, "It's not personal, it's just business," which, in my mind, is simply a poor rationalization to act badly.

Even in business environments that are not considered "cutthroat" and may have some heartfelt elements to them, the definition of success is still primarily money and status—usually in that order. For example, when we see individuals accumulate great amounts of money, regardless of what they do, we generally consider them successful. We don't often ask how they achieved it—ethically, shadily, legally—but seem to applaud them for obtaining it, perhaps even with a wry smile if they "beat the system." Whatever selfishness may have been involved, even at the expense of others, seems to be overlooked or forgiven, as the sole focus is on getting the prize.

Although this model may emanate from a sense of individual survival, it is also selfish, shortsighted, and inconsiderate of others. Perhaps originally experienced by immigrants, it is more of an "us versus them" attitude versus an understanding that we are all in community with each other. Whether consciousness is being expanded or whether research shows it more successful, some organizations are now embracing greater care for employees and incorporating greater concern (at least in their mission statements) for all stakeholders, not exclusively shareholders. Perhaps the definitions of personal success and business success are getting closer.

Present Moment Success

There are some Zen-like philosophies that define success as being in the present moment, and that the present moment contains success. Their mindful meditations help remind us that we are already in the state of joy and success versus living in the state of anxiety always striving to the next level to achieve success and joy. They state:

To feel success, happiness, achievement, fulfillment, satisfaction, or joy, see it where you are today. You do not need to get another job, read another book, evolve just a bit more, or get another degree. If you expend one half that energy to recognize the joys of your current day, then all days will be joyful. Then your journey towards your goals will be joyful, and the accomplishments of your goals will be successful and joyful.

This approach or attitude is clearly one of gratitude and appreciation of what we already have. It does not obviate goal-setting or aspiration, but quells any anxiety of not being enough and/or being dissatisfied with our current conditions. Plus any such anxiety may actually thwart forward movement toward your goals. The message is therefore to see the joy and success in your current situation *and* to aspire to greater goals and accomplishments.

Measuring Success

In business, more than personal, success seems to be defined by an outer measurement such as the number of sales, the revenue goal, the percent of market capture, the P&L of each division, the stock value, etc. I'd like to pose some examples for your consideration—both personal and business.

If your child comes home with the grade of B, is that a success? With only that information and no context, it is impossible to answer. For example, if your child is a straight A student and this particular subject was quite easy for them, you may not consider this a success. Conversely, if your child is a straight C student and achieves a B grade on a subject that has been quite challenging for them, then this is a quite wonderful success. Therefore, the success, in this case, is not based on an arbitrary outer measurement but instead based on the specific situation and the innate/inner ability of your child. And of course, your reaction to them would vary based on the context.

In a similar fashion, if your organization sets a revenue or profitability goal of X, would you consider it a success if you reached it? Although the general answer would be yes, what if the goal was incorrectly set either too low or too high? If too low, and you only achieved the exact goal of X, is that a success? And conversely, if the goal was inappropriately set excessively high, and you achieved 95 percent of X, would you consider that a failure?

Olympians and professional athletes and their coaches know that the best performances result from the prior honing of skills followed by integrating the calming visualization practices during the performance. The Olympic coach does not pressure the athlete to obtain the gold medal or to reach a specific time for that run. It may be helpful to encourage the athlete to visualize a celebratory finish, perhaps even visualizing a certain numerical goal. However, this would not be done with pressure or anxiety but instead with a positive visualization. But even this is not the main message—instead, they are encouraging the athlete to attain an inner calm, to maximize the possibility of reaching "the zone," a "flow" state that will produce their best performance regardless of any numerical goal. **It bears repeating to say they understand that the best performance will result from expert rigorous training followed by attaining a flow/zone state whereby they will perform at their absolute best, and this absolute best may or may not match some outer numerical goal.**

Success then should not be measured by the athlete's ability to reach an outside numerical goal but instead to reach their personal maximum potential.

This application of success can also be applied to business situations. If management measures success solely by its ability to reach a numerical goal, they may be ignoring the abilities of the employees in performing their best, and this numerical goal may or may not correctly relate to the abilities of the employees. And if incorrect, they may be inaccurate either on the low side or the high side. In either case, the measurement of success would be an inaccurate one.

Employers may argue that the numerical goals are appropriate if they are based on the perceived abilities of the employees. Although this appears reasonable, my observation is that the numerical goals are generally more influenced by the financial needs/goals of the organization and that once the goals are set, pressure is generally applied to the employees to reach those goals. Such pressure will generally prevent the employees from reaching the state of flow or zone, thereby preventing them from performing at their highest level. In other words, the emphasis seems to be influenced more strongly by the needs of the organization rather than the maximization or optimization of the performance of the employees.

I imagine this occurs for a few reasons. First, it is easier to measure success against the numerical figure; second, it is harder to determine the maximum abilities of an employee; and third, it takes more time to invest in the employee in a manner that helps them reach their maximum flow capacity. Although we may consider this dynamic to be "lazy" on the part of management, I suspect the greater reason is that most managers are not trained or skilled enough to work with the employees in this manner. Hence, the numerical goal generally remains as the standard.

And since each level of management is generally measured based on such numerical goals, pressure is generally placed throughout, and each level of management will frequently pass their pressures to the levels below them. This behavior fosters higher pressure and anxiety at most levels of management and their employees, resulting in performance levels lower than possible, since no one is encouraging or fostering the inner flow state necessary to produce their best performance. I liken this dynamic to the adult who has a stressful day at work and then comes home to "dump" or transfer this stress to their spouse, children, or pets. It doesn't solve anything and in fact worsened the situation by adding stress to the entire environment.

So what should be done? In the case of family life, the stressful adult can share their problems with their spouse or partner. This sharing will allow their partner to understand what is going on, will likely help defuse the situation, and together they can plan, if necessary, how to speak to their children. In this manner, the partner is there to help them and the stress is insulated from the children allowing them to continue to flourish and flow.

The same approach can be used in business, i.e., to have peers to share, discuss, and strategize regarding the situation while maintaining a positive and healthy relationship with your employees. If generally used, this approach will prevent each level of leadership to simply dump the stresses on the levels beneath them thereby creating anxiety and stress at all levels. This mature approach requires awareness and courage but will ultimately allow your employees the opportunity to perform at their best levels.

Your Calling, Your Awareness, Your Success

For many years of my life, I have heard people talking about a "calling." Perhaps the first time was in grammar school when the parish priest would visit our classroom asking us if we had a calling to become a priest. Although I raised my hand since that was expected of us, I had no such calling and hence did not understand the concept of a calling. In fact, I felt left out that I heard no calling of any kind. I have since heard those words from many others as they described their calling and again, I felt excluded.

What I did hear was a mantra to go to college and get a better job with financial security. I never named this a calling but instead thought of it as an important goal to reach. It made sense to me, was extremely practical, and seemed to be very wise advice. And indeed it was.

I followed that path successfully by going to college, getting multiple degrees, working in a professional career, getting married, and starting a family. The plan and goals were being achieved. During the 1970s, I began studying at the New Jersey Metaphysical Center and a decade later felt the urge to integrate consciousness into the business world. Was this a calling? I think so. How did I know and how is this different from the early goals of achieving financial security?

As I think about it now, my initial goal was more about survival and self-care, while the later goal was more about an internal desire. Although they were different, both were important and both were necessary. The initial goal was more about external needs while the later goal was more about an internal aspiration. Perhaps this is yet another example of duality (internal/external) and the need to honor both.

What is your calling? What are your external needs and what are your internal aspirations?

I think the external needs are more easily defined as they are generally more obvious—whether we see them ourselves, our parents point them out to us, our friends advise us so, or our physical environment demands it.

Internal aspirations may be more concealed. Depending on how we were brought up and what we were taught, we may or may not have easy access to our internal desires. If we were taught to mostly observe external rules, expectations, and "shoulds," we may have little familiarity with our actual internal yearnings. If these teachings were extreme, we may have never had the opportunity to identify our own internal desires and instead followed the paths to which we were directed. As an example, we all know of children who followed the career paths of their parents, married a certain type of person, had a certain number of children, lived a certain lifestyle, all to blow up at a later point in life when their true internal nature erupted like a volcano. And many of their friends would be shocked thinking they had a perfect life, and perhaps even *they* were surprised at their own reactions. Perhaps that programmed lifestyle was perfect for someone else but clearly it did not match their own internal composition. As American jazz legend Billie Holiday put it, "Everyone's got to be different. You can't copy anybody and end up with anything. If you copy, it means you're working without any real feeling. And without feeling, whatever you do amounts to nothing."

Hence, it behooves us to identify our true internal desires and inclinations, and to ensure we clearly incorporate them into our life plans. Of course, this sounds obvious. But if we are unconscious about our internal self, we may easily follow someone else's picture of a fulfilling life plan.

It is therefore necessary to identify both our external needs and our internal desires, and since our society's inclination is toward the external, we generally need to better develop our awareness of our internal needs, aspirations, and inclinations.

Once again, self-awareness is key. Within this book, there are many tools and suggestions to help you become more self-aware and to also be aware of your surroundings. If this is new to you, please be patient with yourself as it is an incremental learning process, not unlike building a muscle. Find the technique(s) that best suits your personality, for it matters not which tool you use. Having greater self-awareness allows you to exercise better judgment and to subsequently make better decisions for yourself.

After self-awareness is established, you will begin to identify your internal aspirations. And as you begin to identify these inner desires, you may experience some fear and uncertainty, since these may be new directions for you – directions that may appear challenging and may disturb your sense of comfort and familiarity. If this occurs, you will need to BREATHE! Use any of the modalities in this book to help your awareness of these discomforts, to breathe through them, and to find a level of clarity. Once processed, and assuming you still wish to move forward, you will be exercising your courage to make this change and move in the direction of your inner aspirations.

This process of developing awareness/identification, overcoming fear/discomfort, and exercising courage/change is a necessary part of major life advancements, and is essentially the hero's journey. After your first conquest of this process, you will begin to build a level of confidence that you can do it again and again. This is the courage of our mission.

Finding Awareness

Awareness is a key ingredient to achieving success. This is true regardless of how you personally define success—whether it be wealth, fulfillment, fame, goal-achievement, emotional satisfaction, money, power, reaching your "zone," achieving a meaningful journey, financial security, loving relationships, expressing courage, finding harmony with others, reaching contentment, or other attributes important to you.

This book does not judge your definition of success but instead focuses on awareness and consciousness, including many practices and exercises to help you expand and clarify your sense of yourself. It is my belief that the more you become self-aware and more conscious of yourself and your surroundings, you will better identify your true personal goals and definition of success. I also believe that you will become more connected to yourself and others, more empathic and open-hearted, more caring of yourself and others, and more desirous of success for all.

The title of this book could have been "Finding Awareness" or "Finding Consciousness" or any variation thereof, as all the content, including the exercises, revolves around these concepts. As such, I have included many and various techniques and practices that relate to awareness and consciousness. In fact, these two words may be considered redundant, as consciousness is essentially the awareness of self and our surroundings.

My general advice is to explore the various exercises and practices within this book and determine those that best suit you. You may select one or several, you will find that some are more effective than others, and those you initially select may change over time. Please be patient with yourself as they are practices, meaning that you will develop them more deeply over time. Even if initial results are quick, the more likely scenario is that these practices will develop within you at whatever speed your system can handle. As an example, when you first learn how to drive a car, you are not yet ready to drive a Lamborghini at 200 mph. But if you practice and receive good guidance and teaching, you can get there—if that's your goal.

> **The key to success is to access our state of flow or zone (inner state) and to integrate it with our specific job skills (outer state). Accessing and utilizing both sides of our dual nature will achieve our best results.**

Awareness Success Stories

There are many professionals of various types who can help you to expand your awareness, your consciousness, your goals, your personal fulfillment ... YOUR SUCCESS. I suggest you find the style of work and, most importantly, the proper individual for your personality and goals. The results can be quite amazing.

I have personally worked with many individuals, executives, and business owners assisting them to better understand their internal self, their talents, their goals and challenges, their aspirations, and other aspects of awareness and consciousness. The two techniques I use frequently are one-on-one personal conversations and group improvisational sessions. Clearly, these techniques are quite different in form, yet personal discoveries are made in each. In both techniques, I work at their speed and within their parameters. It is like a dance between us—a dance of flowing conversation and energy to discover and explore what is important to emerge. Sometimes the smallest discovery turns out to be quite profound. In all cases, there is no forced agenda but instead an attempt to create a flowing exchange that opens the unconscious to creative gifts.

Following are a few examples of awareness success stories derived from these two awareness modalities. A cautious note: if viewed only intellectually with your left brain, you may read these and think these are logical and not remarkable, and that would be reasonable. The secret is that these individuals *felt* the discovery versus simply understanding it with their minds. This then becomes an experience that the entire body understands and remembers—an experience that is beyond a logical conversation. Below are a few stories—first from one-on-one sessions followed by some group improv sessions.

One-on-One Sessions

Finding your true inspiration

In one example, a woman named Joan was a marketing expert whose business was declining during the Covid pandemic. She was naturally upset over the decline in business and somewhat depressed. Although our discussion started by addressing the low level of business, further discussion identified her lack of inspiration, not from the lack of business but, from the loss of the interpersonal connections. In addition, in discussing the various aspects of her business, she had an "aha" moment when she discovered that her greatest joy—perhaps even greater than her marketing design work—comes from connecting organizations that have synergistic needs. Understanding these elements, she began to make changes to better align with the activities that inspire her. Her joy returned and fulfillment returned. This could not be told to her but instead had to be discovered and felt by her.

Exercising leadership through delegation and visionary growth

In another case, Steve was the owner of a small but growing financial management firm. The original purpose of our call was to help him with his discomfort in asking existing clients for referrals. However, and not unusual, we uncovered a more immediate issue that was not thought to be a problem. That issue entailed his feeling overly responsible for personally performing many operational tasks and his discomfort in asking others to perform them. We discussed his feelings of burdening others with such tasks and of the importance of him to delegate them in order for him to perform the more expert tasks unique to him. He released his misconception of burdening others by realizing that the employee's expanded role (with a minor pay raise) was received as a positive endorsement and confidence of their work.

He also realized that he would be activating his leadership role as CEO of a growing company, one that would be required repeatedly at each phase of their growth. His awareness of this allowed for both he and his employee to feel much more satisfied about their work.

Regarding the original issue, we also reframed his original thinking of "bothering" his clients. The positive reframing included his understanding that he would be complementing his clients by telling them he wanted a few additional clients with high quality that they exhibited, that their intended growth with these new clients was to offer additional services to all clients including them, and that the referring client would likely receive praise from the new client once they experienced the quality of his work. His new awareness of these positive qualities essentially eliminated any feelings of bothering the clients. And again, these needed to be discovered and felt by him versus any intellectual advice, even if identical in nature.

Integrating heart and humanity for a more holistic presentation

In another case, John was the owner of an IT firm. His work was pristine, accurate, and reliable. Although his clients totally appreciated his work, his outreach to potential new clients was less successful than anticipated. During our conversation, he was exclusively in his left brain providing clear answers in a relatively robotic conversation. However, during the conversation, there were brief glimpses of the social side of his personality where he actually smiled and laughed in a more relaxed manner. I noted these differences and asked him for his assessment of those differences. They could be noted as business/social, mind/heart, or left brain/right brain. After some discussion, he realized that his perception was that clients were looking only for his technical skills versus any social interaction. He realized this inaccuracy and accepted that most clients would like to additionally connect with his humanity and heart. This connection would bring about trust, caring, and humanity to the already robotic accuracy of his specialty. His awareness showed him that not only was the heart connection not a problem, but it was in fact an asset that presented a more holistic personality to the client. Once this awareness set in, his entire body relaxed and a smile came to his face, and I am certain that this new composition is now naturally shown more frequently.

Improv Workshop Sessions

The power of listening

After some listening exercises in a Philadelphia improv workshop, a participant said, "Listening is key. I always want to talk and give my point of view, in business (sales) and at home. But when I do that, it's tough for me to focus and listen to the other person. I guess I have my agenda. But I see that when I do listen, I better understand what's going on with them and we have a better conversation. The talk may not go the way I planned it, but it goes better."

Listening to the true sentiment

At a workshop in Hackensack, New Jersey, a participant said, "I was amazed by the exercise where someone said one thing but meant something totally different. I experienced that exercise as the giver and receiver, and it impacted me. I now understand that I need to listen more deeply—to the true sentiment under the words."

A manager's awareness

During some YES AND improv exercises, a New York manager said, "I'm so used to saying no to my employees and shutting them down. I'm slowly changing to really listen to them, and I see that there's better teamwork that way."

Deeper communication

After a few connecting and communication exercises at a Stonybrook, New York, workshop, a participant said, "In many conversations, people talk *at* each other without really connecting with each other, and the conversation is frequently flat. When we were guided to make eye contact, I actually 'felt' the other person and the communication was so much better. I see that a real connection is a critical part of a good communication."

Acceptance

A succinct comment was made at a New York workshop, "I was delighted to see how conversations go more smoothly when I am more accepting of the other person."

These are but a few examples of only two modality types from one practitioner—me. There are a plethora of awareness techniques and a wide variety of talented facilitators to help guide you with your process. I suggest you explore, explore, explore—and have fun doing so!

Success? Maybe! (A Personal Story)

There is a Taoist story that is quite poignant, and perhaps even controversial to western culture. I present it as food for thought.

I don't know the author but its title is MAYBE and credit goes to the Taoist philosophies for its wisdom. Here is the story.

Maybe

There was an old farmer who had worked his crops for many years. One day his horse ran away. Upon hearing the

42

news, his neighbors came to visit. "Such bad luck," they said sympathetically. "Maybe," the farmer replied.

The next morning the horse returned, bringing with it three other wild horses. "How wonderful," the neighbors exclaimed. "Maybe," replied the old man.

The following day, his son tried to ride on of the untamed horses, was thrown, and broke his leg. The neighbors again came to offer their sympathy on his misfortune. "Maybe," answered the farmer.

The day after, military officials came to the village to draft young men into the army. Seeing that the son's leg was broken, they passed him by. The neighbors congratulated the farmer on how well things had turned out. "Maybe," said the farmer ...

The takeaway is pretty clear: what seems to be a current tragedy or success may actually be different in the long term. This wisdom speaks to our immediate judgments of good and bad and that perhaps we should simply consider that things *just are*. I realize this is quite Zen and may be difficult to employ in all aspects of our lives. But to the degree that we can embrace this level of non-attachment, we will more easily establish a balanced state of equanimity. We will of course enjoy the victories and be saddened by the defeats but to a lesser extreme, thereby avoiding severe pendulum swings of emotions. And when we place these victories and defeats in perspective with our lives, these reduced extremes seem more appropriate.

I have personally had many of these experiences. In general, I am not a big fan of change yet change seems to be constant in my life. When I studied the Chinese philosophy of *The I Ching, or Book of Changes*, I was awakened to their concepts whereby life consists of *nothing but* changes. Although I was resistant, I began to understand it on at least on an intellectual level. Embracing it more fully is the next step, which I continually pursue.

In my business career I have experienced much change over the years. During my time working for other organizations, I seemed to be either promoted or fired. The separations were always quite painful but I always found a better job afterwards. After seeing this pattern several times, I began to trust that this positive outcome would occur again and therefore was less affected by the separations. Although still quite painful, I saw that they were not necessarily horrific events as the eventual outcomes were always positive.

In my personal life, the separations were far more intense as they involved divorces and financial losses. Although much more intense than the career separations, and requiring much more time for healing, I always ended up in a better place—eventually. Some call this growth through struggle, though I wish there was an easier formula.

My most intense career change happened for me during the period from 1999 to 2015. I had created a software development company in 1986 with a typical American style story. I started my business alone in the basement of my condo, added people as it grew, and got thrown out of the basement by the "condo police" when FedEx trucks arrived daily and my four employees were taking up visitor parking spaces. I then leased my first official office space and seemed to move every three years as the company grew. At its height in 1998, we were fifty-plus people with nineteen international distributors and yielding approximately ten million dollars of annual revenues.

This fast-growing company was attractive to many. One party wanted to take us public—I refused since I did not wish to be subject to the young MBAs on Wall Street questioning my quarterly earnings, especially as I was always strategizing for the long term. **Was that a good decision? Maybe!** (I think yes as we were not quite structured for me to spend time away from the office promoting the firm. But who knows?).

The next structural opportunity occurred when another software company of similar size approached me to merge in order to create a larger organization that would be more attractive to buyers. I found the manner in which they approached me to be insulting and reacted with a clear no. They later sold their company for forty-three million dollars of stock. Although I believe that stock value declined, I understand that the equity executives were all compensated quite well. **Was that a bad decision? Maybe!** (Although I may have been well compensated, I believe I would have lost my organization merging into theirs and perhaps also lost my soul. But who knows?)

The third major structural change occurred in 1997-1998 when I engaged with a merger and acquisition organization to explore the possibilities of a merger/sale. Our company was strong, with excellent products, a strong internal and international structure, thousands of customers including a strong Fortune 500 client base, and an excellent reputation. The company was valued at approximately thirty million dollars. Although there was very good initial interest, time passed and the window of opportunity closed. There is a sweet spot to purchase a company. Although there are exceptions, the company needs to have a product that is proven, a satisfied client base (albeit small), some semblance of a management structure, and a clear vision of high-growth in the near future. If placed on the market too early, the valuations and interest will be low as the risks are too high, and if placed too late, the buyers will miss the growth phase. I basically started the M&A process one and a half years too late, especially considering that one of our major product lines was for Y2K migrations. **Was that a bad decision? Maybe!**

Starting that process too late certainly looked like a very bad decision. The only thing worse might have been if I had gotten a lowball bid (e.g., ten to twenty million dollars) and turned it down! I can't imagine my reaction and level of regret if I had turned down that offer and never received another. Also, if I had achieved those golden millions, where would my life be? I thought I'd consult, but in retrospect, I would have never known failure and would be unable to understand anyone else's. I may have assumed, consciously or unconsciously, that they must be inadequate rather than fully understanding all the controllable and uncontrollable factors, and to understand that contraction is part of the life cycle. But who knows? Perhaps this "failure" allowed me to discover my true mission!

The years that followed were more than challenging. Although we had new products developed for post-Y2K, the business slowed dramatically and layoffs were necessary. Business would level off with the hopes of a resurgence, but it was not to be. After each leveling off, there was another downturn and additional layoffs. Exacerbating the situation included the .com bubble burst, the 2008 economic downturn, and seemingly every other uncontrollable negative influence. The cycle of downturns, layoffs, leveling off, and downturns continued until 2015 ultimately resulting in total dissolution. Some had recommended dissolving the company sooner in order for me to retain some of the revenues, but I could not bring myself to abandoning this office family that we created. **Was that a bad decision? Maybe!** (It certainly seemed so).

Although we did not formally file for bankruptcy, we executed an informal insolvency with legal assistance, and during that period, the deeper principles and personalities of all our stakeholders came to light. For example, our customers understood the situation and were grateful for the help we gave them over the years; our vendors equally understood; our creditors exhibited a spectrum of understanding—all were negotiated, but some were very flexible while others were not. The various partner organizations who helped co-develop software with us understood our situation, felt badly for us, and forgave any debt that was owed them—those were very heartfelt conversations and immensely appreciated. Our employees reflected a wide variety of reactions. One employee demanded full benefits with the threat of legal action; most were concerned but understood the need for pay cuts and the ultimate layoffs; and a few dedicated and special souls worked for no pay with the hopes of a revival—they were not independently wealthy and I will never forget their heartfelt offering and sacrifice. In general, I felt blessed with the responses from almost all of my stakeholders. While some call it karma, I was appreciative of the good relationships that I had with these organizations, professionals, and friends. They were concerned for my welfare and they were there when I needed them. I am more than grateful!

After the dissolution of that firm, I did some business consulting for others while simultaneously engaging in other entrepreneurial endeavors. My consulting wisdom was far better than it would have been had I not experienced the contraction of my company. I have often said that I learned ten times more during the contraction phase of my company than during the growth phase. The challenges are far different in each phase. In a growth phase, there's pressure to stay ahead of the action, to keep up with the growth of clients, employees, operations, marketing, supplies, and general demand for your products/services. There are challenges but there is also excitement in the air since you are reaching your goals and positive activity is abound. The pressures are high, mostly good pressures, frequently related to overwhelm, perhaps chaotic, and perhaps more difficult for those who prefer a steady environment, but generally positive.

In a contraction phase, the challenges and pressures are quite strong since survival is at stake. Fear, disappointment, and failure can be intense emotional responses from all involved. In a sense, you see "what people are made of," you see how they react to adversity, how they handle the challenges of failure. It is generally not pretty. You learn a lot about yourself and those around you. Do you blame yourself or others? Can you see the issues clearly? Can you make decisions from a centered place? Do you attack others? Can you see a way out? Can you see the clear reality and can you accept it? Experiencing a contraction is a profound learning experience that requires deep skills including courage, understanding, grace, creativity, and acceptance—a deep and difficult learning.

My next entrepreneurial endeavor was with a new partner-developer friend of mine. We started a software company that provided tracking information for volunteer ambulance squads. Our product was extremely successful and was growing in momentum until the state provided these ambulance squads with a free version of a different product. Clearly, this was difficult to compete against especially considering that the squads had very tight budgets.

My next endeavor was to partner with a scientist whereby we created a B Corporation offering advanced medical technology for body-mind healing modalities. The product was comprehensive and was catching on in various market sectors, but the developer could not keep pace with the competition and our margins were too small to support two executives. After two years, I left leaving the company to my partner scientist.

Were these bad decisions? Maybe!

To support myself during these explorations, I was using savings including retirement funds. Those funds were totally exhausted by early 2015. At that point, I was down to absolute zero in all accounts and all assets, and I remember thinking to myself that I am living what I used to teach—that "security is an illusion." I used to give an unusual talk in one of the classes in my workshop "Business Success through Inner Wisdom." I would tell the students "security is an illusion," that there is truly no material security—if you work for a company, you could get fired even if you had a contract; if you had a family you could lose them; if you had money in the bank, you could lose it through lawsuits, the economy, and/or bank failures. The only thing you really have is yourself and your connection to a higher source (if you believe in such a source). I realized that I was actually living what I used to teach. It was then that I wished I had taught a different subject! But it was that belief that helped me through this difficult period.

During those years, the stress levels were off the chart, especially as a divorce was in the mix of the business downturn, informal bankruptcy, and anticipated home foreclosure. I used every tool in my bag to manage stress, including every form of meditation that I knew, playing tennis and drumming to release the stress and find joy, being with loved ones, losing my linear mind in a good movie, and more. Despite all that, the accumulated stress reached my physical body requiring six surgeries in a one-year period. Being in such pain, and seeing no relief, there were several evenings when I went to sleep conversing with source saying, "If I don't wake up tomorrow morning, it's okay." Although in a very dark place, I continued with my daily meditations and holding faith in my beliefs of a higher source/ purpose/self or whatever. I just knew there was something more than this. I didn't know if I would succeed in climbing out of this hole but I also knew there was no other option. I forged on. **Was that a good decision? Maybe!** (I believe very much, yes.)

Immediately after reaching financial bottom in 2015, things began to turn around. I obtained a stable consulting gig that allowed me to pay my normal bills including my refinanced mortgage. Normal life was returning and I was now breathing easier. A few years later, I decided to complete my MBA that was missing the required thesis. It was here that I met Professor Farias who, as mentioned earlier, has since become a good friend. I did two independent studies with him researching conscious organizations and also the feasibility of using improvisational principles with those organizations. (I had not been aware of the intersection of improvisation and corporate management.) Once I began that process, many doors opened up amazingly and quickly for me. I connected with people and organizations in the world of improvisation and management, including AIN (Applied Improvisation Network), a volunteer organization consisting of a global community of improvisers who apply improv practices to organizations, nonprofits, and society in general. As a matter of synchronicity, I learned about this organization one week before their annual conference. I attended and met many generous and heartfelt people who promote this work and with whom I expect to remain friends for many years.

I was also referred to several peer advisory organizations. I joined several of these and continue to work with them in helping me define my new message. Again, I find these professionals to be very generous, caring about how to best serve clients and society, and concerned for each other's welfare. It has been during this time and through these discussions that I have reignited **my primary mission—to bring greater consciousness, awareness, and authenticity to the business world, in order to better serve all stakeholders and society in general.**

This was not my original mission. My initial mission from childhood was to get a good job and make good money, i.e., develop financial security. This mantra emanated from my immigrant family who worked in sweatshops and constantly stressed over whether they had enough money to put food on the table. Layoffs were regular and the stress of a weekly paycheck was constant. On the positive side, we had family, love, constant play with our hundred cousins, great food, and great communal fun. The only thing missing was the money and hence that was our mantra. I was so focused on this mantra to the exclusion of all others and to the exclusion of even my primary mission.

During the financially prosperous years before the business contraction, I saw that having the money was satisfying my original mission but didn't bring me greater joy or happiness, and also made my life much more complex.

But now that I have gone full circle, I can see the wisdom in not achieving those millions, not retiring prematurely, and likely becoming a naïve consultant. Instead, I took a circuitous route to identify and reignite my primary mission. I also see that I could not have embarked upon this true mission without having first experienced the business world to the degree that I have, including both the up and down cycles. I am now in a very excellent place.

The universe works in mysterious ways! **Was all this a good decision?** I very much think yes, but the Taoist would say **Maybe!**

PART TWO

MINDFULNESS/AWARENESS—
Tools and Suggestions

Chapter 4

Concepts of Self

"To know thyself is the beginning of wisdom." Socrates

"Man know thyself; then thou shalt know the Universe and God." Pythagoras

---

Chapter Highlights

1. The human system has been described, in frequently similar ways, as being comprised of certain high-level components, such as body, mind, and soul. This presentation allows for easier analysis and discussion.
2. Although our system components can be viewed to each have a different quality, purpose, or expertise, they are all part of the one system.
3. Balance and alignment of these attributes is key.
4. Learn how to identify your personality traits.
5. Authenticity, the basis of genuine communication, requires alignment and courage.
6. Values are a reflection of our deeper selves and a focus of our personal growth.

In this chapter, I will introduce concepts that pertain to our inner, deeper, and true selves. Specifically, these concepts will include our awareness, various interpretations of our human system, our goal for inner balance and alignment, personality traits, the quality of our authenticity, and our internal or core values.

Understanding these concepts is critical as foundational data prior to discussing their importance and effect in applying them in our daily lives.

In subsequent chapters, I will then offer you tools, exercises, and suggestions that have been found helpful to access and understand this deeper self, in order to achieve higher levels of awareness and consciousness.

A variety of practices and techniques will be presented with the goal of connecting you to a few that would be in harmony or alignment with your particular personality and being. The offering will include various forms of meditation to achieve a deeper inner state, mindfulness techniques that can be applied to our normal daily activities, and various psychological modalities—all with the goal of accessing your deeper, authentic, inner selves.

Awareness

The individual human is a complex system of mind, body, and more. Sages over the centuries have analyzed, philosophized, and conjectured about how the human system operates. The medical industry examines the complexities of the human anatomy and all of its interrelated systems; the psychologists analyze the human emotional components; the philosophers speculate on the workings of the mind; and many contemplate our connection to an invisible dimension generally termed as spiritual.

Understanding our human system will help us to maintain and improve it, and as with all complex systems there are different levels of understanding. When studying any complex system, it may be relevant or helpful to analyze other similar systems to understand their internal dynamics as they may be analogous to our own. In engineering schools, we study the similarities between electrical systems, thermodynamic systems, and mechanical systems, noting differences and similar dynamics that may be helpful analogies. Let us look at our understanding of our automobile system as an analogy for how we operate our human system.

Our automobile is a complex system of which we are all familiar and of which we each have a different level of understanding of its operations. At the most basic level of understanding, we know that we must insert gasoline into the tank in order for the engine to operate; we understand that there is a battery that keeps the electrical systems properly charged; we understand that the tires need the proper air pressure to support the vehicle; and we understand that we must take the vehicle to an expert from time to time for more in-depth maintenance and repair. A greater level of understanding of the automobile system might include knowing how to perform certain maintenance functions (change the oil or wiper blades) or being aware of when the system is not operating at peak efficiency (gas mileage dramatically decreasing, wheels out of alignment, engine performance not optimal). Even with this greater understanding, we may likely still need outside experts for more challenging issues.

How do we know when an issue arises and attention is needed? There are two major factors to help us with this: first, the depth of our knowledge of the system and its components and, secondly, our attentiveness and awareness of the system. The greater the knowledge and awareness, the sooner the issue can be identified and addressed, thereby minimizing negative effects, and elevating the system back to optimal efficiency. If you are unaware of these warnings, the system will continue to deteriorate until awareness eventually occurs (as per the expression, "He needs to be hit over the head with a two-by-four before he sees it"); and if awareness never occurs, the system will fully break down. As an example of that, I know of a situation where there was no awareness of oil leaking out of an automobile engine that ultimately caused it to seize and die, rendering the automobile totally useless.

Therefore, we can see that the earlier detection would allow us to better maintain the system in its healthiest condition. We also note that it does not matter if we fix the problem ourselves or get expert help to bring the system back into its fullest health. The keys to this early detection are *knowledge* and *awareness*, and the key to maintaining optimal health is to take the necessary *action* to address the issue.

Clearly this analogy is also true for our own human system. The keys are *knowledge* and *awareness* of when our system is not optimal and taking appropriate *action* to address the issue. Just as with our automobile, the sooner we become aware of our situation, the sooner we can address the issue minimizing negative impacts, and it is knowledge and awareness of our system that will help communicate this information to us. Therefore, it behooves us to understand certain basics of how our system operates and perhaps more importantly, to develop and practice the *awareness* and sensitivities to the various components of our human system.

Our Human System

The human system has been described, in frequently similar ways, as being comprised of certain high-level components, such as body, mind, and soul. These can be considered macrolevel components where much greater detail is studied and available within each of those components. Following are some common examples of these macrolevel definitions:

Mind/Body—This is one of the most basic and simplest descriptions of the human system denoting us as being comprised of two major components. There is a separate study of each: medical professionals studying the body, and psychologists and philosophers studying the mind, with some studying the integrated mind/body connection. This mind/body connection has been a major source of study in this last century, offering better understandings of how one affects the other.

Mind/Heart—This is another pairing of components that describes the human system. Although we may have been taught that the mind is superior or more intelligent, studies from *HeartMath, Inc.* have determined "that the heart actually sends more signals to the brain than the brain sends to the heart. Moreover, these heart signals have a significant effect on brain function—influencing emotional processing as well as higher cognitive faculties such as attention, perception, memory, and problem solving."

Their research also explains how decisions made under a stressful condition may not be optimal, stating, "During stress and negative emotions, when the heart rhythm pattern is erratic and disordered, the corresponding pattern of neural signals traveling from the heart to the brain inhibits higher cognitive functions. This limits our ability to think clearly, remember, learn, reason, and make effective decisions." This research corresponds to the common statement that "high emotions cloud clear thinking," or the advice to not make any major decisions when you're highly emotional. They also note the converse stating, "In contrast, the more ordered and stable pattern of the heart's input to the brain during positive emotional states has the opposite effect—it facilitates cognitive function and reinforces positive feelings and emotional stability."

This revelation relates to the questioning of the optimal decision-making process. Do we include the heart, in addition to the mind, in our decision-making process? If so, to what extent? And what about conflicts? How often have we heard, "My heart wanted XYZ, but my brain knew it was not good for me"?

This seeming conflict is akin to the dynamics of polarities common in our universe. Relating to the human system, we can discuss a polarity of the two hemispheres of the brain—commonly called the left brain and right brain. (I understand there are studies denouncing the previous understandings that the left hemisphere of the brain is primarily dedicated to logical and linear thinking while the right hemisphere of the brain is dedicated to intuitive and creative thinking, and that the connection between the two occurs via the corpus callosum. Rather than denounce or debate our evolving sciences, let us accept the premise of the existence of attributes of linearity and nonlinearity, and, for the sake of this discussion, let us use the term "left brain" to generally refer to linearity and the term "right brain" to generally refer to nonlinearity, as these attributes exist regardless from where they emanate.)

Getting back to our example of the mind/heart, some have compared the mind to the left brain and the heart to the right brain. Whether this comparison is fully accurate or not, it allows us to look at a pairing of polarities within a system. In the system of left/right brain, I have always maintained that the best decision-making results from the activation and use of *both* polarities of the brain. For example, if an idea spawns from the intuitive mind, that it be verified and consulted by the left brain, and conversely, if the logical mind initiates a thought and proves it to be logically positive, that the intuitive right brain be activated for review and consultation, and that only when both sides of the brain agree should one move forward with that idea. In this sense, we are making the decision on a proposed idea by utilizing two different aspects of ourselves: the linear aspect and the nonlinear aspect. The linear aspect would likely take the form of "checking out the numbers," i.e., performing all the numerical and business analysis appropriate for this idea. The nonlinear aspect would likely consist of intuition, creativity, getting a "feel" for the idea. These are clearly different aspects, each of which are important to the review of the idea, and each having an expertise and offering that is critical to the decision-making process.

In general, we have been well trained in the linear aspect of the decision-making process (formal education as well as on-the-job training) and I will in this book present several practices for the nonlinear component of our system (awareness, mindfulness, meditation, etc.).

Mind/Body/Soul—This is a very common description that adds an invisible etheric component to the visible body and the tangible mind. There is a range of meanings of the word "soul," from the very religious concept of an invisible spiritual element residing somewhere in, or connected to, the physical body that lives forever and is the connection to the creator, to the nonreligious philosophical references of "the soul of a man/woman" referring more to his/her essence or values.

Physical/Emotional/Mental/Spiritual and *Physical/Emotional/Mental/Intuitive/Spiritual*—This is a more refined or detailed description of the human system, delineating the system into more detailed components for analysis and review.

In all the examples above, the purpose of delineation is to allow us to look more closely at, and bring more awareness to, certain components of our human system. The more detailed the delineation, the more separately we can study and refer to the individual components. As an example, if we wish to discuss or study the subject of temperature, it would be easier for us to communicate via certain subdivisions. If we wish to study a temperature range from zero to one hundred Celsius, we could make a simple dualistic division of temperatures above and below fifty degrees, define each component as cold and hot, and use the words hot and cold for easier communication. If we wish to study and communicate ranges finer than fifty degrees, we would declare additional ranges, e.g., we could denote nine temperature ranges and name them boiling hot, very hot, hot, warm, tepid, cool, cold, very cold, and ice cold. We would define the exact temperature range for each category and use the category names for easier communication. And of course, if nine ranges were too many, we could define fewer, as needed. The point is that the number of components defined is a matter of personal preference based on the intended study, analysis, and need. The systems are not any different whether we define one category or nine categories. As such, in the example of nine components, the components are not truly independent from each other—they interrelate and coexist with each other and are truly all part of the one system.

In summary, the delineations in all the above examples are arbitrary; the components defined are equally arbitrary and used for analysis and understanding; that consequently you cannot separate one from the other; and that they are truly all one. (This understanding of oneness can be applied to many other systems—perhaps all.)

Balance/Alignment

The components of our system noted above can be viewed to each have a different quality, purpose, or expertise. Whichever component system we review, we can see that different activities require and involve a greater emphasis on certain components over the others. For example, if we are running, gardening, or painting a house, our physical subsystem is engaged to a greater extent; if we are joyful over the birth of a newborn, or mourning over the loss of a loved one, our emotional body is more activated; if we are performing a mathematical problem, our mental body is more engaged; if we are walking the beach relaxing and opening toward inspiration, we are accessing our intuitive component; and if we are in deep prayer or meditation, our spiritual self is predominantly engaged.

Although, in these situations, there is one component that is primarily active, our other components are still part of the process. The example above—analyzing temperature ranges in nine categories—demonstrates that although our attention may be narrowly focused on a certain component, that component is part of the greater whole. Using another analogy, if we are running, our legs and lungs may be considered more active than other parts of our being, although all parts are appropriately engaged in, and fully supporting, the activity.

It then becomes important to utilize the various components in the appropriate way for our specific activities, i.e., activate them to the appropriate extent in order to produce the optimal results. When we have these components available to us and use them appropriately, we are in alignment and our system is in balance.

In any of our activities, we may experience or cause an "out of balance" condition whereby certain components are out of balance with the whole depending on the intended activity. For example, we would not wish to activate the physical leg movement required for running when we are in a place of worship intending to pray or meditate; or it would not make sense for us to sit in a meditative position while attempting to run a marathon; or we would not wish to be in a highly emotional state while attempting to solve a challenging mathematical problem. Conversely, a dissonance would occur if we are at a funeral of a loved one and focusing on our mental component, preventing the natural opening of the emotional body; or if we focus on our work issues (emotional and/or mental) during a spiritual worship, preventing us from activating spiritual component; or if we totally focus on the physical body with incessant activity preventing us from feeling painful emotions. These examples reflect out of balance conditions of the components that make up our human system. If our awareness is developed and active, we will notice these conditions and will have the opportunity to take appropriate action to resolve the issues and recreate an aligned, balanced state of being.

In her book entitled, *Training to Imagine*, Kat Koppett discusses the importance of alignment as follows, "As we strengthen our physical and vocal instruments, align our bodies with our minds, and raise our awareness to the effects of our behaviors, we augment our communicative prowess."

Our system is intelligent—we know what a successful run feels like, i.e., we know which components are more active and which components are quieter; we know what a successful business meeting feels like; we know what a good cry feels like; we know what a successful prayer/meditation feels like. In these cases, our system is in balance, our components are active, interact and interrelate appropriately, and there is a natural overall positive flow to the process. This is a state of balance or flow, and when we are in a state of balance and flow, we are in alignment with our optimal self.

Mary C. Gentile PhD is the Creator/Director of Giving Voice to Values and Professor of Practice at the University of Virginia, Darden School of Business. In her book entitled *Giving Voice to Values*, she states, "… the fundamental stance we are taking in the Giving Voice to Values approach to values-driven action is one of alignment, of moving *with* our highest aspirations in our deepest sense of who we wish to be, rather than a stance of coercion and stern judgment, or of moving *against* our inclinations."

Personality Traits

Personality traits are characteristics and qualities that make us unique individuals. Since childhood, we have likely been told that we are either funny, stubborn, anxious, lazy, active, extroverted, introverted, open, secretive, or more. Hopefully, these were not told to us in an overly critical or malicious manner, but instead as observations of our tendencies that were totally acceptable (unlikely, but one could hope!). As children, we were likely sensitive to these comments and reacted in a variety of ways. Our reactions could have caused us to feel pride or shame and may have caused our behavior to be modified based on these comments, perhaps to the degree of requiring introspection and discussion with a friend or a professional.

Understanding who we are, our tendencies, and how we operate in the world is important self-awareness that we include in our decision-making processes. An introvert and an extrovert would react and operate differently in the same situation; similarly an open person and a secretive person would react differently. The important point is to honestly understand our personal tendencies and traits and to utilize them appropriately in our interactions and decision-making processes.

In *Giving Voice to Values*, Gentile offers several options for employees to voice to their true values based on the situation and based on their personality traits. Two quotes from her book demonstrate this. First, "There are many different ways to express our values (for example, assertion, questioning, research, and providing new data; persuasion, negotiation, setting an example, identifying allies); that some may work better in some circumstances than others; that we may be more skillful or simply more likely to use one approach than another, and so our ability to see a way to use that particular approach may be the most important determining factor in whether or not we speak." The second quote states, "Giving voice may mean simply asking a well-framed question allowing people to think in a new way about a situation; or ensuring that certain information is included in a proposal for decision-makers to see the longer-term impact; it may mean speaking quietly behind the scenes with someone who is better positioned to raise the issue; or it may mean simply finding another ethically acceptable way to accomplish an assigned task." In these quotes, Gentile presents a range of actions—to voice one's true values—based on the situation and based on your specific skills, and the more self-aware you are, the better you can manage and succeed in these situations.

There are many ways that will help you identify your personality traits. Comments and observations from parents and friends may be helpful but also possibly subjective and interlaced with their personal traits thereby biasing the information. Feedback from a professional therapist will likely be more accurate and objective. In addition, there are formal tests aimed at being more objective that have become popular.

Many professionals speak of the Big Five—openness, conscientiousness, extraversion, agreeableness, and neuroticism—commonly abbreviated as OCEAN. Developed in the 1970s by two research teams, one from the National Institute of Health and one from the University of Michigan, it is said that each person possesses these qualities in various amounts, and the different ratios is what makes each of us unique from the others.

Formal personality tests have become popular in the business world for hiring purposes and attempt to identify a variety of personal qualities. In a March 30, 2017, article entitled "Top 10 Most Popular Personality Tests," Michelle Liew lists the top ten tests. These include Meyer-Briggs Type Indicator, DISC, Winslow Personality Profile, Process Communication Model, Holtzman Inkblot Technique, Hexaco Personality Inventory, Neo Pi-R, Personality Assessment System, Birkman Method, and Enneagram.

In the world of improv, Billy Merritt and Will Hines describe three personality traits in their book entitled, *Pirate Robot Ninja, An Improv Fable*. Their theory is that every improv student has traits and things that are good and some things that need to be learned. They wish to celebrate your strengths while remaining humble about what's left to learn. They use the categories of pirate, robot, and ninja to describe three overall qualities required in an improv scene. The pirate is visual, demonstrative, physical, brash, and dangerous; they feel and react. The robot is logical, witty, intelligent, and fast to find a pattern; they think, remember, and see the absurdity. They then state that if the pirate is all "heart" and the robot is all "head," the ninja expertly blends both characteristics. Ninjas move with flexibility and precision to serve the highest good of the scene and the choices have an elegance that can be unappreciated to the untrained eye. These three traits are needed in an improv scene as they each bring something positive to the scene that is different and unique from the others, and the creative balance of utilizing these different traits is what the performers strive for. Although each of these traits lives within each of us, there is generally a predominance of one over the other and hence we may become identified, or even over identified, by one trait even as we are nurturing and growing the others.

I find it fascinating that they describe the pirate and robot as heart and head, a dichotomy that is discussed previously in this chapter. This is yet another example of duality and of the importance of each pole of the duality, and the constant search for the balance and blend of the two. The key again is to be aware, to learn, to integrate, and to balance these characteristics within ourselves, and within the improv scene, thereby enhancing the performance—in the improv scene and in life.

Then there are other systems that define unique personality traits that are less scientific and also controversial, such as astrology that identifies the effects the stars and planets have on us at the time of birth, and numerology that identifies our personality traits based on a numerical calculation of our birthdate. At this time, I will admit that my original profession was as a mathematician and, as such, I always looked for the proof of any situation. After all, we ended all of our papers with Q.E.D., the Latin abbreviation of *quod erat deomonstrandum*, which means "that which was demonstrated (proved)." Therefore, if it couldn't be proven, it didn't exist, or at least it wasn't worth our consideration. However, considering that the moon can dramatically affect an entire ocean on a monthly basis, can I conclude that there is no effect on the human body that is composed of over 50 percent water? I have no Q.E.D. for that argument, and by extension, for possible effects of other planets. I leave this controversy for your consideration.

Whether you choose a formal personality test, or whether you study with a therapist, or whether you receive information from friends and relatives, or whether you seek alternative advice, or whether you explore meditation, mindfulness, or psychology to better understand your personal traits, I believe we each have the responsibility to learn about ourselves and to grow and evolve in a positive manner. It is important to be self-aware of our personal traits and how we operate in the world. Self-understanding and self-awareness are critical, foundational information that will bring clarity to your life situations allowing you to make better decisions, advantageous to your well-being.

To help this process, in subsequent chapters, I will present many techniques, tools, and suggestions aimed to enhance your self-awareness.

Authenticity

Authenticity is a principle quality in all walks of life—in relationships, business, improvisation acting, international alliances, and more—as it is the basis of genuine communication.

Although the term genuine communication should be considered redundant, we have all seen situations where the verbal communication does not match the sentiment beneath the words, hence, ingenuous communication. A simple example of this occurs on a very frequent basis when one asks, "How are you?" and receives a curt reply of "Fine." Although this reply may be utilized because of time constraints, it is also frequently used outside of such constraints. Both in personal relationships and business relationships, inauthentic replies are often used to avoid speaking the truth. Whether this occurs because of fear of consequences or the unwillingness to be vulnerable sharing one's truth, inauthentic communication seems to occur regularly.

Fascinating is the belief that such a reply is frequently accepted as truth, i.e., that the speaker believes the listener is accepting the inauthentic comment as truth, and perhaps that belief is strengthened by the silence that may occur in response to the inauthentic comment.

How often have we said, "She said XYZ to me but I didn't really believe her"? In this case, we are savvy and sense that the verbal communication did not match the underlying sentiment. Have we ever watched a movie and said, "He's a bad actor"? This usually occurs when the actor's words are not matching their belief or underlying sentiment. In other words, we frequently have a sense when someone is not being authentic. Yet conversely, the person speaking inauthentically may somehow imagine that the listener is believing them. This is quite a disconnect.

In fact, there may be two disconnects in this process: one between the parties and the other within the person who is speaking inauthentically.

The disconnect between the two parties would certainly result in ineffective communications with consequences varying from incidental to catastrophic. We have certainly seen such disconnects in our personal relationships and in our workplace environment, with a corresponding range of consequences. There has been much written about improving such communications through the use of workshops, professional instructions, training practices, mediation, communication training, and more, as it is clear that better communications would yield positive and more effective results.

More difficult is to accept and analyze any disconnect within oneself. A major reason for this challenge is that there is no second person to witness and argue a different point of view. Instead, we must be honest with ourselves to identify any non-truths, and this is quite challenging as it requires both awareness and acceptance of the inauthenticity.

Such inauthenticity would generally relate to a misalignment within ourselves. For example, if you have a deep feeling of love or anger toward another, but are not fully aware of it or incapable of admitting it, you are out of alignment within yourself and any subsequent words that do not reflect the truth would easily be sensed as inauthentic. Your heart and mind are misaligned and out of balance.

If you are not self-aware, you could easily be speaking inauthentically unconsciously, i.e., you are not even aware of the disconnect within yourself. To further confuse the issue, the listener may in fact sense the speaker's truth of which the speaker is not even aware. How would you solve this dilemma?

To address issues of inauthenticity, you need to do the following three things:

1. Better understand yourself and be more self-aware
2. Be vulnerable in reviewing and accepting the truth of yourself
3. Be courageous to evolve and speak that truth

Only then will communications be authentic.

The importance of authentic communications cannot be overstated as its absence causes a wide range of challenging consequences.

Authenticity is an absolute requirement to perform improvisation effectively. In *Training to Imagine*, Kat Koppett states, "If you are conscious, aligned, and authentic, your nonverbal behaviors can catapult your effectiveness to increasingly higher levels of mastery. Although stretching in these ways might feel unnatural at first, these ways of expanding your performance range can have deep impact."

Within this book, I will discuss the criticality of authenticity and will provide several tools and exercises to assist you in the attainment of self-awareness, authenticity, and consciousness.

Values

The word values in this context refers to your internal or core virtues as described by philosophers, psychologists, and other thought leaders. When discussing the definition of these values, some list what they feel are the top ten virtues, while others list as many as fifty or more. Although the lists differ, they all present virtues and positive human qualities that are generally accepted as definitions or examples of personal values.

In *Giving Voice to Values,* Gentile offers definitions of values from two esteemed researchers—Martin E. P. Seligman and Rushworth M. Kidder—with Seligman noting six virtues of wisdom, courage, humanity, justice, temperance, and transcendence, and Kidder defining values as honesty, respect, responsibility, fairness, and compassion.

These values are clearly positive attributes of our human system and are best accessed and expressed when we are aware, authentic, and conscious. Therefore, it behooves us to develop self-awareness, understanding of our human system, balance, alignment, and authenticity. I believe that if these attributes are not at least moderately developed, it would be challenging to access and express core positive values, as there would likely be blockages (emotional or otherwise) preventing us from such access.

Values are not cognitive attributes but instead are reflective more of our inner or deeper selves. I do not believe we can point to a specific human subsystem as the exact location from which values emanate. Values seem to be more ethereal, or at least the location of these values. If I point to my body as I say the word values, I will likely point to my heart area but would also sense that it is more than the heart—bigger than the heart. Perhaps, therefore, our values emanate from our greater being centered around the heart. What is clear is that it is not centered around the mind; it is not cognitive. We can then say that values emanate from our heart-centered being and relate to our deeper or inner self.

Our deeper or inner self may also be a mystery to us as it is ethereal and unavailable to our physical touch. As such, it does not reside in the physical body; it does not reside in the emotional body as it is a quiet energy; and it does not reside in the mental body as it is not a cognitive attribute. Yet, we understand what wisdom, courage, respect, responsibility, and compassion are. Accepting that values are part of our being and a reflection of our inner or deeper self, our focus can then be to better understand our deeper self and to develop these inner qualities and values to become the best version of ourselves and to express our deepest, truest values.

Chapter 5

Meditation

"To a mind that is still. The whole universe surrenders."
Anonymous

"The soul loves to meditate, for in contact with the spirit lies its greatest joy." Paramhansa Yogananda

---

Chapter Highlights

1. The benefits of meditation are well documented and reviewed within.
2. The styles of meditation have been categorized as Sitting, Moving, and Guided.
3. For simplicity, I summarize a few suggestions for each category in this chapter. All styles are presented in Appendix B.

In this section, I will discuss the deliberate and separate activities of meditation emanating from various ancient and current traditions.

Historically, most meditation techniques emanated from Eastern philosophies thousands of years ago. Until recently, they were practiced almost exclusively by select groups of spiritual sects. In the last few decades, these techniques have become popular in the Western world for the purpose to access higher levels of consciousness and spirituality, while also to generate relaxation and inner calm in society's general population.

Although there are many forms and types of meditation, most sources agree on the general definition of what meditation is, regardless of its type or form. Below are a few examples:

Merriam-Webster

"To engage in contemplation or reflection. To engage in mental exercise (such as concentration on one's breathing or repetition of a mantra) for the purpose of reaching a heightened level of spiritual awareness."

NCCIH—The NIH National Center for Complementary and Integrative Health is the Federal Government's lead agency for scientific research on the diverse medical and health care systems, practices, and products that are not generally considered part of conventional medicine. They state, "Meditation is a *mind and body practice* that has a long history of use for increasing calmness and physical relaxation, improving psychological balance, coping with illness, and enhancing overall health and well-being."

Wikipedia

"*Meditation* is a practice where an individual uses a technique—such as mindfulness, or focusing the mind on a particular object, thought, or activity—to train attention and awareness, and achieve a mentally clear and emotionally calm and stable state."

Mosby's Medical Dictionary

Meditation therapy is *"a method of relaxation and consciousness expansion by focusing on a mantra or a keyword, sound, or image while eliminating outside stimuli from one's awareness."*

Psychology Today

"Meditation is a mental exercise that trains attention and awareness. Its purpose is often to curb reactivity to one's negative thoughts and feelings, which, though they may be disturbing and upsetting and hijack attention from moment to moment, are invariably fleeting."

I suspect that none of us are surprised with the similarity of these definitions, with the essence of each to go deeply within in order to achieve higher states of awareness and consciousness.

Benefits

The benefits of meditation span from the basic advantages of stretching our physical body, to calming our emotional state, to achieving an enlightened state of being, and to all variations in between.

There is much scientific and medical documentation regarding the benefits of meditation that demonstrate positive effects on the health of the body and its ability to access deeper levels of creativity and consciousness.

The *Mayo Clinic* suggests that the emotional benefits of meditation can include:

- gaining a new perspective on stressful situations
- building skills to manage stress
- increasing self-awareness
- focusing on the present
- reducing negative emotions
- increasing imagination and creativity
- increasing patience and tolerance

Additionally, they state that some researchers suggest that meditation may help people manage symptoms of conditions such as:

- anxiety
- asthma
- cancer
- chronic pain
- depression
- heart disease
- high blood pressure
- irritable bowel syndrome
- sleep problems
- tension headaches

Psychology Today states, "Practicing meditation can help clear away the mind's chatter. Studies show that meditating even for periods as short as 10 minutes increases the brain's alpha waves (associated with relaxation) and decreases anxiety and depression." They further state that "Meditation acts on areas of the brain that modulate the autonomic nervous system, which governs such functions as digestion and blood pressure—functions heavily affected by chronic stress. Many people find meditation an effective stress-reliever. Through its physiological effects, meditation has been found to effectively counter heart disease, chronic pain, and other conditions."

In an article by Emma Seppala PhD, she lists twenty scientific benefits of meditation, grouped into seven categories:

Health:

1. increases immune function
2. decreases pain
3. decreases inflammation at the cellular level

Happiness:

4. increases positive emotions
5. decreases depression

6. decreases anxiety
7. decreases stress

Social life:

8. increases social connection and emotional intelligence
9. makes you more compassionate
10. makes you feel less lonely

Self-control:

11. improves your ability to regulate your emotions
12. improves your ability to introspect

Your brain:

13. increases gray matter
14. increases volume in areas related to emotional regulation, positive emotions, and self-control
15. increases cortical thickness in areas related to paying attention

Your productivity:

16. increases your focus and attention
17. improves your ability to multitask
18. improves your memory
19. improves your ability to be creative and think outside the box

Wisdom:

20. gives you perspective

NCCIH—The NIH National Center for Complementary and Integrative Health, noting various studies conducted from 2009 to recently, investigated meditation for different conditions, and discovered evidence that meditation may reduce blood pressure as well as symptoms of irritable bowel syndrome and flareups in people who have had ulcerative colitis. They also discovered that it may ease symptoms of anxiety and depression and may help people with insomnia.

They state that some research also suggests that meditation may physically change the brain and body and could potentially help to improve many health problems and promote healthy behaviors.

Certain specifics they discovered based on the research were as follows:

- People who practiced meditation for many years have more folds in the outer layer of the brain. This process (called gyrification) may increase the brain's ability to process information.
- Meditation may slow, store, or even reverse changes that take place in the brain due to normal aging.
- Meditation can affect activity in the amygdala (a part of the brain involved in processing emotions), and that different types of meditation can affect the amygdala differently even when the person is not meditating.
- Research about meditation's ability to reduce pain has produced mixed results. However, in some studies scientists suggest that meditation activates certain areas of the brain in response to pain.

Positive Psychology notes five health benefits of daily meditation according to science:

1. meditation enhances empathy
2. meditation improves cognition
3. meditation is a natural stress stabilizer

4. meditation promotes emotional health and well-being
5. meditation increases the tension by inducing a state of flow

They offer scientific research in areas of pain and disease:

Pain:

- A study by the National Center for Complementary and Integrative Health (NCCIH) found that mindful meditation reduces pain sensations in the body without using the brain's natural opiates (Cherkin, Sherman, Balderson, Cook, Anderson, Hawkes, Hansen, and Turner, 2016). The research suggested that combining meditation practices with medication for treating pain conditions like osteoarthritis, headaches, and other chronic pains can be useful for providing long-term remedies.

Diseases:

- The NCCIH conducted studies to explore the impact of meditation on disorders like pain, fibromyalgia, stress disorders, migraines, hypertension, psoriasis, anxiety, and depression. Most of their research and reviews show that committing to a daily practice improves the overall quality of life and has long-term benefits for staying emotionally and physically healthy.
- Studies show that meditation had similar effects as medications in treating depression, anxiety, and other emotional problems.
- Meditation practice helped in reducing the anxiety associated with IBS and improved the individual's

quality of life to a large extent (Gaylord, Palsson, Garland, Faurot, Coble, Mann, and Frey, 2011).

In *Quantum Leadership*, Tsao and Laszlo discuss the benefits of meditation and offer explanations from the viewpoint of psychology, neuroscience, and quantum science. They state, "When we engage in sense-making or presencing practices, we are connecting to something greater than ourselves. In the perspective of quantum science and consciousness research, we are synchronizing in some way to the cosmos, not only loosening our frames of mind and quieting our automatic ways of thinking but also connecting to a generative field that underlies everything and helps heal and make us whole. When we connect with this field, we have instant (also called "nonlocal" in quantum physics and "transpersonal" in consciousness studies) direct-intuitive experiences that help us meet the challenges we face in life. A psychologist and leadership expert might say that the practices help us let go of our attachments ... or help us 'see what we are seeing' and become more aware ... A neuroscientist might say that the practices do this by strengthening the neural networks associated with positive emotions and reducing activity in the part of the brain that account for our sense of separateness and individuality and that they enable our brains to access quantum-level information ... A quantum scientist would suggest that the practices may be helping us connect to a universal vibration field of energy that helps make us whole (if we just slow down a little and let it) and increases our sense of oneness with others and all life on earth."

Meditation Styles

There are many styles and forms of meditation originating from the Hindu/Yogic tradition, the Buddhist tradition, the Chinese tradition, the Sufi tradition, the Christian tradition, and other forms presented as guided meditations.

The various traditions and styles would appeal to various personalities. In Appendix B, I describe each style and include a personal comment about each. In this section, I offer suggestions regarding which tradition and style may best suit you.

The specific meditation styles from these various traditions I will review are as follows:

Hindu/Yogic Meditations

- Transcendental Meditation (TM)
- Mantra Meditation (OM)
- Gazing Meditation
- Chakra and Third Eye Meditations
- Kundalini Meditation
- Tantra Meditation
- Pranayama and Kriya Meditation

Buddhist Meditations

- Zen (Zazen) Meditation
- Vipassana Meditation
- Mindful Meditation
- Loving Kindness Meditation (Metta Meditation)
- Walking Meditation

Chinese Meditations

- Taoist Meditations
- Qigong (Chi Kung)

Sufi Meditations

- Meditation of the Heart
- Muraqabah (Watch Over)

- Sufi Mantra Meditation
- Sufi Gazing Meditation
- Sufi Walking Meditation (Nazar bar Kadam)
- Sufi Whirling
- Sufi Zikr

Christian Meditations

- Christian Prayer
- Christian Reading
- Centering Prayer
- Sitting Meditation

Guided Meditations

- Relaxation and Body Scans
- Guided Imagery
- Sound Bath (Singing Bowls)

Yoga

- Classical Hatha
- Ashtanga/Vinyasa
- Iyengar
- Bikram
- Kundalini
- Yin/Restorative
- Integral Yoga

Mind Body Medicine

- Relaxation Response

Suggestions

- Sitting/Still Meditation
- Moving/Active Meditation
- Guided Meditation

Enthusiasts will generally explore and practice several of these meditative techniques, after which they will likely focus narrowly on a specific few. It is not my suggestion that you necessarily study or experience many of these practices, but instead explore them to match your personal preferences.

As I have been practicing meditation since 1970, I have personally experienced most, if not all, of the meditation styles listed in this section. I will first present you with my suggestions and recommendations for three different styles of meditation. The recommendations will include a brief description of the meditation with the fuller description of these and all the forms presented in Appendix B.

Suggestions

Since the meditation styles listed in Appendix B are many, and may be confusing, I suggest a categorization of these established traditions and styles into three distinct forms allowing you to select the form that is most suitable to your personality. And within each form, I will offer a few suggestions of specific styles for your consideration.

It is my goal that this simplification will help you determine the form that suits you best and the style within that form you most easily resonate.

The three forms or categories that I have organized for your consideration are:

1. Sitting/Still Meditation
2. Moving/Active Meditation
3. Guided Meditation

Sitting/Still Meditation

The sitting or still meditation would include those meditations that I consider most traditional, e.g., Zen or TM. In all of these meditations, you would sit in a comfortable seated and still position while performing the meditation. I offer three suggestions for sitting meditations (info on each is found in Appendix B):

Suggestion #1:

Zen, Mantra, or TM. Each of these meditations is straightforward and easy to learn. However, the difference is that the Zen meditation searches for emptiness, suggesting that your thoughts pass through your mind while both the Mantra and TM meditations focus specifically on a particular mantra. Therefore, if you find the emptiness of the Zen meditation difficult, you may find the focus of the Mantra or TM meditations more amenable to you.

Suggestion #2:

Gazing Meditation (Trataka or Sufi). The Gazing Meditation is one that is likely known to you already, as we have all stared at a vision of beauty, be it a sunset or a fire flame or the ocean waves breaking, at some point in our lives. This meditation basically extends that activity for a likely longer period of time and with the discipline of quiet and mindfulness.

Suggestion #3:

Loving Kindness Meditation (Metta Meditation). I suggest this meditation as it is also likely familiar to you, as we have all focused on a loved one whether it be a parent, child, spouse, or friend in a loving manner. Similar to the Gazing Meditation, this meditation basically extends an activity for which we are familiar by adding a longer time and a mindfulness discipline.

Moving/Active Meditation

In the moving meditations, you are not in a seated or still position but instead moving the physical body in a meditative and conscious manner. I suggest this style of meditation for those who have difficulty sitting in a still position (info on each is found in Appendix B):

Suggestion #1:

Sufi Walking Meditation (Nazar bar Kadam). I suggest this meditation because of its familiarity. It is likely that you have experienced this practice already—perhaps walking along the beach in solitary with peaceful silence, fishing alone on a quiet lake, or hiking alone in the woods. The Sufi Walking Meditation would focus on a walk in quiet solitude, noting sounds and smells, noting the reaction of the ground as you place your foot upon it, noticing your breath as you take each step, noticing the wind and other physical elements as you walk with discipline and intention in this meditative practice.

Suggestion #2:

Yoga. I suggest yoga as a full-body practice helpful to the body, emotion, mind, and spiritual centers of the body. Classes are provided at various levels, are generally easy to find, and the facilitators are generally very attentive to the students. The depth of this practice is quite scalable, i.e., applicable to the beginner as well as the expert, and from a very physical level to a much deeper meditative level. For beginners, I would recommend Classical Hatha yoga, Yin yoga, or Restorative yoga as they are relaxing and easy to follow. Noting yoga's popularity, it is likely that you have already tried a yoga class at some time. If so, and you did not enjoy it, I would recommend you try a hatha yoga or yin yoga class at a yoga center. Alternatively, you could try Qigong or Tai Chi, both of which would require a greater time investment to learn the movements.

Guided Meditation

In the guided meditations, there is a facilitator—live or recorded—who is guiding you in a variety of ways to help access the deeper levels of your consciousness. I suggest the following meditations (info on each is found in Appendix B):

Suggestion #1:

Body Scan Meditation. In this meditation, you need only follow the direction of the facilitator. It is quite easy, quite relaxing, and quite beneficial to your overall health. Any meditation or yoga center would likely offer such a meditation.

Suggestion #2:

Sound Bath (Singing Bowls). I suggest this guided meditation as it requires nothing of you except to lie down and enjoy it. The sounds and the beauty that emanate from the instruments are quite fascinating, relaxing, and intriguing. It is an experience that is generally extremely well received regardless of your level of meditative attunement or experience.

Suggestion #3:

Guided Imagery. I suggest this form of meditation if you are a bit more adventurous or curious. It is safe and the facilitator will take you on an imaginary journey, which will generally be quite pleasant and may also prove to be quite useful to you. Many yoga and meditative practitioners would offer this meditation.

Chapter 6

Mindfulness in Daily Activities

"The feeling that any task is a nuisance will soon disappear if it is done in mindfulness." Thich Nhat Hanh

"Be where you are, otherwise you will miss your life." Buddha

"Just don't give up trying to do what you really want to do. Where there is love and inspiration, I don't think you can go wrong." Ella Fitzgerald

---

Chapter Highlights

1. Mindfulness can be integrated into our daily activities without requiring additional time.
2. The "zone"—What is it, what's its benefit, and how do I achieve it?
3. Elite athletes use mindfulness and visualization in addition to rigorous physical training.
4. Businesses use creative visualization when they post sales goals, strategy directions, and corporate mission statements.
5. Music and art are natural arenas for mindfulness and can be used to induce the intuitive mind.

> 6. Mindfulness and flow can help you reach transcendence.
> 7. How to reduce stress at work.

Integrating Mindfulness

In the previous section, I discussed several activities including meditation and yoga that are deliberate activities aimed to achieve mindfulness, and are separate activities from our normal day's routine, i.e., you must carve out a specific amount of time from your schedule to perform the mindful activity, whether it be at home, at a meditation class, or a yoga center.

Let us now look at activities that we normally perform that do not require an additional and separate unit of time, i.e., our normal daily activities, and let us explore the possibility of integrating mindfulness into these activities. I believe that the integration of mindfulness into your normal activities would produce a higher quality activity, greater effectiveness, and a feeling of general well-being. For example, you can practice mindfulness during sports activity, singing, driving your car, walking, dancing, shopping, or any activity in your normal routine.

Experiment with these activities by observing yourself prior, during, and after the activity, and simply note your experience. Avoid the temptation of self-criticism or judgment, but instead just observe the experience. Follow this same process during subsequent visits to this activity. Simply watching yourself in this manner will cause you to be more mindful during the activity and likely have a more meaningful, effective, and positive experience.

I then suggest you further deepen the quality of the activity by being more mindful of each component of the activity, noticing every detail, focusing more deeply, and noticing each reaction to your actions. This focus will generally produce a deeper level of consciousness during the activity, a deeper satisfaction during the process, better self-understanding, and greater awareness.

We have all likely experienced these deeper mindfulness qualities at certain times during some of our personal activities. It may have happened while walking the beach, listening to your favorite music, dancing, playing tennis, reading a book, fishing, watching the sunset, etc. Mindfulness is therefore not unfamiliar to us. The goal, then, is to consciously apply mindfulness to additional areas of our lives, thereby facilitating a deeper and more fulfilling experience.

You may ask if these dynamics also apply to the work environment. There are some, perhaps older, systems of thought that carry the belief that work activities are generally challenging and stressful while personal activities are generally positive and fun. I feel that this belief does not serve us, and that positive outcomes will generally prevail—even in our work environment— if we are sincere, mindful, authentic, and genuine in all phases of our life. This in turn will provide the best possibility for success.

Let us now look at some examples of these regularly performed activities with the goal of understanding how we may have achieved that depth and consider how we may create it more frequently. We will explore these qualities as they pertain to our various sporting events, music/arts activities, mindfulness attitudes, and daily life activities, including our job.

Sports

There are many stories of athletes reaching a heightened state of awareness, a deeper level of consciousness, feeling "out of their body," being in "the zone," whereby their performance is at a level much higher than usual. In this state, they are almost "watching themselves" as they partake in the activity. They know they are performing at an incredibly high level and also feel that their body is on "automatic," and that some deeper level of ability and consciousness is in charge directing the body in this optimal performance.

It sometimes feels like a dream, is generally euphoric, and there is understandably a desire to have that state of consciousness continue for as long as possible. If fear or other emotions get interjected into this experience, it is likely that they will involuntarily lose that "zone." There is therefore a sense that they must remain calm and not disturb this supernatural feeling for it may easily leave them. It's quite a unique experience that is welcomed as frequently as possible.

We will explore these phenomena in sports activities in three categories:

1. Runner's high
2. Playing in the "zone"
3. Creative visualization and inner balance

Runner's High

In this section, I will review the runner's high and offer various opinions on the "what, why, and how" regarding this sensation in order to facilitate your understanding and pursuit of this phenomenon.

What

The term "runner's high" is one of the most popular terms referring to this state of consciousness and likely the most experienced by amateur athletes. The definitions and descriptions of the runner's high are quite consistent across medical, educational, and sports settings. Below are some such definitions from these various organizations.

Road Runner Sports defines a runner's high as "the feeling of pure elation, reduced stress, and a decreased ability to feel pain due to a flood of endorphins released by exercise .... Extreme happiness, serenity, motivation, and gratitude are all emotions commonly reported by athletes when the runner's high finally kicks in."

Scientific American describes runner's high as "a feeling of euphoria coupled with reduced anxiety and a lessened ability to feel pain."

WebMD quotes Jesse Pittsley, PhD, president of the American Society for Exercise Physiologists as saying, "Psychologically, runners may experience euphoria, the feeling of being invincible, a reduced state of discomfort or pain, and even a loss in sense of time while running."

Sarah Willet of Lehigh University states, "Many runners have had the opportunity to experience a state of euphoria while running .... Runners typically say that it is a pleasant state they might experience after a certain distance .... The body and mind are both highly stimulated and seem to elevate a person's senses ... when the environmental stimuli around you is near perfect and you are feeling good you are actually feeling a type of 'high' ...."

Why

The obvious question is why does a runner get this high, euphoric feeling? Below are some explanations by athletic and medical experts that discuss the age-old suggestions of release of endorphins and also subsequent understandings, or at least theories, of connections to endocannabinoids.

Runner's World refers to a statement made by David A. Raichlen PhD, a professor of biological sciences at the University of Southern California noting that "recently, researchers studied how the brain responds to running and found that the ability to get 'high' might be hard-wired within us, and that years ago, our ancestors' survival likely depended on chasing down food. The desire to live was probably their motivation to run and run fast, and the feel-good brain chemicals released when they did so may have helped them achieve the speed and distances required. The runner's high may have served (and serves today) as a natural painkiller, masking tired legs and blistered feet."

Road Runner Sports notes, "When you run for a consistent period of time at moderate intensity, your body produces the stress hormone called cortisol, which then stimulates that fun stuff (AKA endorphins and endocannabinoids)." They add, "Both endorphins and endocannabinoids are produced as a response to stress. Prolonged running puts stress on your bodily functions (no matter how well-trained you may be), which causes you to then pump out endorphins and endocannabinoids."

WebMD quotes Cedric Bryant, PhD, chief science officer for the American Council on Exercise as saying, "Runner's high is a phrase that we use to describe the feelings of psychological well-being that are associated quite often with long-duration, rhythmic-type exercise, and marathon running ... For a long time, people believe the answer lay within the whole endorphin argument—with long-duration exercise you release endorphins, which have a morphine-like effect on the body and therefore may be responsible for the feelings of well-being ... While our circular levels of endorphins might be up, whether that impacts a person's psychological outlook output directly is probably not that likely. In some studies when the effects of endorphins have been blocked chemically, people still experienced this high, so the whole endorphin argument has been called into question."

Bryant also states, "Norepinephrine secretion, dopamine, and serotonin have all been shown to help to reduce depression and these neurotransmitters also tend to be released and produced in higher concentrations during exercise, so people think that it may be some of these other biochemical substances, aside from endorphins, that might be responsible for this effect."

Scientific American notes that, "For decades, scientists have associated runner's high with an increased level in the blood of b-endorphins, opioid peptides thought to elevate the mood." They then note that "German researchers have shown the brain's endocannabinoid system—the same one affected by marijuana's THC may also play a role in producing the runner's high." *(Proc. Natl. Acad. Sci. USA 2015, DOI:10.1072/pnas.1514996112).*

They quote Johannes Fuss, at the University Medical Center Hamburg-Eppendorf as saying, "Researchers hit upon the endocannabinoid system as possibly being involved because they observed that endorphins cannot pass through the blood-brain barrier."

David A. Raichlen, also expert in human brain evolution and exercise, then at the University of Arizona, notes that research team's findings suggest that endocannabinoids such as anandamide help runner's high stating, "The authors have moved the field forward by providing such a complete view of how this key reward system is involved in allowing exercise to improve psychological state and pain sensitivity."

There are yet more experts suggesting that the runner's high is caused not just by endorphins but that endocannabinoids are involved. *RunnersConnect* refers to B. P. Sparling and colleagues at the University of California-Irvine who suggest this additional involvement of endocannabinoids. *RunnersConnect* also refers to a study published in the journal *Cognitive Neuroscience* where Sparling studied well-trained college students running and then taking blood samples to measure endocannabinoid levels, as endocannabinoids **do** cross the blood-brain barrier unlike endorphins and are therefore easier to measure.

Sparling subsequently indicated that runner's high is more than a simple surge in one chemical in the brain but rather a complex dance of psychoactive compounds released in response to exercise that boost your mood, raise your energy level, yet also relieves anxiety, and makes you feel calm and relaxed. Additionally, a 2007 study even found that an exercise program was just as effective as prescription anti-depressants in patients with major depressive disorder.

How

Since the runner's high is such a euphoric state of consciousness, many have asked for the formula to achieve such a state. Although most experts may not be able to provide the exact formula, most recommendations are quite similar. Below are a few of these recommendations.

Runner's World references Matthew Hill, PhD, an associate professor at the University of Calgary's Hotchkiss Brain Institute who recommends "you push yourself hard, but not too hard, noting that endorphins are painkillers produced in response to physical discomfort." He continues saying, "But that doesn't mean your runs should be excruciating; you need to find a sweet spot where they are comfortably challenging (think tempo run)."

Cindra S. Kamphoff, PhD, director of the Center for Sport and Performance Psychology at Minnesota State University states, "Most runners I have worked with experience endorphins when they are pushing their bodies, but not usually at max effort."

Road Runner Sports suggests these techniques in attempting to achieve a runner's high:

1. Run at 70 percent to 85 percent of your maximum intensity
2. Run for an extended period of time

3. Run consistently
4. Add intervals
5. Get enough sleep
6. Schedule days of rest
7. Zone out

RunnersConnect offers suggestions that expand beyond technical instructions and includes environmental and more holistic recommendations. They offer the following seven steps to increase your chances of experiencing a runner's high:

1. Make sure your easy days are slow enough
2. Run with others
3. Explore a new place to run
4. Soak in the achievement of others
5. Find what food works for you
6. Eat a good pre-run or race meal
7. Take a moment to reflect post run

As you can see, much has been written about runner's high—its effects on the body, the scientific theories discussing the reasons it occurs, and suggestions offering the highest likelihood of achieving such a state. In general, the information regarding the "what, why, and how" of the runner's high have great similarities and consistencies.

Playing in the "Zone"

The expression "playing in the zone" refers to the performance of an athlete who is playing at a level beyond their norm. For the athlete, it is a dream state of being, in that they are performing in a flawless manner, essentially playing their sport at their ultimate best. They are not necessarily performing beyond their abilities but instead executing each of their abilities flawlessly and with absolute precision. Clearly, this is a situation that is an extreme rarity, as imperfections are generally a common aspect of every performance. As such, playing in the zone is an extremely exceptional occurrence that athletes experience rarely, if ever.

We have all seen such ultimate performances by professional athletes including basketball players Bill Russell, Michael Jordan, Wilt Chamberlain, and Lebron James. We have seen quarterbacks in football playing "out of sight," we have seen baseball players hit "out of their minds," and we have seen tennis players striking the ball with astounding power and unbelievable precision, making little to no errors. These athletes were playing in the rarefied air called the "zone." Regardless of the sport you watch, it is very likely that you have witnessed athletic performances of this kind.

At the amateur level of sports in which we and the general public participate, it is expected and usual that we have experienced various levels of performance in our sporting events. As such, we can easily understand that the body and mind behave differently on different days. We can easily explain these differences based on levels of rest, physical fatigue, stress, distractions, and more. If we are fortunate, we will have experienced a special day where every physical and emotional component are at their maximal peak thereby allowing us to play our "A" game. And if we are extremely fortunate, this "A" game will rise to the level of "being in the zone." As those who have experienced this phenomenon tell us, you cannot force the "zone" or predict when it will occur, as it involves a multiple of criteria including peak physical condition, peak emotional condition, peak mental condition, and a deep connection to an inner self that allows all components of your being to coordinate in absolute perfection. Most will state that they were playing beyond their body and mind, in a "zone" of seemingly another dimension.

Dr. Jay Granat, sports psychologist describes this phenomenon as, "The zone is a state of mind which is marked by a sense of calmness. In addition, there is a heightened sense of awareness and focus. Actions seem effortless and there is an increased belief that your dreams or goals can become achievable and real. In addition, there is also a sense of deep enjoyment when the person is in this unique, special and magical state of being."

Comments from athletes in the "zone" include:

- Tennis professional Andy Murray stating, "I don't remember a thing about it," referring to an outstanding tennis match just played.
- Basketball great Kobe Bryant stated, "Everything just slows down; you have supreme confidence. You get in the zone and just try to stay there. You don't think about your surroundings, or what's going on with the crowd or the team. You're kind of locked in."
- Tennis star Serena Williams states, "If you can keep playing tennis when somebody is shooting a gun down the street, that's concentration and ultimately being in the flow."
- Legendary basketball coach Phil Jackson states, "In basketball—as in life—true joy comes from being fully present in each and every moment, not just when things are going your way. Of course, it's no accident that things are more likely to go your way when you stop worrying about whether you're going to win or lose and focus your full attention on what's happening right this moment."

- Former New York Yankees Mark Teixeira states, "It's just about being in the zone, in any sport, be it football, basketball or baseball."
- Tennis star Venus Williams states, "I didn't hear anything today. I didn't hear anyone. The only people I could hear were maybe in my box, but other than that most of the time I don't hear anything. I am in the zone."
- **"… being in the zone is like being in harmony with the universe, where the mind and body become one." Unknown author**

Flow

The terms "flow" or "zone" have been used interchangeably and have been applied to various fields of life, perhaps especially to sports performance. As discussed, they pertain to that optimal state of being that allows one to perform at their highest level.

In the article entitled, "FLOW: The Psychology of Optimal Experience" by Mihaly Csikszentmijalyi, the author describes flow as a state of concentration so focused that it amounts to absolute absorption in an activity. He discusses the merging of action and awareness, clear goals and feedback, concentration on the task at hand, the paradox of control, the loss of self-consciousness, and the transformation of time.

He also states that one typically experiences strength, alertness, effortless control, unselfishness, and operating at the peak of their abilities. Both the sense of time and emotional problems seem to disappear, and there is an exhilarating feeling of transcendence.

The obvious question becomes, "How does one achieve this flow?"

Exactsports.com references several authors as they discuss "flow" and how to achieve it. They reference the ten essential elements to achieve the flow as identified by Jackson and Csikszentmihalyi (1999). They present it as summarized by Weinberg and Gould (2011) as follows:

1. Balance of challenge in skills—For flow to occur it is imperative that the athlete believes they have the skills to successfully meet the challenges faced.
2. Complete absorption in the activity—The participant has total focus in the activity and that nothing else matters.
3. Clear goals—The goals are so clear that the athlete knows exactly what to do and enabling them to fully concentrate.
4. Merging of action and awareness—The participant is fully aware of their actions but not of the awareness itself.
5. Total concentration on the task at hand—The performer has total concentration to the point that crowd noise, their opponent, or other distractions do not affect them.
6. Loss of self-consciousness—Performers report that the ego is completely lost in the activity itself.
7. A sense of control—Although not actively aware of control, the participant is simply not worried about any lack of control.
8. No goals or rewards external to the activity—The performer participates purely because of the activity itself without seeking any other reward.

9. Transformation of time—Time is distorted for the participant, either speeding up or seemingly standing still.
10. Effortless movement—The athlete is performing well (extremely well) but is not thinking about it, nor appears to be trying too hard.

Although many references to "flow" and "zone" are made relating to the extremely high performance in a sports activity, this state of being can also be applied and experienced in the business environment.

In an article entitled, "Moments of Greatness" by Robert E Quinn, Quinn infers that the state of flow is what assists business managers to obtain the greatest moments of greatness.

He attempts to identify and seek the means to obtain these moments and states that these moments generally occur during a crisis but may also be developed as a skill to be accessed at any point in time. He notes that many leadership schools study the behaviors of those who have been successful and teach people to emulate them. But they have discovered that when leaders do their best work, they are not copying anyone, but instead being their deepest and truest self—quite unique from anyone else. Therefore, they have determined that to achieve the greatest moments of leadership depends not on how one emulates another leader, but instead occurs when any leader reaches their deepest fundamental state of mind.

He defines four characteristics for reaching this fundamental state:

1. to move from being comfort centered to being results centered
2. to move from being externally directed to being more internally directed

3. to become less self-focused and more focused on others
4. to become more open to outside signals or stimuli, including those that require us to do things that are uncomfortable

Summary

In the sections above, I have reviewed thoughts and experiences of various experts and athletes, some of which were relatable to our own personal experiences. As we review the totality of this information, we can easily see that to achieve the state of optimal flow, we must eliminate outside disturbances and find our deepest truth. We must quiet our emotions, quiet our mental chatter, and allow our consciousness to sink into its deepest and truest state of being. In this state, we are free from distractions, free from outside and inside voices, free from criticism, free from pressure, free from fears or concerns of achievement, free from anticipation, free from judgment, free from anticipated results, and basically free from any outside or inside criticism or influences that would keep us from accessing our deepest and truest self.

If this sounds familiar, it is because this process is quite similar to the process of meditation that we have previously described, and as such, those who have a regular meditation practice will likely have a higher probability of achieving these desired states.

My "Zone" Experiences

I have had the good fortune to experience the "zone" on a several occasions. I would like to describe three different experiences:

1. Finding and keeping the "zone"
2. Finding and working hard to maintain the "zone"
3. Finding and losing the "zone"

Finding and keeping the "zone"

I am an avid tennis player who never knows how I will play on game day, regardless of how good I may feel physically, emotionally, or mentally. I have a general range of performance that is assisted by preparation that includes proper rest, food, stretching, meditation, and visualization. Although the preparation may raise the range of performance, I still will never know what to expect on the court.

I am not an "A" player but have had a number of games where I played at my best (*my* "A" game) that spanned across the spectrum from my lower level "A" game to "A+," which is being in the "zone" for me. I will relay one such game when I was clearly in the "zone."

It was a normal morning game as many of us played multiple times a week in the indoor early bird tennis leagues of northern New Jersey. I was playing my good friend Jerry, I was calm and relaxed, with no remarkable sensations prior to playing. However, what happened during play was remarkable as I seemingly hit every shot exactly how and where I wanted, with one winning shot after another. Throughout the match, my body felt totally coordinated and smooth, and I was totally calm and relaxed. Fortunately, I did not get excited with the winning shots as that could have taken me out of the zone. While playing, I noticed my tennis coach was giving a lesson on the next court and watching me from time to time. Little did I know that in those moments he was incredibly proud of what he was seeing. After the match he came up to me and said "very impressive" to which I said that I didn't think I did anything extraordinary, i.e., that each shot I played I have hit before. The difference, of course, was that I hit *every* shot I tried, which resulted in a flawless game. My friend Jerry, after the match, said that I played "out of my mind" and that I would have beaten any of the guys that day. I will never forget the level of inner calm and total coordination I had during that match and that I was sufficiently deep into the "zone" that there was no emotional excitement during, or even after, play that could have taken me out of that state. It was calm and magical.

Finding and working hard to maintain the "zone"

On another occasion, I was bowling for my insurance company where I held a summer job during my college days. Again, I felt calm and relaxed prior to the game with no remarkable sensations or any feeling of an exalted state. We began to play and after the first few frames, it was clear that I was bowling an exceptional game. My teammates were getting excited and I knew I did not want to have my calmness affected by their excitement. As such, after each frame that I bowled, I sat in a seat well behind the team in my attempt to remain calm. I could feel my heart begin to beat with excitement and was working quite hard to remain inward and quiet. It was quite a challenge. Most of my teammates respected my need and quietly supported me. As I got up ready to bowl the last frame, I picked up my ball slowly, endeavoring to remain calm. As I did that, my captain yelled out at me for some reason, breaking my calmness. He noticed that interruption of my calmness and quickly quieted himself. Now I had a greater challenge to remain calm. I took a little extra time, did some deep breathing, and focused inwardly. I bowled this last frame well but not great (a spare and a high count versus a strike and potentially two more). I ended that game with a score of 247, which earned me trophies for high game and high series, and trophies for our team for a first-place finish. I was quite proud and excited, but to this day I wonder if I would have had a better last frame without that interruption. That will remain life's mystery. This is an example of finding the zone and working hard to stay in it.

Finding and losing the "zone"

I have had many experiences of dropping into a "zone" when drumming. Rhythmic hand drumming, ala African or Afro-Cuban drum circles, can easily bring me into a zone of meditation and inner calm. In that state, I and others will flow smoothly and easily, and frequently play at an incredibly high level. Also, we will more easily blend in harmony with other drummers and musicians thereby creating a group orchestration that is phenomenally good, even compared to a detailed orchestrated planned chart. This essentially is improv at its best.

Although most of my musical zone experiences have occurred with hand drumming, I wish to tell you about a zone drumming experience I had on a jazz drum kit. My dear friend Barry was a drummer, pianist, and all-around musician. When alive, he would invite me and other workmates to jam at his home after work. None of us were great except for Barry, but he was so generous for he saw how much we enjoyed playing these instruments or singing even though we were mediocre at best. I was playing his drum set (his primary instrument), he was playing keyboard, someone was singing, and another playing guitar. As I said, except for Barry, the three of us were only mediocre on these particular instruments. On one occasion, we were playing an upbeat number, which was getting better by the moment. After playing well into this piece, we were truly humming—each of us doing quite well on our respective instrument. I was playing "out of my mind" as if I were an expert on the drum kit while Barry watched in utter joy at what I was accomplishing. I was frankly so amazed at what my hands and feet were doing, I was in awe. Being curious, I started to watch my hands more closely to see exactly what I was doing. That, of course, was the beginning of the downfall as my mind got involved looking at the intricacies of the movements. As soon

106

as my analytical mind got involved, amazed that "I didn't really know how to do *what I was already doing*," I lost the rhythm and the flow. Lesson learned—when you're in the flow, surrender to it and don't get your mind involved with analysis or your emotions involved with excitement. Overall, it was a highly exceptional experience, with the zone developing slowly over time, remaining while I maintained my inner flow, and departing as I lost my inner calm—quite a lesson in entering and losing the "zone."

Creative Visualization

We have all heard of the expressions "creative visualization" or "guided imagery." Although its use has been practiced for many years, the terms became popularized in the New Age movement in 1978 with the book entitled *Creative Visualization* by Shakti Gawain. Other cohorts including psychologists, sports trainers, business leaders, and more, have made use of these powerful tools to facilitate their respective goals. Whichever of these factions you view, the definitions and usage of creative visualization are quite similar.

I should first mention that the one-word term "visualization" may technically refer to creative visualization, mental imaging, information graphics, music, science, and more. As some of these terms have different meanings, we will use and consider "visualization" and "creative visualization" to be synonymous, denoting the mental imagery process used to facilitate the manifestation of one's goals.

Wikipedia defines creative visualization as "a cognitive process of purposely generating visual mental imagery ... simulating or re-creating visual perception in order to maintain, inspect, and transform those images, consequently modifying their associated emotions or feelings, with intent to experience a subsequent beneficial psychological, physiological, or social effect, such as expediting the healing of wounds to the body, alleviating ... anxiety and stress, improving self-confidence ...." They add that it is also used in a way, "by which the participant envisions themself in desired circumstances, commonly evoking prospective images that depict abundance of wealth, success, achievement, health, and happiness."

A definition provided by Elizabeth Quinn in her article "Visualization Techniques for Athletes" is much more concise while still capturing the essence of the meaning. She states that "Visualization is the process of creating a mental image or intention of what you want to happen or feel in reality."

In her article entitled, "Visualize It," Jennifer Baumgartner Psy.D. states, "Visualization is a cognitive tool accessing imagination to realize all aspects of an object, action, or outcome. This may include re-creating a mental sensory experience of sound, sight, smell, taste, and touch."

We will look at creative visualization from several points of view—from authors such as Shakti Gawain, to sports trainers, to psychologists, and to business leaders. The authors will give us the principles behind creative visualization, the psychologists will demonstrate its use to help ease emotional and psychological pain, and the sports trainers and business leaders will utilize it to achieve certain performance goals. As such, the authors will focus on the "what and why" while the others are more concerned with the "how."

Authors

Shakti Gawain discusses her book, *Creative Visualization*, and related thoughts in an interview entitled *Thinking Allowed with Jeffrey Mishlove* in 2010. She discusses the creative process as being comprised of two components or polarities—the active and the receptive, where the active component is the thinking process and the process of setting goals, while the receptive component is the process whereby we listen, receive images, and note our intuitive feelings. She compares this to the esoteric, and now universal, principle of yin and yang.

The yin/yang concept, also presented as male/female, positive/negative, represents the duality or polarity of life's dynamics in the universe. Simply put, the concept describes seemingly opposing forces, views, or dynamics—(polarity)—and also the nature of these opposing forces to simultaneously be complementary, interdependent, and interconnected. If you view the Chinese symbolism of the yin/yang diagram, you will see that in this black-and-white colored diagram that one element flows into the other, and that in each half resides a piece of the other. Although distinct from each other, they are not separated by a solid wall but instead share a flowing divider while each element contains a small portion of the other. Basic views of this concept teach the acceptance of opposing views, the understanding of self and the other, the flowing integration of two separate elements, and the wisdom to find the proper balance.

In the case of creative visualization, it is important to acknowledge both the active (yang) and receptive (yin) components of the process. As such, Gawain suggests that we actively plan, think, set goals, visualize, energize, and create that which we seek while also being receptive by allowing yourself to listen, attract, and receive what comes forth from the active component.

She also notes that there is a higher intelligence at work in this process, an intelligence that is part of us not outside of us, one that knows what is best for us, and one by which we can feel a level of protection—at least with respect to the activity of goal setting. If, for example, our active mind visualizes ourselves in a situation that is truly unhealthy for us, our higher or deeper intelligence will understand its lack of wisdom, and that visualization will likely not manifest. In this case, the receptive part of the process would likely be sending such a signal in response to the active request, but it would have been necessary to be receptive and open to hearing the message.

Exercising and acknowledging only one of the two components would generally not yield positive results. In the United States, there are many examples of those who actively sought and perhaps achieved great wealth and material goods only to discover that this "outside stuff" did not bring them joy or happiness. The disappointment for those individuals resulted because of an out of balance condition, i.e., they sought only exterior goals, perhaps at the expense of deeper and more meaningful internal endeavors. Gawain states that if we listen deeply, we will see that our source of happiness is more associated with being connected to ourselves, our higher self/intelligence, and our loved ones; that we are creative beings and that the process of creation is what will give us joy and satisfaction. It is therefore imperative to understand that the process of creative visualization includes an active component and a receptive component.

Her suggestions for performing this creative visualization are quite straightforward:

1. Relax the body and mind as completely as possible in order to achieve a quiet state of mind that will open and easily access the intuitive states of our being.

2. Create the experience you want. It can be external such as a new house or job, or it may be internal such as improved self-confidence, the ability to express feelings better, or the activation of your creativity; and, of course, it may include a balance of each.

In this process, the idea of visualization is to create an internal reality (imagining it as already existing), which in turn tends to attract that reality. This, of course, does not guarantee that it will occur, but it greatly improves the probability. And lastly, it is important to accept the results, especially if different than requested.

Sports Trainers

Visualization has become an important part of sports and sports psychology, with many believing that the outer performance is directly related to the inner attitudes and beliefs.

As sports has become big business and big events in our culture, interest and wealth have sought the help of sports psychologists to improve the performance of their team members. Perhaps the past may have generally seen mostly a macho attitude toward the sport and its performance, the current day athlete is trained both in the physical rigor as well as the mental or inner elements in order to produce optimal results.

Elizabeth Quinn, in her article entitled, "Visualization Techniques for Athletes," summarizes that, "there are many stories of athletes who have used visualization techniques to cultivate not only a competitive edge but to create renewed mental awareness, a heightened sense of well-being, and confidence. All of these factors have been shown to contribute to an athlete's sports success."

Quinn later adds that, "Research is finding that both physical and psychological reactions in certain situations can be improved with visualization. Such repeated imagery can build both experience and confidence in an athlete's ability to perform certain skills under pressure, or in a variety of possible situations. Guided imagery, visualization, mental rehearsal or other such techniques can maximize the efficiency and effectiveness of your training ... [especially] in a world where sports performance and success is measured in seconds [or less]."

Common themes amongst all articles are the need to relax, concentrate, and focus, as well as to visualize the event in a sensory manner with as much detail as possible, e.g., noticing or creating the smell, the light, the colors, the atmosphere, the environment, and most importantly your positive emotion in the scene.

In his article "The Power of Visualization," Matt Neason provides five tips to improve your performance via the power of visualization:

1. Practice makes perfect—suggesting that visualization may be a struggle, they suggest practicing in a consistent manner and staying positive throughout the practice
2. Visualize what you want—they suggest that one of the most powerful effects of good visualization is that it programs the subconscious brain in a positive rather than negative manner, which is vital to success
3. Determine/shift perspective—see yourself performing the activity in an associated manner, i.e., looking out from your body just as you would if you were really there

4. Pump it up—maximize the emotional sensory of the visualization as its level of intensity will directly relate to the outcome

5. Follow a system—based on your research and various recommendations, define a protocol that works for you and utilize it consistently

Patrick Cohn, in his article "Sports Visualization: The Secret Weapon of Athletes" notes the difference that separates elite athletes from average athletes: "Elite athletes utilize the power of guided imagery or visualization. Imagery has long been a part of elite sports and many Olympic athletes have mastered the skill with the help of sports psychologists and mental game coaches." They provide examples from several Olympic athletes:

Canadian bobsledder Lyndon Rush:

"I've tried to keep the track in my mind throughout the year. I'll be in the shower or brushing my teeth. It just takes a minute, so I do the whole thing or sometimes just the corners that are more technical. You try to keep it fresh in your head, so when you do get there, you are not just starting at square one. It's amazing how much you can do in your mind."

Emily Cook, veteran American freestyle skier and three-time Olympian:

"I'm standing on the top of the hill. I can feel the wind on the back of my neck. I can hear the crowd, kind of going through all those different senses and then actually going through what I wanted to do for the perfect jump. I turn down the in-run. I stand up. I engage my core. I look at the top of the jump. I was going through every little step of how I wanted that jump to turn out."

Michael Phelps and his coach Bob Bowman:

> Bowman instructed Phelps to visualize every aspect of swimming a successful race starting from the blocks and culminating in a celebration after the race was won. He states, *"We figured it [imagery] was best to concentrate on these tiny moments of success and build them into mental triggers ... It's more like his habits had taken over. The actual race was just another step in a pattern that started earlier that day and was nothing but victories. Winning became a natural extension."*

Nicole Detling, a sports psychologist with the United States Olympic team explains the importance of having a multi-sensory approach when visualizing. She states, *"The more an athlete can image the entire package, the better it's going to be."*

Finally, Cohn suggests the following protocol for sports visualization:

1. Visualize the outcome you want
2. Use all your senses from a first-person perspective
3. Practice frequently
4. Consult with a mental game coach

Psychologists

Psychologists and other mental health therapists use visualization to help relieve emotional and psychological pain from their clients.

Dr. Cathryne Maciolek, a DC area psychotherapist, utilizes visualization in a clinical practice. In the "Visualize It" article, she elaborates on the power of visualization and its concrete benefits by stating, "With a patient experiencing depression with suicidal ideation, I created a treatment plan including setting future positive goals. Although the patient had initial difficulty imagining purchasing a house, getting married, and starting a family, with the help of pictures from magazines, the patient could literally hold on to his dream. He carried these images of a woman, a home, and children in his wallet. During times he fell down, he would take the pictures out of his wallet as a concrete reminder of what he wanted for his future."

For patients battling anxiety, Dr. Maciolek uses visualization to create "mental vacations." She states that, "This technique involves imagining a place that is calm and comforting. With one patient who suffered from severe anxiety, using pure visualization to imagine a serene vacation spot was almost impossible. With the aid of a concrete visual, a picture of the spot depicted on poster board, the image calmed the patient when she was feeling anxious."

In another example in "Visualize It," Baumgartner highlights Mandy Lehto, PhD, owner of Bravura Coaching and Image, who uses visualization with clients to allow their subconscious to work freely without inhibitions. In addition to the common aspects of visualization, Dr. Lehto believes that "clothing is a critical part of visualization … and that the client should align their personality with their wardrobe." This is an excellent example of creating detail in your visualization. Experimentation with visualization and the details within it will guide you to the optimal process for yourself.

Dr. Sheri Jacobson, founder of Harley Therapy, states that "the point of guided visualization is to harness the brain's positive response to images to help you manage your emotions and life challenges more effectively." She adds that, "visualization is not hypnosis, nor is it about being forced to do something or told what to do, and it can be used for pain management, habit control, getting motivated, releasing stress, coping better, changing moods, improving relationships, and psychological health conditions such as depression, anxiety, PTSD, phobias, eating disorders, panic attacks, and insomnia."

Business Leaders

Many business leaders have discovered the art of creative visualization as it pertains to improved performance in the workplace. The simplest example of this are goals set by the organization, perhaps the mission statements that may be placed on the office walls, the sales goals that are continually burned into the minds of the sales team, and/or the corporate personnel goals developed as part of the corporate strategy.

Whether creative visualization was a known process or not, business leaders intuitively knew that by stating and repeating the goals, they would expect a higher likelihood of their achievement. Once the evidence of positive results of visualization became known, business leaders increased their use of such techniques.

In an article entitled "Creative Visualization: A Tool for Business Success," Diann Daniel tells a story of Brian Nielsson, the founder of a mobile-solution supplier *HandStep*, who utilized visualization in his organization because of his successful experience with these techniques as a kayak racer during his teenage years. Nielsson stated that he counts visualization as one of the most important tools in his success toolkit.

In another example, Daniel speaks of Thomas Koulopoulos, founder of innovation consultancy Delphi Group, who states that, "For some reason visualization is a concept that many business folks tend to dismiss, perhaps due to the preponderance of left-brain thinking in business." His statement reflects back to the yin/yang principles of balance discussed previously. In this case, the left (yang) brain is associated with analysis and logic, which historically has been the overriding criteria in the business world.

In more recent times, we see an increased use of the right (yin) brain function of creativity and intuition. Just as the athletic organizations have added creative visualization to give them an aid to improve their performance (adding right brain activity to the existing left brain activity), the addition and inclusion of right brain activity is critical for the full potential of individuals and organizations to fully emerge and therefore optimize their performance.

In the same article, social psychologist, author, and president of Next Level Sciences, Stephen Kraus, states that, "Visualization helps people get clear about aims and objectives ... people with clear non-conflicting goals accomplish more and are healthier." In his book *Psychological Foundations of Success*, he says vision is a cornerstone of success and points to the words of Harvard marketing guru Ted Levitt, who says, "The future belongs to people who see possibilities before they become obvious." This is a clear statement regarding insight, intuition, and creativity—aspects associated with the right brain and aspects developed through the use of various forms of meditation. In short, visualization drives creativity.

Mark Suster confers with the importance of creativity in the workplace. In his article "How I Use Visualization to Drive Creativity," he includes some of the following points in the executive summary:

- Almost all business success relies on creativity.
- Despite the importance of creativity, there seems to be almost no focus on teaching it, encouraging it, training it, or incorporating it into our daily routines. The need for creativity extends well beyond product design.
- Since many people are visual thinkers, visual brainstorming is necessary to drive creativity.
- You need to find what works for you regarding these concepts.

- I learned about the "creative brain" by reading Betty Edwards's book called *Drawing on the Right Side of the Brain* where she shows how an artist's mind gets "into the zone."
- Adding structure to creativity is not an oxymoron but it's how you codify your ideas.
- All people are creative, but creativity takes practice.
- Visualization is a well-known technique in professional sports and if it could work for them, it can work for you.

As we can see from these articles, the business world is employing visualization techniques in their business plans with the goal of optimizing performance. The creative visualization process is directly related to creativity; creativity is directly related to the right brain functionality; and meditation and mindfulness practices activate the right brain, the inner self, creativity, and the spiritual aspects of our being.

Music/Arts

There are excellent possibilities for you to practice mindfulness in the areas of music and art. Chronicles show that both professionals and amateurs have experienced such a state of mind while performing their art form.

For example, it has been well documented that professional jazz artists play at their peak levels when they are relaxed and flowing. Many have discussed being "in the zone" and reaching incredible levels of performance resulting in sheer joy, supreme satisfaction, and euphoria—a state of transcendence.

In the arts, performers of dance and acting may also get in the "zone" when they focus so deeply on their practice that nothing else exists. They are so concentrated on their art and its beauty that they feel they are existing on another dimension—again, transcendence.

Some may feel it is easier to achieve the "zone" in the areas of music and art because of their intrinsic beauty. However, we have seen that this state can also be achieved in the area of sports performance, and we perhaps wonder if this state of mind can be achieved in the business arena.

If we consider that the pathway to reaching the zone is relaxation and creativity, and if we consider that those qualities are more aligned with the intuitive or right brain functionality, and if we consider that music and the arts are more aligned with the right brain, and if we consider that business (at least up till now) has been largely guided by the left brain functionality, then we can easily see how reaching the "zone" may be easier with music and the arts, rather than in business.

In the cases of music and art, as well as in sports mindfulness, there is an important criterion for reaching the zone that includes the active/receptive, yin/yang, male/female dynamic that must be incorporated and exercised. Specifically, the active or left brain functionality requirement is that the fundamentals and rudiments of the specific craft be learned at a level acceptable to you. Then you may fully employ the right brain functionality of creativity and surrender, allowing your being to move into a state of ultimate flow. In these cases, there is total confidence (no stress or concern) in the technical capabilities of the craft and that confidence allows you to fully relax and flow during the performance, facilitating a high-level experience possibly reaching the "zone."

It is my goal to further expand use of this active/receptive dynamic in the business world with techniques offered in this book and many others that will further activate the right brain creativity aspect of each person in the organization. I recommend that the leaders of our corporations exercise and foster these qualities within themselves and their organization, and I also encourage each individual to independently develop these practices. Once a critical mass is reached, the entire organization may operate in a state of flow and creativity. Some call this a conscious organization.

Not only are conscious organizations more principled, aware, and ethical, but they have shown to perform financially better as reported by John Mackey and Raj Sisodia in their book *Conscious Capitalism*. And most importantly, in addition to improved creativity and performance, these organizations will contribute to society in an exemplary fashion.

Jazz

Jazz musicians speak frequently of being in the "zone," "pocket," or "groove." It is the time when their individual and group performances reach a level beyond excellent, to the point where they may not even know what they are playing. Again, this can only occur if they have first mastered the rudiments and technicalities of their instruments after which they allow the flow to occur, potentially resulting in them playing in a "zone." Composer, pianist, and bandleader Geri Allen put it succinctly when she said, "Playing with freedom can only come after a certain amount of foundational study."

Frank J. Barrett in his Coda paper entitled, "Creativity and Improvisation in Jazz and Organizations: Implications for Organizational Learning," speaks of the goal of musicians to reach dynamic synchronization, commonly called a groove or the zone. He states, "this experience of groove that [jazz] improvisers hope for seems to involve a surrender of familiar controlled processing modes; they speak of being so completely absorbed in playing that they are not consciously thinking, reflecting, or deciding on what notes to play, as if they were able to simultaneously be inside and outside of their bodies and minds. Controlled thinking is depicted sometimes as an obstacle ....."

We again see the dynamics of active/receptive, yin/yang play out—once you have completed the active component of learning your craft (yang), it is imperative that you activate the receptive (yin) component by totally letting go in order to get into the flow. In this example, it is emphasized that once you are in that flow, it would be counterproductive to return to any active thinking. He acknowledges that this is a point of paradox whereby if musicians strive too much to attain the zone, they actually obstruct it.

He also notes that musicians speak of these moments as ecstasy, divine, transcendence, and spiritual dimensions associated with being carried by a force larger than themselves, and he compares these experiences to FLOW as written by Csikszentmihalyi in his 1990 book entitled *FLOW: The Psychology of Optimal Experience*.

Playing beyond one's perceived capacity, Frank Barrett notes that pianist Fred Hersch stated, "Buster [Williams] made me play complex cords like Herbie Hancock sometimes plays—that I couldn't even sit down and figure out now." Buster, in turn quoted his experience with Miles Davis saying, "With Miles, it would get to the point where we followed the music rather than the music following us. We would start with a tune, but the way we played it, the music just naturally evolved."

In all these examples, we can see how the concept of mindfulness is employed and how powerful the results can be. Although these musicians are masters at their craft, mindfulness and flow can be achieved at any level. It is a common goal to be better than we are. This is true for the amateur and the master professional who is always seeking an improvement in their performance, a new outlet for their creativity, and more. Accepting this premise, you can select whatever instrument for which you might be familiar, learn even a single chord or pattern, and then play that learned chord in a mindful manner, i.e., forget the technicality and allow yourself to surrender into the flow as you play it. It is important to ensure that the selected pattern is simple enough to master, for then you can more easily surrender the technical component and allow your being to surrender into the flow. Any of the meditation practices presented in this book will assist you in this endeavor.

Notable quotes from Miles Davis:

In improvisation, there are no mistakes.

Do not fear mistakes. There are none.

If you're not making a mistake, it's a mistake.

If you hit a wrong note, it's the next note that you play that determines if it's good or bad.

Don't play what's there; play what's not there.

Play what you know, and then play above that.

If you're not nervous, then you're not paying attention.

It's not about standing still and becoming safe. If anybody wants to keep creating, they have to be about change.

Anybody can play. The note is only 20 percent. The attitude of the motherf****r who plays it is 80 percent.

When you're creating your own s***. Man, even the sky ain't the limit.

Dancing

Dancing seems to exist in most every culture on the planet and has generally played an important role since the origins of these cultures. Their forms may be quite different, their goals and intentions vary, but one thing seems to be very common—the effects on their entire beings are generally very positive.

In our current culture, we experience dance at weddings, parties, and public dance clubs. Whether we are avid dancers or shy wallflowers, we have all taken part in this cultural experience. Perhaps you are so free on the dance floor that you forget everything around you and enjoy the activity with extreme joy, or perhaps you are so self-conscious that it is literally painful to dance in public for fear of being harshly judged. If the latter, it is likely that you have looked upon those "free-flowing" dancers with envy, seeing their joy, freedom, and lack of self-consciousness (I know I have).

Their ability to dance so freely requires a quieting of the mental critic within them combined with an absorption of being in the moment and surrendering to the musical rhythms. These qualities are natural for some, while learned or perhaps nonexistent for others. In all cases, it is likely that advances can be attained on both fronts, i.e., quieting the inner critic and reaching a deeper state of mindfulness or being in the moment.

DancingMindfulness.com states that *"Dancing Mindfulness* uses the art form of dance as the primary medium of discovering mindful awareness. Dancing through seven primary areas of mindfulness in motion: breath, sound, body, story, mind, spirit, and fusion (of all elements), with a respect to the attitudes of mindfulness, participants tap into their body's own healing resources and realize that we all have a unique creativity just waiting to be cultivated!"

Since we have previously discussed how the various forms of meditation and mindfulness involve breath, sound, and movement, we can see how these meditative techniques can be applied to the movement of dance. This activity can therefore become a "meditation in motion," and as you employ this practice into your dancing, you will find that you will be less self-conscious and that you will be more in the moment, dancing more freely and more joyfully—and others may envy *you!*

In a *New York Times article,* David Gelles quotes Jamie Marich saying, "Dancing isn't about escaping the stressors of daily life. Dancing offers us a way to embrace them. By being present while dancing, we can learn about ourselves and our bodies. You don't need to be perfect as a dancer. Instead, we can come home to the present moment through the practice of mindful dancing."

In this quote, there is an important note about not needing to be perfect, but instead to be present and notice ourselves and our bodies. The strive for perfection in each of us may serve us to improve the technical components of our craft. However, once we have learned that specific technical component, we must let that go and practice our craft with a sense of surrender and mindfulness. This active/receptive process will provide you with your optimal outcome and likely a more joyful dancing experience.

Drumming

The drum is likely one of the earliest of the musical instruments, originally used as a form of communications between tribal villages. It is perhaps the most primal of all instruments. Tribal drumming also included various rhythms designed to support dancing, singing, and a variety of cultural ceremonies.

In Africa, tribal drummers used a hand drum called a *djembe* for healing ceremonies, warrior rituals, to accompany dancers, and to support singers. In India, ancient cultures have for thousands of years used a hand drum called *tabla*, which is performed with the hands and fingertips. China also has a very long history of drumming in their culture, using a large tubular barrel drum with two heads called a *tanggu*. Although frame drums have been used in many cultures, including for certain Sufi ceremonies, the Irish/Celtic community uses one called *Bodhran*, which had possible ancient roots in Africa or Spain. The origin of *bongos* is traced back to Cuba and *congas* have roots in South America and Cuba. The Kodo drummers of Japan have made *taiko* drumming quite popular and middle Easterners generally play on a *darbuka* drum. These native drums were made by hand and out of natural materials. Although drum manufacturing today is quite sophisticated, many of these native hand drums are still quite popular and used for various ceremonies and also in today's drum circle gatherings.

Whether drumming on original native creations or on currently manufactured products, the rhythmic beat of a drum is akin to the heartbeat of a human, and as such, can entrain you into a meditative mindful state of being. This entrainment, in addition to one's intention to be mindful, allows you to more easily reach a state of mindfulness, rhythmic meditation, and possibly a "zone."

Inrhythm.com states that, "Drumming with a hand drum like a djembe, is a fantastic way to achieve mindfulness. You can focus on your hands or the drum or the beat and be fully in the present. Many people report that when they drum, they actually 'lose' themselves in the moment and forget about everything else. When the drumming session is over, these individuals reveal that they feel refreshed, energised and happy because they were so 'in the zone'."

In a *Psychology Today* article, Canadian sound therapist Gary Diggins states: "We moderns are the last people on the planet to uncover what older cultures have known for thousands of years: The act of drumming contains a therapeutic potential to relax the tense, energize the tired, and soothe the emotionally wounded."

Since the rhythm of the drum is akin to the rhythm of the heart, the practice of drumming may be one of the easiest forms to practice mindfulness. And whether you are a beginner or advanced drummer, if you have not tried drumming in a group session, you might find it surprisingly invigorating as well as meditatively mindful.

Acting

There are many forms of acting including performances in television, film, live theater, stand-up comedy, and improv, with each having their own form requiring subtly different talents from the actors. Many would say that acting requires a certain set of talents including good memorization skills, clear communications ability, a good stage presence, the ability to access a range of emotions, and a fearlessness (or at least the courage) to be showcased before large audiences.

For various reasons, we have glamorized award-winning actors, whether because of their natural beauty or their superb acting skills or the lifestyle we believe they lead. Perhaps one of the reasons we admire actors is because of the courage they demonstrate—a courage that we may secretly covet. We certainly see this admiration and respect in the field of improvisation, where the audience members cannot fathom how one can get onto a stage and perform extemporaneously with no script or prepared lines, having no idea where the scene may go. It is truly an extreme test of vulnerability, courage, trust in yourself, and trust in your fellow improvisers.

There are a vast number of professional actors who have stated that they would never try improvisation. As one example,

Jimmy Carrane, improv teacher and workshop leader, notes that, "Actors are often skeptical of taking an improv class. I can't tell you how many actors tell me 'I am a serious actor. Why do I need to take an improv class?' Or they say, 'I'm not funny,' 'It scares me,' or 'I wouldn't be any good at it.'"

Improvisation requires that the improviser surrender to themselves, their partners, and to the scene, and also requires total attention and mindfulness to all that is happening within themselves, with their partners, and in the scene.

All forms of acting are aided by this level of surrender, as this level of surrender allows the actor to reach a deeper part of themselves thereby providing the audience with a more compelling performance. However, since the acting forms—other than improvisation—consist of a script and lines to be memorized, it is possible that the actor may focus and rely more on the lines versus the surrender and emotion associated with the underlying sentiments of the lines. Of course, the ratio of reciting lines mentally versus the emotional depiction of the meaning of the lines would likely affect the quality of the performance. In the best case scenario, one would have the lines memorized so deeply that they are fully able to express the emotional component associated with those lines, and this quality is key to the ultimate determination of the actor's performance. Improvisation removes this concern as there are no lines to rely upon, and therefore requires only the surrender and the depths of truth in order to perform a scene.

In her article "Mindfulness and Acting," Thalia R. Goldstein PhD speaks of an 80/20 ratio rule stating, "For the moment of performance, mindfulness may be the key to what actors are 'doing,' because what they are 'doing' is 'being.' Or perhaps 80 percent of their selves are. The other 20 percent is remembering lines, finding light, and facing the audience. Or as Spencer Tracy said, 'Just learn your lines and don't bump into the furniture.'"

In all variations of acting, you can consider and practice it as a form of mindfulness. In mindfulness, you do not pass judgment, but instead you simply observe what is happening physically and emotionally. And as you understand that the active/receptive dynamic is in play, and that the receptive component relates to a surrendering to yourself and to your partner (once necessary lines are memorized), then this art form can be used to help you practice and attain a high degree of mindfulness.

Daily Life Activities

In addition to sports and music/arts, mindfulness can be practiced and experienced in routine daily life activities like going to the grocery store or waiting on a line at the bank. Let us look at a few of these examples to understand the process of mindfulness that can be applied to any activity.

Food Shopping

Food shopping is a universal activity performed by most all of us in our society. To apply or practice mindfulness to this seemingly mundane task, it is best to approach the task with a sense of calm. For some, that would mean to take clear inventory at home as to what is needed and to create a corresponding list to take to the store. This would be considered the preparation necessary to enable a sense of peace and calm as the shopping is performed. For others, it may be stressful to prepare such a list and instead be a more joyful experience to simply go to the store selecting items seemingly more randomly. In each case, a sense of calm is attained allowing the experience in the grocery store to be an enjoyable and mindful one. In that state of mind, one would not be anxious or stressed, which would be obstacles to mindfulness. Instead, the sense of calm would more easily allow one to focus and enjoy each moment of the shopping experience—whether that be the joy of seeing the different varieties from which to choose or the satisfaction of finding exactly what you are seeking. The mindful process would include being fully aware of yourself and what is happening around you, noticing all the details of your physical environment, of the products you are selecting, of the items in your cart, of the remaining items on your list, etc. The sense of inner peace and calm prior to shopping, combined with the sense of joy and awareness while performing the activity, would naturally create a state of mindfulness where you are fully engaging in the activity, and without distraction.

It is interesting to note that for some the calm state would be achieved with the precision of identifying what's needed—perhaps more of a left brain function, while for others that calm state of mind is better achieved with the spontaneity—perhaps more of a right brain function. It is critical to understand that you can achieve a state of mindfulness in either case, the difference being that there may be different preparations required in order to relax and surrender into the state of calm.

Waiting on a Bank Line

Waiting in a queue for any reason can be a source of frustration and stress, especially in a fast-paced society. Although perhaps challenging, this situation gives us plenty of opportunity to practice patience, consideration, and mindfulness. I suspect there are times when we have been calm in these situations and other times where we have been quite anxious, perhaps even experiencing both polarities in the same waiting line experience.

There are those who espouse that we can determine or select our feelings, and I imagine it is frustrating to hear comments like, "You can choose how you feel," especially when you are in the state of anxiety or emotional discomfort of any kind. Although

I believe this is a false choice, I do believe that being mindful can help change our feelings, and waiting in a queue presents an excellent opportunity to practice mindfulness. To do so, we can begin by observing ourselves (without judgment)—are we antsy, are our feet moving nervously, are we looking around erratically, is our breathing shallow and quick, etc.? By simply noticing these characteristics, we will change them as quantum physics demonstrates. Without effort, you will see that each of these characteristics will begin to quiet as you observe them; you are becoming more mindful of your own bodily attributes. Once your system calms via this observational process, you may then begin to observe those around you—their level of anxiety or calmness, their presence or stature, their attitudes, openness, etc. By observing others, you will remove the focus from yourself and you will continue to further calm. To take this further, you may then observe the physical structure of the store that you're in or perhaps the outside environment if it can be seen.

Observation of yourself, others around you, and the environment you are in will become an exercise in mindfulness that will help allow you to focus on the present moment.

Paying the Bills

Paying the bills is sometimes a task so arduous and stressful that people literally groan when speaking of this common task. As seen from the shopping example above, preparation can be an important key in setting up your attitude prior to the task, and we can easily see that a stressful groan may not be the best preparation, unless its purpose is to release tension.

It is difficult to generalize what might work for you and how you can infuse mindfulness into this process, since financial conditions and attitudes vary to such a large degree. For example, we all know of people who are quite wealthy yet stress about money, and we know of others with moderate means who are at peace with their financial situation. These represent two distinct attitudes prior to the actual activity of paying the bills. The next step—actually paying the bills—is a major component that might evoke yet different emotions. Understanding and addressing the intensity of these emotions are beyond the scope of this book, but to provide the possibility of mindfulness during this process, I respectfully offer these suggestions.

First, I would suggest you simply observe, without judgment, your attitudes toward money. This is essentially a personal assessment, not an analysis, criticism, or judgment. An honest assessment would provide you with an awareness of your attitudes and feelings, which is an extremely important step in the process of mindfulness. What you do with this awareness is a personal choice and not a subject of this writing nor a requirement to achieve mindfulness. Divergent attitudes certainly exist spanning from those who hate to pay their bills (whether or not they could afford to) to those who joyfully pay their bills because they can afford to. Again, I suggest you simply observe and become aware of your attitudes.

Secondly, when paying each bill, you may feel anger toward the recipient or the amount required by the recipient, or you may feel pleasure in knowing that that payment would provide you a service or product that would give you great joy. (I have personally experienced both and have learned to adjust to the latter, most of the times.) Once you observe and are aware of your personal attitudes and understand there are choices, you may find yourself adjusting your attitude. This is not a requirement and there is no goal to make such a change, but clear awareness may organically help to produce such change.

Paying the bills may be one of the most challenging activities at which to perform mindfulness but, as such, may produce great satisfaction and possibly surprising results.

Walking the Dog

In contrast to paying the bills, walking your dog may be one of the easiest activities to apply mindfulness. Although this can be performed under stressful conditions such as inclement weather or time pressure, it is more frequently a pleasurable experience as you are caring for a being who you love. If the outside elements such as good weather add to the positive experience, then mindfulness may be more easily achieved.

The application of mindfulness here would consist mostly of your focus, connection, and love for your dog. Simultaneous activities such as speaking on the phone or to a neighbor may either enhance or detract from the overall experience. We can easily understand how these other activities could be a distraction and degrade the mindfulness experience. However, if these other activities result in a more positive experience, then you are basically redefining the experience as something greater than mindfully walking your dog, e.g., having a social event with both your dog and your neighbors.

Maintaining the original activity of walking your dog, the mindful approach would be to focus more deeply on that particular activity and moving more deeply into the enjoyment of walking your dog. This would include noticing your dog's reaction to the various elements in the environment (smells, tastes, etc.), his/her reaction to people who may be walking by, their joy and appreciation of being outdoors and walking with you, the way they turn to look at you with their wagging tail, and their loving connection to you that you both enjoy. This is a mindful experience you would both appreciate.

Doing House Chores

Since routine household chores vary in size and scope, it is likely that our attitudes also vary for each of these chores. Whether the chores are easy or difficult or enjoyable or stressful, we can apply the same mindful techniques discussed above. Awareness of our feelings and attitudes towards the chore should be observed; we should focus on the task at hand rather than other thoughts or distractions; and we should think about the resulting effect the completed chore would have on us and our family; and as we perform the chore, we should observe what is happening in each moment of time.

Again, observation of our attitudes before, during, and after, and awareness of everything that is happening during the performance of the chore are important ingredients in creating the atmosphere of mindfulness.

Exercising

There are various reasons why we exercise, ranging from purely healthful, to honing a specific skill, to rehabilitating a particular body part, to joining a group activity, to engaging in a physical competition, or to playing a favorite sport.

The attitudes that we carry into the activity and the attitudes we exhibit during the activity may vary greatly based on which type of exercise we are performing. For example, it is likely that our attitude may be very positive before and during playing a favorite sport and may consequently result in a mindful experience because of the desired and enjoyable focus we place on that activity. However, we have all seen those who partake in their favorite sport only to exhibit great stress and frustration, leading us to wonder why they do it. Perhaps it is not the performing of the sport that brings them joy but instead some measured achievement in that sport. In this example, we can see that mindfulness is not being achieved, for the mind is attached only to some specific result rather than the focus and awareness of every element of the activity. When you are mindful of each element of your activity, you are living in the present moment, which is a state of mindfulness that does not carry the stress of accomplishment.

To apply mindfulness to any of your forms of exercises, we suggest you expand your awareness of your activity by noticing your emotion when you are originally planning the activity, e.g., does planning it put a smile on your face or does it stress you in some way. Simply notice and observe this reaction. In the same fashion, notice your attitude of anticipation immediately prior to the activity, and of course notice your level of enjoyment and engagement during the activity. If these moments are not positive, in a general sense, you may wish to reassess the reason you are participating in this sport. In this case, awareness and mindfulness will help you to determine if partaking in this activity is truly harmonious to your being, versus some other potentially unconscious reasoning for your participation.

Therefore, mindfulness is your friend for possibly different reasons—primarily to bring further depth, meaning, and enjoyment to your activity, and possibly to bring clarity and awareness to a potential disharmony with your being.

Working at Your Job

We have reached the activity that may be the most stressful and/ or the one most challenging to practice mindfulness. Most of us work as a requirement to pay our bills, with only few working voluntarily without the need for a paycheck.

Those working voluntarily would be in a similar category to those who exercise their favorite sport, i.e., it should be an enjoyable experience with the ability to practice it mindfully. For the majority of us who must work, we aspire to find a job that is creative, meaningful, satisfying, and generally fulfilling. There is much written about attracting and acquiring such a position. And we have all heard the phrase, "Do what you love, and the money will follow." If you are fortunate to love what you do, it will be easier to practice mindfulness since there will be little stress in the process and fewer obstacles to the goal of reaching mindfulness. Following the suggestions from the above examples would guide you to the highest likelihood of achieving that mindfulness in your already satisfying job.

Working a job that is unsatisfactory and/or stressful creates a much greater challenge to achieving a mindful state of being. One suggestion to help the overall situation would be to segment your job into several meaningful components thereby allowing you to address each one separately. You may find that there are certain segments that are quite stressful, other segments less stressful, some segments unremarkable, and hopefully some segments satisfying. With this awareness, I suggest you experiment in various ways. Perhaps you can expand the satisfactory segments of your job and minimize the most stressful; perhaps you can move, or request to move, the most stressful to someone else, within or outside the organization; perhaps you can share that stressful segment with another, thereby sharing that load. Once you have done all you could regarding who handles these tasks, you could then consider the environment within which this task is accomplished. For example, can you define a circumstance where that stress is at its least, e.g., is it less stressful to perform this task on a certain day, at a certain hour, in a certain way, with a certain person, at a certain location, etc. Analyzing the stress effect during different circumstances may allow you to perform or manage the task in a way that carries somewhat less stress.

Once you have optimized these "outer" elements, you can then look inward and apply mindfulness to this aspect of your job. I recommend you start by aligning yourself using some form of meditation you enjoy. This could simply be a two-to-three-minute breathing or movement exercise (perhaps in private) that will help center and align you. Once you are performing the task, I suggest you mindfully focus on each small activity or movement of the task—simply observe it and notice its effect. Do this for all aspects of the task. As you do this, you will have placed yourself in a mindful and more peaceful state of being. The task will likely be accomplished smoothly, with less stress, and time will likely pass quickly. The Zen masters apply this level of mindfulness to all tasks, however mundane, like washing dishes. The Sufi Walking Meditation described within may be a good exercise to help develop the muscle memory needed for this situation. You too can then bring your Zen-like attitude to your job.

In summary, this technique will help you identify certain segments of your job that could be reviewed for possible modification and will help you reduce stress levels using the mindfulness techniques you have learned and practiced. If upon analysis, you determine that all segments are unsatisfactory, and the mindfulness techniques are not improving the situation, then this may be important feedback information for you to incorporate into your career planning and decisions.

Chapter 7

Psychological Exploration

"The first half of life is devoted to forming a healthy ego; the second half is going inward and letting go of it." Carl Jung

"Yesterday I was clever, so I wanted to change the world. Today I am wise, so I am changing myself." Rumi

"The good life is a process, not a state of being. It is a direction, not a destination." Carl Rogers

"It isn't where you came from, it's where you're going that counts." Ella Fitzgerald

---

Chapter Highlights

1. The psychology of the human mind has been a subject of interest since ancient civilizations.
2. There are numerous forms and styles of psychological assistance—both formal and informal—that are aimed to help reduce stress, manage anxiety, and cope with depression.

> 3. Informal styles include self-reflection, journaling, speaking with clergy/friends, and more. Formal styles are generally facilitated by a trained professional and are briefly described within.
> 4. All are presented for your exploration.

Introduction

Interest in the human mind and behavior dates back to philosophical interests in the ancient civilizations of Egypt, Persia, Greece, China, and India.

The history and development of modern psychology is vast and has taken evolutionary turns with each new, brilliant mind or groups of minds. Today, there are many forms and styles of psychological assistance—both formal and informal—and are identified with diverse nomenclature, such as psychology, counseling, psychotherapy, self-help, and even coaching. These and other disciplines share the goal of understanding and assisting the behavioral and mental processes, including managing anxiety, reducing stress, coping with depression, and more.

Informal styles include journaling, speaking with clergy, sharing with friends, walking the beach, singing, and self-reflection, while formal styles—listed below—are generally facilitated by a trained and licensed professional.

There are many who discuss the benefits of inner transformation as it relates to business success. In one such book, Tsao and Laszlo state the following in *Quantum Leadership*, "Quantum leaders embrace the inner transformation of people ... Such inner transformation brings out one's intrinsic care and compassion, inspiring us to do good from a more authentic place. A holistic approach to the well-being of self, organization, stakeholders, community, and the environment is the only route to a full-spectrum flourishing that includes financial benefits."

Relating to the work in this book, all these various psychological practices can provide you with the means to better understand yourself, to improve your self-awareness, to allow your unconscious to become conscious, and to develop self-truth, a clearer inner voice, and authenticity. Since there is such a wide variety of these specialties, you may wish to experiment with one or another to determine what style best fits your personality. I will present several of these various formal practices that reflect differences in breath and style.

Psychological Therapies

There are many types of psychological therapies—clinical, modern, popular, established, esoteric, recent, and/or exploratory. Although all are essentially designed to bring you awareness, reduced pain, greater joy, and enhanced consciousness, each therapy has its own foundational beliefs and related practices designed to produce its intended goals. Following are brief descriptions of a variety of these therapies for your consideration.

Positive Psychology

Many believe that the term positive psychology was introduced by Abraham Maslow in the 1960s but was brought to the forefront by Martin Seligman of the University of Pennsylvania in the late 1990s as president of the American Psychological Association.

PsychologyToday.com discusses positive psychology as follows, "Positive Psychology focuses on the character strengths and behaviors that allow individuals to build a life of meaning and purpose—to move beyond surviving to flourishing ... In focusing on how people can become happier and more fulfilled, positive psychology stands in contrast to a focus on psychopathology." It continues, "In positive psychology, there is an emphasis on meaning, not just on fleeting happiness. Martin Seligman, often regarded as the godfather of positive psychology, has described three paths to happiness: the Pleasant Life (Hollywood's view of happiness), the Good Life (focused on personal strengths and states of 'flow'), and the Meaningful Life (aimed toward a higher purpose) .... We should strive for *eudaimonia*—Aristotle's concept of flourishing—rather than *hedonia* (pleasure)."

We should note here that this evolution toward positive psychology and flourishing begins to blend with the flourishing aspects presented by modern-day business thinkers such as Emily Smith, John Ehrenfeld, Mihaly Csikszentmihalyi, and others.

Research shows there are many suggestions and techniques offered to achieve a positive state of mind, or positive psychology. I will present a few of the more common techniques recommended and also note a general caution perceived by some in the field.

Techniques

- *Gratitude exercises*—It is natural to get accustomed to our way of living, whether it be wealthy, middle class, or impoverished, as we humans have an amazing ability to cope and accept the conditions of our lives. Whether we strive for more, or become complacent with what we have, it may become easy to lose sight of our current conditions and overlook the positive aspects of our lives. As such, we may be focusing more on what we *don't* have rather than what we *do* have, thereby not appreciating our current circumstances. Gratitude exercises consist simply of listing our appreciation of what we do have—in our health, our friendships, our housing, our career, our family, etc. These exercises can be performed verbally or in writing, in the mornings or evenings, or however they will be more meaningful to you, with the essential elements being that the sentiments are genuine, authentic, and meaningful.

- *Acts of kindness*—It has been shown that performing an act of kindness to another actually increases your own self-happiness. "The beauty is in the giving" is a familiar phrase. Volunteers, service workers, adults caring for children or loved ones have reflected on this dynamic. The act of kindness can be quite simple such as carrying a package for someone or even simpler like conveying a loving smile, as it is the authentic loving gesture behind the action that is the essential element.

- *Fostering relationships*—It is often believed that love and relationships are the most important aspects of life. It therefore follows that connecting with those we love (ourselves, in addition to our loved ones), as well as discovering new relationships, would add to our levels of happiness.

- *Mindful meditation*—As discussed in previous sections, mindful meditation has been shown to reduce anxiety and depression, improve physiological functions such as heart rate and blood pressure, connect us more deeply with our inner selves, connect with a higher power (based on our beliefs), and improve various cognitive functions.

Cautions

- In general, the cautions or concerns by certain psychologists revolve around the use of positive psychology as a possible means to avoid or deny negative feelings. Although they believe that positive psychology has its uses, especially for those who consistently carry a negative outlook on life and/or who specifically look negatively upon themselves, they do not believe that it is "one-size-fits-all" therapy. As past psychological therapies may have over-focused on the difficulties of our lives, perhaps to the point of reinforcement rather than healing, they warn of caution of the other extreme, i.e., focusing only on the positive without at least acknowledgment of the difficulties. Such avoidance or denial could cause one to bury the issues only to surprisingly erupt at a later point in time with perhaps greater intensity.

- Psychologist Julie Norem discusses "defensive pessimism" in her book, *The Positive Power of Negative Thinking*. *She notes that there are those who use pessimism as a defensive mechanism to maintain an environment of safety. They worry about future challenges as a way of life, which is, for them, a healthy means to prepare for such an adversity. She states that it has been* shown that when defensive pessimists are deprived of their pessimism by being forced to look on the bright side of life, their performance on tasks plummets. For defensive pessimists, positive psychology has a decidedly negative side.

Cognitive Behavioral Therapy (CBT)

Many experts state that CBT is one of the most popular forms of talk therapy today, and that its solution-based treatment helps clients overcome issues by revealing and changing their thinking and behavioral patterns. *Psychology Today* notes that, "CBT was founded by psychiatrist Aaron Beck in the 1960s, following his disillusionment with Freudian psychoanalysis, and a desire to explore more empirical forms of therapy."

The American Psychological Association defines CBT as "a form of psychological treatment that has been demonstrated to be effective for a range of problems including depression, anxiety disorders, alcohol and drug use problems, marital problems, eating disorders, and severe mental illness."

They state that CBT is based on both research and clinical practice and that there is ample scientific evidence showing its positive results in clients. Based on faulty or unhelpful ways of thinking, and learned patterns of unhelpful behavior, CBT usually involves processes to change one's thinking patterns and ultimately behavioral patterns.

To change one's thinking patterns, the client is taught to recognize distortions in their thinking and to reevaluate them based on current conditions; they are taught to better understand the behavior of others; and to better cope with difficult situations. To change behavioral patterns, the client is guided to face their fears; to relax and be mindful; and to role-play in preparation for challenging situations.

The overall emphasis of CBT is to help clients develop their own coping skills whereby they can learn to change their own thinking and behavior patterns, thereby learning to be their own therapists. To support that concept, the therapy sessions focus on the clients' current life conditions rather than past events.

This form of therapy minimizes the emphasis on early life events and focuses on practical present-day solutions. The technique of role-playing would certainly be enhanced with the practice of improv.

Dialectical Behavioral Therapy (DBT)

DBT is a modified form of CBT originally developed to treat borderline personality disorder and is now used to treat a wider range of issues. Psychologist Marcia Linehan is credited with the founding of DBT to improve the effectiveness of CBT.

The term "dialectical" refers to the interaction of two conflicting concepts—acceptance and change. Most experts state that a key difference is that DBT emphasizes that your experiences are real and therefore teaches you self-acceptance regardless of the level of difficulties.

Kristalyn Salters-Pedneault, PhD, writes in a *VeryWellMind.com* article that, "It [DBT] focuses on skills like mindfulness or living in the present, regulating emotions, tolerating distress, and effectively managing relationships with others. DBT is the only empirically supported treatment for borderline personality disorder."

Inner Child Therapy

The inner child is a term used in popular psychology to define the childlike aspect of ourselves. It is considered to be a subpersonality, i.e., one component of our overall personality, and is frequently unconscious to our waking mind.

We have likely all experienced this quality when expressing a temper tantrum or other childlike behavior, and we have likely been told to grow up and stop that behavior. In many cases, that voice needs to be brought out of the unconscious and be heard to determine its importance.

A professional therapist is trained to help you understand the purpose of that behavior and voice, i.e., help you understand the value of that voice. This process would help you to have greater awareness of yourself by bringing the unconscious to your consciousness, and by better understanding your behavior patterns that were based on childhood experiences.

This type of therapy would provide a greater awareness of yourself and your personal dynamics that are key ingredients to authenticity and clearer decision-making.

Hypnosis

WebMD provides this explanation of hypnosis, "Hypnosis—or hypnotherapy—uses guided relaxation, intense concentration, and focused attention to achieve a heightened state of awareness that is sometimes called a trance. The person's attention is so focused while in this state that anything going on around the person is temporarily blocked out or ignored. In this naturally occurring state, a person may focus his or her attention—with the help of a trained therapist—on specific thoughts or tasks."

They add that, "the hypnotic state allows people to explore painful thoughts, feelings, and memories they might have hidden from their conscious minds." In this regard, it is a tool of psychotherapy to help bring the unconscious to the conscious mind, thereby increasing awareness and understanding of self.

Accessing a deeper part of our psyche is also the goal of various meditation techniques as discussed earlier. The advantage of hypnosis would include having a professional therapist guiding you, as well as accessing the deeper hypnotic state, which might be too painful to otherwise access.

Dream Therapy

Since ancient times, tribal elders have analyzed and interpreted dreams as they were often considered to be spirit communications or divine intervention. Today, the psychological study of dreams is aimed to bring greater awareness of the subconscious mind and a healthy integration with the conscious mind.

Most dream experts believe that dreams reveal our subconscious thoughts and are frequently symbolic yet could be realistic or even prophetic.

Carl Jung felt that dream therapy helps us to confront unconscious contents as they are projected into our relationships and that relationships improve as we become more conscious.

If you can recall your dreams (immediate notetaking is advised to capture the dream), and especially if you have recurring dreams (where your subconscious continues to badger you until you listen), you may discover clarity and/or answers revealed through a dream therapy session.

Ultimately, this is another tool to provide greater self-awareness.

NLP

NLP is a personal development therapy that is one of the most difficult to define. Developed in the 1970s, it was originally marketed as a tool for people to learn how others achieve success and, as such, has found interest in the fields of counseling, medicine, law, business, the arts, sports, education, and more.

GoodTherapy.org describes NLP as, "a psychological approach that involves analyzing strategies used by successful individuals and applying them to reach a personal goal. It relates thoughts, language, and patterns of behavior learned through experience to specific outcomes."

Modeling, action, and effective communication are key elements of NLP, the belief being that if an individual can understand how another person accomplishes a task, that process may be copied and communicated to others so they too can accomplish the task.

Although difficult to define, we can see that this process involves the study and awareness of others, the awareness of ourselves, and the attempted assimilation of certain successful qualities observed in others.

Somatic Therapy

In 1969, Peter Levine, PhD, experienced a singular event resulting in his interest in mind/body healing and eventually the healing of trauma and other stress disorders. Dr. Levine created Somatic Experiencing® and explains that, "the traumatic event isn't what caused the trauma, but instead it is the overwhelmed response to the perceived life threat that is causing an unbalanced nervous system, and our aim is to help you access the body memory of the event, not the story."

This therapy is designed to unpack traumatic disorders, including PTSD, in a manner that does not retraumatize the patient. Dr. Levine states, "Trauma is a fact of life, but it doesn't have to be a life sentence."

This is yet another tool for self-awareness and healing, specifically designed for those who have experienced trauma.

Mindfulness Therapies

There are several therapies that integrate traditional psychotherapy techniques specifically with mindfulness, where mindfulness practices are an essential component of the therapy. Below are listed a few of these healing therapies.

Mindfulness-based stress reduction (MBSR)

Wikipedia describes MBSR as "an eight-week evidence-based program that offers secular, intensive mindfulness training to assist people with stress, anxiety, depression and pain. Developed at the University of Massachusetts Medical Center in the 1970s by Professor Jon Kabat-Zinn, MBSR uses a combination of mindfulness meditation, body awareness, yoga, and exploration of patterns of behavior, thinking, feeling and action."

Will Baum discusses the core of this therapy—that there are decisions we can make between a stimulus and our response to that stimulus. He quotes psychiatrist and Holocaust survivor Viktor Frankl who said, "Between stimulus and response there is a space, in that space lies our power to choose our response, in our response lies our growth and our freedom."

Baum notes that the MBSR program helps us to become more aware of our habitual reactions to stimuli and helps us relate to ourselves in a new way to interrupt the cycle and to create more choices in our reactions.

As with most therapies, MBSR helps to create greater self-awareness but specifically focuses the awareness on our habitual behavior patterns to various stimuli, thereby allowing us greater conscious choice in our decisions.

Mindfulness-Based Cognitive Therapy (MBCT)

Psychology Today describes MBCT as, "a modified form of cognitive therapy that incorporates mindfulness practices such as meditation and breathing exercises. Using these tools, MBCT therapists teach clients how to break away from negative thought patterns that can cause a downward spiral into a depressed state so they will be able to fight off depression before it takes hold."

This form of mindful therapy fosters self-awareness and is specifically designed to help people who suffer repeated bouts of depression and chronic unhappiness.

Mindfulness-Based Relapse Prevention (MBRP)

MBRP is an integration of other mindful therapies (RPT, MBSR, MBCT) and is the core foundational teaching of The Center for Mindfulness at the UC San Diego Medical Center.

Specifically designed for substance abuse clients, MBRP integrates mindfulness meditation practices with cognitive-behavioral strategies to help prevent the clients' relapse. The program guides participants with their discomfort (rather than searching for a "fix"), internal and external triggers, and a healthy lifestyle for recovery.

This is a program that utilizes mindfulness practices as a key element and is clearly specialized for substance abuse clients.

Acceptance and Commitment Therapy (ACT)

ACT is an action-oriented approach to psychotherapy where clients learn to stop avoiding, denying, and struggling with their inner emotions and, instead, accept that these deeper feelings are appropriate responses to certain situations that should not prevent them from moving forward in their lives.

ACT is not about eliminating difficult feelings, but rather to be present with what life brings us and to move forward with valued behavior.

This form of therapy has been used effectively to help treat workplace stress and other traditional disorders such as anxiety, depression, and more.

Voice Dialogue

Voice Dialogue was developed in the early 1970s by Drs. Hal and Sidra Stone as a method for working with subpersonalities. Their work evolved over the next quarter of a century into a complex methodology for working with selves and a complete theoretical system, which they called the Psychology of Selves and the Aware Ego Process.

Although comprehensive, Voice Dialogue can be easily described as a method to enter into dialogue with our inner voices, voices that reflect the various parts of our personality: "our selves." Each of these selves has its own way of thinking, feeling, behavior, and observation. Often, we identify with one or more subpersonalities, our so-called "primary selves," while we repress or disown their opposites. Voice Dialogue is a facilitation process that invites "ourselves" to speak freely and express themselves honestly.

An important component of this process is the concept of the Aware Ego that gets strengthened and developed each time we disidentify from our primary selves and begin to reclaim our repressed or disowned selves. Prior to the development of the Aware Ego, one's behavior is generally guided by the ego identified with one or more of the subpersonalities—sometimes even fluctuating from one opposing subpersonality to another. As these subpersonalities are uncovered, heard, and understood, greater awareness and consciousness are developed creating a healthy Aware Ego. The Aware Ego Process combines awareness and connection without judgment. This gives greater insight into these opposing issues and will be able to make more conscious and intentional decisions.

When I think of this "committee" of subpersonalities in my head, it reminds me of committees in organizations that are comprised of committee members with a single committee chairperson. The analogy would be that each committee member is a subpersonality with different opinions and views, and the chairperson represents the aware ego.

In this case, if the chairperson is weak with little understanding of the workings of the committee, the committee may effectively be directed by the individual members. And since each member has their own opinion and agenda, the committee will likely be directed chaotically and in a flip-flop fashion bouncing from one member to another. This chaos would result because of a weak chairperson. However, if the chairperson is more aware and conscious, they would listen to and understand each member's position, including opposing member's views, and make more conscious decisions based on a more complete understanding of all the information. This concept of a competent chairperson is analogous to a developed Aware Ego where understanding of the subpersonalities occurs and is not hidden or unconscious.

Once we understand there are multiple subpersonalities within us (some loud, soft, strong, weak), we will then begin to see how we were possibly operating out of one of those subpersonalities rather than from an Aware Ego; and once we acknowledge and hear each of the subpersonalities, we will then be able to make a more conscious decision from our Aware Ego. Again, this process is analogous to organization leaders and their members, i.e., it is critical to acknowledge all members (strong, weak, loud, squire) in order to make an informed, conscious, and aware decision.

Reichian

Reichian therapy is a form of personal growth work based on the principles of Dr. Wilhelm Reich. It is a body/mind approach that includes breathing and physical energetics.

The Reichian Institute describes the observation and discovery made by Dr. Reich stating, "Dr. Reich observed that for every neurosis, every illness, any problem that a person might bring to a psychiatrist, there was always some impediment in that person's breathing. He noted that how we are breathing at any given moment corresponds precisely to the emotions and physical state we are experiencing."

A description of the dynamics and benefits of Reichian therapy is presented on the *Reichian.com* website stating, "The emphasis is on deeper, more natural breathing and on increased energy. Patterns of chronic holding in the organism are identified, and their meaning is clarified. As these patterns are loosened, the free flow of feeling and awareness is fostered, and the capacity for self-expression is stimulated. At the same time, a greater degree of self-understanding and self-possession is established, facilitating an enhanced responsiveness to the challenges of life."

This is one form of mind/body therapy that includes breathing and physical energetics in addition to traditional talk therapy.

Gestalt

Gestalt therapy focuses on the present moments versus analysis or examination of the past or projections of the future. This focus on the present requires an awareness of self.

In the *Introduction to Gestalt Therapy* by Gary Yontef and Lynne Jacobs, they state that, "Since Gestalt therapy is an experiential and humanistic approach, it works with patients' awareness and awareness skills rather than using the classic psychoanalytic reliance on the analyst's interpretation of the unconscious."

They continue, "the active methods ... of Gestalt therapy are used to increase the awareness, freedom, and self-direction of the patient rather than to direct patients toward preset goals ... therapists and patients are encouraged to be creative in doing the awareness work. There are no prescribed or proscribed techniques in Gestalt therapy ... From this present-centered focus, one can become clear about one's needs, wishes, goals, and values."

In his book, *Gestalt Therapy Theory of Change*, Gary Yontef states, "Rather than aiming to move the patient to be different, the gestalt therapist believes in meeting patients as they are and using increased awareness of the present, including awareness of figures that start to emerge (thoughts, feelings, impulses, etc.) that the person might or might not allow to organize new behavior. With this present-centered awareness, change can happen without the therapist aiming for a preset goal.

And finally, in his book *Awareness, Dialogue, and Process,* Gary Yontef states that, "Gestalt therapy focuses more on process (what is happening) than content (what is being discussed). The emphasis is on what is being done, thought, and felt at the moment rather than on what was, might be, could be, or should be.

I find it fascinating that the practice of improv, which requires and helps develop self-awareness, could be a very useful skill helpful to the effectiveness of Gestalt therapy.

Bioenergetics

Bioenergetics, also called Bioenergetic Analysis or Bioenergetic Therapy or BioEnergy, is a form of mind/body therapy with a focus of healing through the body. It was developed in the 1950s by Alexander Lowen, an American physician and psychotherapist, and a long time student of Wilhelm Reich.

Massachusetts Society for Bioenergetic Analysis, on their website *MassBioenergetics.org*, describes this therapy as follows, "Bioenergetic Therapy allows a person to get in touch with the self through his or her body. The goal of this therapy is a more alive body. The deeper one's connection is to one's body, the greater one's capacity to breathe deeply, to accept and respect the self, and to love and accept others."

The Academy of Bioenergetics (*AcademyOfBioenergetics.com*) makes a stronger connection to the energy body stating, "Bio-Energetics is the study of energy transfer and relationships between all living systems. As the body is exposed to toxins, viruses, emotional stress, etc., the tissue's normal electromagnetic frequency becomes abnormal. When the energetic imbalance is left undetected, undesirable chemical changes begin in the tissues. As the imbalance continues, chronic and degenerative diseases such as arthritis and cancer can occur."

The New York Society for Bioenergetics Analysis describes what to expect in Bioenergetic Therapy by stating, "Bioenergetic Therapy is both verbal and physical. The verbal work consists of an exploration of an individual's past, dreams, associations, and current issues. Work with the body gives people a chance to become aware of their emotional issues on a tangible body level to facilitate change."

The essence of this therapy is that there is a strong and clear connection between the physical body, the emotional system, and the mind, and that to relieve stress, trauma, or pain in the emotional or physical body would require an exploration and understanding of the interrelationship of the mind and the body.

Individual Bioenergetic therapy sessions may include physical movements, postural changes, expressive movements, breathing, and grounding exercises, all designed to evoke impulses, feelings, memories, or insights to effectuate self-awareness and change.

Core Energetics

Developed in the 1970s by John Pierrakos, MD, Core Energetics is a synthesis of body-oriented psychotherapy and spiritual development. It brings consciousness to how we block our life energy by perpetuating defensive patterns adapted in childhood which keep us limited and disempowered.

Core Energetics helps us understand how our life and worldview is to a large extent a function of these blocked energy patterns. These patterns keep us recreating similar life situations and relational dynamics, leaving us trapped and frustrated.

Core Energetics helps identify and dissolve these blocks, allowing us to experience more freedom and aliveness.

Rolfing®

Named after its founder, Dr. Ida P. Rolf, Rolfing is a form of bodywork that reorganizes the connective tissues, called fascia, that permeate the entire body.

Rolf.org states, "Rolfing works on this web-like complex of connective tissues to release, realign, and balance the whole body, thus potentially resolving discomfort, reducing compensations, and alleviating pain ... Rolfing aims to restore flexibility, revitalize your energy, and leave you feeling more comfortable in your body. Rolfing is a way to ease pain and chronic stress and improve performance in professional and daily activities."

The traditional protocol for this therapy involves a ten-session series whereby the therapist will systematically balance and optimize the structure and function of the entire body.

Although Rolfing may seem to be exclusively a physical therapy, we understand there is an integral connection between the body and mind, whereby one affects the other, and the subsequent healing of one will include healing and support of the other. For example, we know that emotional traumas may manifest into physical maladies. Common examples of this dynamic would be ulcers, stress-induced pain, and certain heart conditions. To fully heal the malady as well as its source, it will generally be necessary to address both the physical and emotional.

RolfingByAnne.abmp.com makes the direct connection of the body/mind/emotional connection by stating, "Rolfing is a scientifically validated system of restructuring the human body. It releases the body from life-long patterns of tension and allows gravity to naturally realign them. This therapy is highly effective for improving posture, reducing or eliminating chronic pain, and releasing long-term emotional and mental stress."

This therapy may be appropriate for you if you feel physical stress in your body or if you feel the structure or alignment of your body is not optimal. This therapy can be used alone or in conjunction with other emotionally based therapies.

Family Constellation

Founded by Bert Hellinger, Family Constellation is a therapy method to help release your entanglements from family dynamics allowing you to fully be yourself rather than be guided behaviorally by ancestral family patterns.

Hellinger.com states the basic issue and its solution as follows, "Frequently, it is beliefs that we have inherited from our parents that keep us imprisoned ... They were created in the subconscious and are now in our way, preventing changes in behavior. Family Constellation brings these hidden beliefs to light in order to be questioned, released, and overwritten. By releasing the old unconscious bonds, our focus is directed toward true love, care, mindfulness and respect, and dreams become reality."

HellingerInstitute.com describes this therapy as, "Family Constellation is a groundbreaking methodology to free yourself from the damaging repetitive patterns, behaviors, and emotions that are limiting your life in some way today but **did not originate with you**." They clearly are emphasizing the words they bolded to identify the behaviors and patterns that are not truly yours but instead were inherited, likely unconsciously, from your ancestral family.

To identify whether your issues are appropriate for this therapy, the Hellinger Institute posits the question, "What if it was not just about you? What if some of it came from something much deeper, from unresolved traumas or unprocessed emotions from your family system that you had picked up subconsciously out of a very powerful love and loyalty to them?"

It can be quite a difficult investigation to determine if our issues emanate from our personal core or from unconscious inherited family dynamics. One general suggestion to help make this determination is to observe whether our behaviors seem consistent with our core beliefs. If not, we may feel that we are not being "ourselves" and such a discordant alignment may be an indication to investigate the Family Constellation method.

Couples Therapy

Couples therapy is also known as marriage therapy, marriage counseling, or couples counseling and is aimed to improve romantic relationships as well as to help resolve conflicts between two people in a non-romantic relationship.

Although some couples prefer to keep their issues private and work through their issues themselves or with their clergy, peers, or elders, many choose professional therapists to assist with these conflicts.

The therapist will guide each of the couple to identify their own values, positions, opinions, and boundaries, and then to hear, understand, and hopefully accept the values, positions, opinions, and boundaries of the other. To facilitate this communication process, the therapist would ask each participant to do their best to listen deeply to their partner, without judgment, as they respectively share this information—a listening that may not have occurred on their own. This back-and-forth process of clear communication and deep listening alone may create certain discoveries unknown beforehand.

The therapist would not only guide these communications but also act as referee should either client deviate from open, civil, and effective communications. As the communications unfold, the therapist would act as mediator and help guide the clients towards clarity and understanding, necessary to determine the best direction for both.

The goal of the therapist is to foster positive mental and emotional health for both clients—a task that is sometimes quite difficult. The therapist will not be aiming for a particular outer result, as they will not know what outer result is optimal for both—that result will hopefully be revealed during the process.

Although there may be several styles of such therapy, the goal to provide mental and emotional health to both parties is the same.

Family Systems

In previous sections, we have discussed the mental health of the individual, and various therapies available to the individual to improve their personal health. In Family Constellation, we saw the interconnection of the individual and their family dynamics; and in couples therapy we saw the interactions of two individuals and how they can affect each other. Family systems is an extension of these and includes multiple individuals in a family dynamic whereby each affect, and is affected by, the other in a family setting.

In *Encyclopedia of Human Behavior* (Second Edition), W.H. Watson describes family systems as, "... an approach to understanding human functioning that focuses on interactions between people in the family and between the family and the context(s) in which that family is embedded." He continues stating that, "According to a family systems perspective, an individual's functioning is determined not so much by the intrapsychic factors as by a person's place in the system, subject to the pushes and pulls of the system, including competing emotional demands, role definitions and expectations, boundary and hierarchal issues, conditions and conclusions, loyalty conflicts, family and institutional cultural and belief systems, double binds, projective identifications, and systemic anxiety. In addition, self-correcting and self-reinforcing feedback loops in a system can either facilitate or hinder pathology or health, break down or resilience."

I suspect we are all familiar with certain family dynamics such as the different behavior patterns commonly observed with the oldest child versus the youngest child, or with the only child, or perhaps with gender differences, or perhaps the behaviors and reactions to the sibling who excels in some life area. Our place in our family tree naturally gives us a starting point of who we are, how others may treat us, and how we may see ourselves.

Family systems analysis would help us to understand certain behaviors based on these positional family patterns.

Multigenerational

Multigenerational or Intergenerational family therapy is an extension of Family Systems as it also considers the dynamics and differences between generations. In a sense, it can be thought of as a cross between Family Constellation and Family Systems.

In short, Multigenerational therapy would acknowledge generational behaviors, differences, and influences on the individual and family behavior. We have all had casual discussions about the various generations in our culture and the differences we each observe in these various generations. Although not scientific, of course, it is clear that each generation brings a different, or at least modified, view of themselves and the world within which they live.

In *The SAGE Encyclopedia of Theory in Counseling and Psychotherapy* edited by Edward S. Neukrug, Amanda A. Brookshear states that, "psychiatrist, Murray Bowen, developed multigenerational family therapy to explain an individual's dysfunction or pathology with consideration to the individual's family .... Multigenerational therapy has Bowenian theory as its foundation and seeks to identify how the family's current dysfunction is a result of generational patterns. The multigenerational family therapist focuses on the facts related to the family rather than the family's thoughts, feelings, and emotions."

Transpersonal Psychology

There are certain subsections of psychology that take a broader and more holistic approach to therapy by integrating traditional psychological techniques with spiritual beliefs and paradigms. These are called spiritual psychology, transpersonal psychology, or psycho-spiritual therapy.

Wikipedia states that, "Transpersonal psychology, or spiritual psychology, is a subfield of psychology that integrates the spiritual and transcendent aspects of the human experience with the framework of modern psychology. The transpersonal is defined as 'experiences in which the sense of identity or self extends beyond (trans) the individual or personal to encompass wider aspects of humankind, life, psyche, or cosmos.'"

In an article by Steve Taylor PhD, Taylor suggests that transpersonal psychology was an outgrowth of humanistic psychology with Abraham Maslow being its pioneer. He states that transpersonal psychology is "an attempt to integrate the ideas and insights of Western psychology with the insights of Eastern spiritual traditions, such as Buddhism and Hindu Vedanta and yoga, particularly their examination of higher states of consciousness, and higher stages of human development. In Abraham Maslow's words, the role of transpersonal psychology was to explore the 'farther reaches of human nature.'"

Mindfulness is a component of transpersonal psychology and there are aspects of positive psychology that interact with these dynamics.

Transpersonal psychology is therefore a wide holistic approach that includes psychology, behaviorism, cognitive therapies, humanistic psychology, Eastern and Western philosophies, mindfulness, and spirituality.

PART THREE

IMPROVISATION—The Freedom to Experiment

Chapter 8

The Improv Environment

"A person who never made a mistake never tried anything new." Albert Einstein

"Mistakes have the power to turn you into something better than you were before." Anonymous

---

Chapter Highlights

1. The improv environment is safe, accepting, free of criticism or judgment, fosters creativity, and ripe for experimentation and testing new ideas. It is hence perfect for personal exploration.
2. In improv, there are no mistakes, only happy accidents.
3. Improv is more about feeling and surrender vs. thinking.
4. This chapter discusses short-form vs. long-form improv, improv vs. standup, the YES AND principle, the Conscious Communication Cycle™, and the applications in business.

No Mistakes

Now that you have discovered more about your inner selves through meditation, yoga, mindfulness activities, and psychological self-exploration, let us now experiment with this new awareness in an environment that is safe and accepting.

Improvisational acting is a perfect format for such experimentation as it fosters creativity, speaking with few limitations, trying new ideas, thinking out of the box, and making mistakes. Yes, making mistakes is a very acceptable part of the learning process. In fact, a basic tenet of improv is that there are no mistakes, only "happy accidents," and that everything we say and do is worth expressing and exploring to see what results would occur.

Thomas Edison knew this well in his creative and inventive life saying, "I have not failed. I've just found 10,000 ways that won't work." If we fear making mistakes, we will constrain ourselves and prevent our inner expressions to emerge. This would limit our creativity and self-expression, both of which are key components of improvisation, and one may argue, even to life. During an improv workshop in Edison, New Jersey, an employee expressed a recent realization and shared, "Mistakes are okay, and even normal, as long as I speak to them and learn from them."

Improv is about accepting our feelings and perceptions and expressing them authentically. It is about surrender—to let go of the limiting voices within that speak of many "shoulds" learned in our lifetime and allowing our inner freedoms to emerge.

To facilitate such a release of our inner selves, it is important that we have a safe environment, an environment that encourages such a release, and one that is caring and accepting of you as you are. Unfortunately, such an environment does not generally exist in many places of our lives. On the contrary, we are generally taught to behave in a certain way, be a certain person, and to even have specific feelings as an appropriate response. Each of these teachings create limitations and renounce our authentic feelings. After many years of this type of training, it may be difficult to actually know our true preferences and ultimately ourselves.

Hence, the various practices to explore our inner selves, as reviewed in previous chapters, become quite essential, and the experimentation with our new awareness in a safe setting, such as improvisation, is equally important. We must "try on" our new characteristics and traits of which we have become aware. We may feel joyful with our new expressions or perhaps awkward as they may feel foreign to us. Over time and with practice, we will become more comfortable in these new expressions, may see some evolution of these traits, and will be more confident in ourselves.

With this in mind, we will delve into the principles and characteristics of improvisation and demonstrate how your newfound awareness can be explored and developed in this art form.

I wish to note that there are many excellent books that describe the principles, techniques, and exercises of the improvisational art form. While some focus on the history of improv, many focus on the particular exercises or "games" that are to be utilized in the improvisational exercises. In this book, I will not focus or present the specific improvisational games but rather focus on the principles and benefits of improv, and how they may be applied to workplace situations.

The principles will generally be presented in three subsections: first, *Improv*, where I will discuss the principle as it pertains to improvisational acting; secondly, *Exercises*, where I will present exercises to help you understand and practice that particular principle; and thirdly, *Workplace,* where I will reflect upon the application of this principle in the workplace.

The objective is to help you understand these principles and benefits, to become more aware of how they operate in you, and to practice them for your assimilation, with the ultimate goals to improve awareness, leadership, and consciousness in the workplace.

Structure

Generic

When one hears the word "improv," one might first think of the major city theaters where improvisation is performed. Most of these improv clubs present the traditional "YES AND" technique of improvisation whereby the actor accepts their partner's statement (offer) as true, and they then expand upon it in some improvisational manner. The expansion is generally designed to offer more information to their partner that becomes helpful for the scene to be engaging, interesting, and artful. This entertaining banter moves back and forth between the actors and frequently ends in some outrageous place of comedic entertainment. Of course, there is no script and the scenes may move in directions surprising to even the actors.

The structure of the improvisational scene is quite sparse. This is purposely intended to allow the actors to be freshly creative, i.e., to provide the possibility for the actors to create something special and unique. During the improv scene, the actors create a connection with their partner; the actors consider the situation to be real; and the connection will likely spur emotions and words that may not be imagined by a script writer. It exemplifies the concept of WE versus ME, where WE create something unique to this moment.

The structure is therefore designed to be as minimal as possible. At most, each actor would know who they are, how they are related to the other, and some general physical setting. However, in most cases, the actors would have totally no such information, and they would create even this minimal structure live on stage.

Short Form Improv vs Long Form Improv

There are two distinctive forms of improvisation—short form and long form. Although the generic structure noted above applies to both forms, there are clear differences between the two. In long form improv, the audience will usually provide one suggestion and the improvisers would create a twenty-to-thirty-minute set based on that suggestion, whereas in short form, there is more frequent interaction with the audience as there are multiple shorter games (a few minutes each) that are independent of each other. The TV program, *Whose Line is it Anyway*, is an example of the short form improv and is likely what the general population thinks of when they hear the word improv. These games are quick, gimmicky, and fun. In long form improv, there are structures within which the improvisers perform and relate the subject matter to the suggestion of the audience, a common of these forms being called The Harold. The scenes are clearly longer than in short form, are more grounded, develop relationships more deeply, and create a storyline. Humor will generally emerge as the scene is cleverly heightened by the improvisers.

Improv vs Standup

A common misconception of improv is that it is the same as standup comedy. Although both provide audience entertainment, these art forms are quite different. In standup, the performer is generally presenting prepared jokes and stories with the main purpose of attaining humor. The communication is unidirectional, i.e., they are speaking *to* the audience, not conversing *with* them. In improv, there is no scripted material, the connection of the actor to their partner is critical to the development of the scene, deep listening and patience are critical, and the goal is to provide dialogue that is engaging, interesting, and authentic, versus strictly humorous. The skills needed for each of these art forms is quite different and in fact can sometimes be an impediment to performing the other. Comedian John Oliver succinctly says, "In improv, the whole thing is that it is a relationship between the two people, as a back-and-forth. In standup, you don't really want to be listening to what somebody else is saying, you want to project your jokes into their face."

Conscious Communication Cycle™

The next chapters will detail the improv principles and benefits. In this section, I would like to describe the basic cycle of communication that is required for a successful improv, and for a successful communication in general. I aim to describe a simplistic exchange that is at the foundation of all clear and conscious communications. The subsequent chapters will then delve more deeply into principles, benefits, exercises, and relation to our workplace.

The Conscious Communication Cycle™ is a communication dynamic between two people that incorporates deep listening, self-assessment, and authenticity. It is one of awareness, perception, and true connection. Foundational aspects of this communication cycle are caring, openness, vulnerability, and honesty, and can only be performed if both the heart and mind are involved. This Conscious Communication Cycle is a foundational requirement for a successful improvisational scene.

I would like to describe how this cycle pertains to specific emotions and actions that occur when an improviser—specifically me—steps out on the stage.

Prior to walking out on stage, I am both nervous and excited. I look at the audience and I see people with smiles on their faces ready to be entertained and ready for laughter. I typically know a couple of them but the majority are strangers. Although I attempt to not be attached to the outcome of the improv, I am hoping the audience will enjoy our offering.

Depending on the improvisational form we have decided to offer the audience, we will generally ask them for a suggestion or word that we will incorporate into a specific type of opening. The purpose of this opening is to develop several ideas from which we will create improvisational scenes.

After these ideas are identified, one of us will step out from the back line to perform the first improv scene. To support this brave initiator, someone immediately steps out to join and support them. When I am that supporting person, the following happens. I am still nervous and excited; I have no idea what my partner will say; no idea what the scene will be about; and I expect that my partner has an idea since they came out first. Therefore, at this point I am there ready to support my partner and engage them with what will hopefully be an entertaining scene. As I first step out there, my heart is beating and my entire body (mind, heart, and more) is totally 100 percent focused on my partner since I have no idea at all what my partner will say or do. My eyes and ears are wide open and my entire body is at 100 percent attention ready to receive whatever my partner is offering, since if I don't listen, I will have nothing to say in response. I not only listen to their words but I am listening to their tone, watching their facial expressions, and noticing their entire body language. I am looking at everything—are they excited, are they sad, are they angry, are they pensive, are they playing the role of an adult, child, animal, or other character? I need all this information in order to fully understand not only what they're saying, but what they're really conveying to me, e.g. what is the context, the message, the environment, and the true sentiment. Only then will I be able to truly understand the offering and be able to subsequently respond appropriately. If I miss an essential element of their offering, I may respond with something that is disconnected from their true offering. This may confuse my partner and, equally important, will confuse the audience. For my partner, they will have to process this disconnect and determine what direction to take the scene, i.e., do they double down on the initial offering or do they follow my disconnected tangent? For the audience, their confusion may be conscious or unconscious, but they will not fully connect with the scene and therefore be unsatisfied—again this may be unconscious but it will occur.

Assuming my deep listening to my partner was successful, it is now my turn to accept their offer and add to it (YES AND), offering them something in return. At this point, I can certainly go to my mind to respond with something I believe to be appropriate. However, a much better approach would be to first perform a self-assessment, i.e., how do I *feel* about my partner's offering? Am I shocked, am I delighted, am I angry, am I joyful, or do I feel betrayed or elated? Assessing these feelings would help to provide a more authentic response. Once these feelings are identified, I will incorporate them somehow into my authentic response, making my response much more meaningful. If I fail to do this, my verbal response may not match my internal emotions, resulting in a disconnected response. Again, both my partner and the audience may perceive my emotional reaction (perhaps unconsciously) and expect my response to relate to that emotion. If it does not, both my partner and the audience will feel that disconnect.

Once I have successfully performed the deep listening from my partner's offer, identified my emotional response to that offer, and somehow incorporated that emotion into an authentic response to my partner, I will have then completed one half of the Conscious Communication Cycle. My partner and the audience will be clear as to the interchange that just occurred.

As you may expect, it is then my partner's turn to complete the cycle by performing deep listening of my offer, performing a self-assessment of their emotional reaction to my offer, and returning with an authentic response. Once this occurs, we have completed a full cycle of a conscious communication.

The diagrams below depict this Conscious Communication Cycle. Notice that to perform this cycle requires both the mind and the heart.

DIAGRAM A

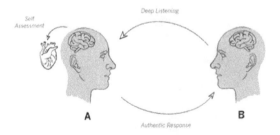

Conscious Communication Cycle™

A Cycle

In this A Cycle diagram, person B initiates the conversation with an opening line. Once this occurs, person A would first perform deep listening, then perform a self-assessment of their emotions, and then reply with an authentic response.

DIAGRAM B

Conscious Communication Cycle™

B Cycle

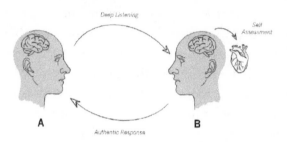

In this B Cycle diagram, person A initiates the conversation with an opening line. Once this occurs, person B would first perform deep listening, then perform a self-assessment of their emotions, and then reply with an authentic response.

DIAGRAM C

Conscious Communication Cycle™

A/B Cycle

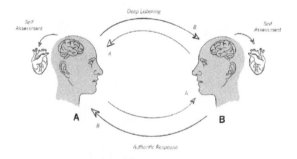

This A/B Cycle diagram depicts the full Conscious Communication Cycle, whereby, after every comment, the receiving person first performs deep listening, then performs a self-assessment of their emotions, and then replies with an authentic response. This pattern continues to cycle throughout the conversation.

A more advanced option to this cycle would include the aspects of incorporating reflection and discretion into this process. In the diagram above, they would occur after the self-assessment and before the authentic response. The reflection would consist of a quick mental review of what just happened, i.e., the offer from my partner and my emotional response to that offer. (The caution here is to avoid using this mental review *instead* of the self-assessment of your emotions). This reflection may reveal that there are multiple possible responses, each equally authentic. In this case, your discretion would select one of those authentic responses—perhaps the one you believe is more entertaining, or has more "runway" for the scene to grow. Note that this review would happen instantaneously and organically.

This reflection/discretion option is not recommended if you are a newer improviser as it may interfere with your training of shifting your focus from thinking mode to feeling mode that helps to unleash your deeper creativity. As you become more advanced, these attributes will organically integrate into your improv scenes, i.e., it will take little to no effort to include them—they will just happen. Hence, I recommend you ignore them for the moment and watch them naturally appear as you become more proficient.

It is obvious to note that this type of conscious communication should be employed in all areas of our lives including personal and business. How often have we seen or heard someone say, "you're not really listening"? Or how often have we seen people in business too busy and only half listening to what is being said? In improv, the consequences are quickly apparent if we are not listening—hence the 100 percent focus. In both our business and personal lives, the consequences may not be immediately apparent as there is no audience to react—there is only one person who may not immediately respond. However, the ultimate consequences may in fact be problematic, but not revealed until a later time. Therefore, it behooves us to listen deeply at each communication interchange and to assess the importance of this dialogue. If deemed unimportant, it could be terminated noting the reason; if deemed less important, it could be prioritized for discussion at a future time; and if deemed important it can be addressed immediately. However, to make this assessment, it is necessary to perform the focused, deep listening.

Improv in Business

Although the word improvisation comes up most frequently in the entertainment world, interest in improv has grown over the past decades in the business world as well, in part because organizational life is changing fast. Technological and social innovations are emerging at an unprecedented rate, and in these circumstances, detailed plans and existing routines may be inadequate or impossible, leading people to improvise. Research suggests that improvisation can generate novel and useful solutions in organizations, such as real-time problem-solving by managers in fast-paced industries, entrepreneurs dealing with unexpected problems and opportunities, or responses to life-threatening crises that go beyond the scope of people's training. In short, improvisation can be an important source of creativity at work that can have positive and lasting consequences for organizations.

Colin M. Fisher and Frank J. Barrett in their manuscript entitled, "The Experience of Improvising in Organizations: A

Creative Process Perspective," describe improvisation occurring in organizations when one encounters unforeseen obstacles, fumbling through potential solutions extemporaneously, working with materials at hand, to come up with new insights or alternative courses of action or product innovations. They note that, "improvising evokes simultaneous exhilaration and fear, as well as experiences of nongoal-directed action. In many organizational contexts, however, improvisation is normatively discouraged, which heightens the fearful aspect of the experience. This leads many workers to avoid improvising, using it as a method of last resort and even hiding its use."

Edgar H. Schein in his book entitled *Humble Inquiry* notes, "There is growing recognition that the complex work of today is better likened to improvisation theater and jazz bands than to formal bureaucratic models of organizations."

Frank J. Barrett proposes improvisation is "fabricating and inventing novel responses without a prescriptive plan and without certainty of outcomes; discovering the future that action creates as it unfolds." David Bastien and Todd Hostager defined improvisation as "the invention, adoption and implementation of new ideas by individuals within the context of a shared awareness of the group performance as it unfolds over time." Cunha, Cunha, and Kamoche review several definitions and compile them as, "Conception of action as it unfolds, by an organization and/or its members, drawing on available material, cognitive, affective, and social resources."

Patricia Ryan Madson, in her book entitled *Improv Wisdom,* states, "Clearly, the ideal of teamwork is what fuels countless workshops, seminars, and wilderness experiences. It's possible to train ordinary people to work like improvisers. The improv "talent," which involves listening carefully, observing the actions of others, contributing, supporting, leading, following, filling in the gaps, and looking for the appropriate ending, can be taught and learned."

Chapter 9

Improv Principles

"Just say yes and you'll figure it out afterwards." Tina Fey

"The improviser has to understand that his first skill lies in releasing his partner's imagination." Keith Johnstone

---

Chapter Highlights

1. The primary principle of YES AND, plus many other improv principles are described.
2. Each principle notes the relationship to improv, is followed by exercises designed to help you develop these attributes, and relates them to the workplace environment.

Although the essential fundamental principle of improvisation is "YES AND," there are many more supporting principles or attributes that improvisational actors must embody in order to produce a successful improvisational scene. Below I will present several of these principles noting their relationship to improv, followed by exercises designed to help you develop these attributes, and lastly relating them to the workplace environment.

YES AND

Improv

There are many excellent books written exclusively on the YES AND improvisational format and include many exercises or "games" for use by improvisational teachers or other practitioners. Although in this book, I will not duplicate the presentation of "games," as others have superbly done, one of the earliest being *Improvisation for the Theater* by Viola Spolin, I wish to acknowledge the foundational YES AND principle of improvisation. I will therefore include a description of the YES AND principle, recognizing it as a fundamental improvisational principle and affirming its essential underlying foundation.

Although there are different types of improvisation, the most common form embodies the fundamental and essential principle of YES AND. This basically means that whatever your partner says must be accepted as truth (the YES part). For example, if your partner thanks you for picking up the groceries, you cannot reply "I did not pick up the groceries." Instead, you must accept your partner's statement or "offer" as truth, by saying, for example, "you're welcome " or "sure, no problem " or something that denotes your acceptance of your partner's statement, versus any sort of negation.

To take this to the next step, you must now offer your partner something in return—this return offer is the AND part of YES AND. In this example, you can respond in a number of ways, e.g., "Sure thing, and I saved a lot with those coupons you gave me ..." or "No problem, and I was really surprised to see your brother John there as the new manager." In these statements, you can see that in addition to accepting your partner's offer (YES), you are adding something (AND) to the conversation. This is your offer back to your partner to continue the conversation and providing them with additional information upon which they will accept (YES) and add their corresponding offer (AND). This volley exchange will continue and build between the actors and hopefully heighten to some entertaining peak or climax.

Izzy Gesell describes the goals of YES AND in his book entitled, *Playing Along,* as follows, "The goals of YES AND are to foster cooperation, to improve interpersonal relationships and listening skills, and to demonstrate the basic improv principle that 'agreement is the one rule that can never be broken.'"

In her book *Training to Imagine,* Kat Koppett states that, "YES AND means that not only must I, the improviser, accept an offer, I must build on it. I must contribute. I must make an offer of my own in response to my partner's. It is this process that harnesses the power of collaboration. Everyone offers and accepts. Each team member is responsible for both contributing to and supporting the group's activity. Through the implementation of this method, brainstorming sessions lead to innovative solutions. Even the smallest spark can be fanned into illuminating flames."

Charna Halpern, Del Close, and Kim "Howard" Johnson in *Truth in Comedy* state that, "*Agreement is the one rule that can never be broken*: the players must be in agreement to forward the action of the scene." They continue by saying, "When improvisers meet on stage, they agree to accept each other's initiations; they must completely commit to the reality they create for each other without a moment's hesitation." They note that this is a very relaxing way in which to work since, "A player knows that anything he says on stage will be immediately accepted by his fellow player, and treated as if it was the most scintillating idea ever offered to mankind. His partner then adds on to his idea, and moment by moment, the two of them have created a scene that neither of them had planned."

Pat Shay is a veteran New York/Chicago improv teacher (IO Road Show, UCB, Second City, PIT (Gut Improv, Faculty), TV, author *Fifty Grades of Shay: An Academic Fantasy*) and my Level 2 instructor at The PIT. In his book entitled, *The Heart of the Scene*, he provides an astute explanation of the consequences of YES AND and NO as follows. "When we say NO, we control our endpoint, attempting to define the edges of the scene. We get into an argument/negotiation, and we have a lot better idea what we're going to be talking about until we are edited. NO then becomes an attempt to script the rest of our scene." He continues and describes the consequences of YES, "YES [extends] from being a simple act of politeness to becoming a doorway to adventure. YES keeps us in a spot where we don't know what's going to happen next—that's the absolute best spot to really make discoveries. The early sensations of feeling lost are replaced with sensations of being surrounded by unlimited opportunities, a feeling you may start to crave. YES keeps us in a mode of discovery. YES is the thing that keeps us improvising."

Patricia Ryan Madson states in her book entitled *Improv Wisdom*, "When the answer ... is yes, you enter a new world, a world of action, possibility, and adventure. Yes starts the juices rolling. Saying yes is an act of courage and optimism; it allows you to share control. It is a way to make your partner happy. Yes expands the world." She notes a reality check by saying, "it is undoubtedly an exaggeration to suggest that we can say yes to everything that comes up, but we can all say yes to more than we normally do."

Caveat—The nature of improv challenges our self with the unknown—the unknown script, the unknown emotional reaction we may have, the unknown dialogue we will engage in, and the unknown outcome. There will likely be anticipation, fear, and discomfort because of these unknowns. In general, the challenge is to face these discomforts and move through them, thereby exercising our courage, facilitating self-growth, and exploring new opportunities. This occurs when we exercise the YES AND basic principle of improv, as we will have no idea what will be said or offered, or where the scene will go.

Although self-growth will generally occur with this exercise, it is important to accept self-responsibility and to know our own personal safe boundaries. For example, if our partner says something that is quite triggering and saying YES would be harmful or traumatic for us— beyond self-growth—then we must find a way to deny our partner's offer. We would be then exercising our self-choice and self-respect, and honoring our self in this manner may actually be our exercise in self-growth. In either case, these aspects of self-choice and self-honoring are paramount to maintain our truth, integrity, and inner alignment.

Therefore, we say YES AND until we must say NO THANK YOU, and saying no thank you acknowledges the offer but refuses the sentiment or intention. Chris Griggs, (veteran NY comedian, improviser (Second City, UCB, PIT), actor with numerous TV appearances, founding member of the Baldwins improv team, and my PIT Master Class improv instructor), explains this concept as follows, "I want to accept the reality of what my scene partner is saying but I don't have to say yes to something that makes me feel compromised or triggered as a person."

This action is a rare exception to the traditional YES AND principle but necessary to acknowledge as a possibility.

Exercise

Perhaps a useful exercise to demonstrate YES AND would be one that brings awareness to the frequency with which we say "yes," "no," or "yes, but," which is essentially a "no." The "no" response seems to be an easy default, perhaps one ingrained in us during childhood.

Saying no, or blocking, is discussed by Madson in *Improv Wisdom*. "Blocking comes in many forms; it is a way of trying to control the situation instead of accepting it. We block when we say no, when we have a better idea, when we change the subject, when we correct the speaker, when we fail to listen, or when we simply ignore the situation. The critic in us wakes up and runs the show. Saying no is the most common way we attempt to control the future. For many of us the habit is so ingrained that we don't notice we are doing it. We are not only experienced at blocking others, we commonly block ourselves."

To demonstrate this, I suggest three parts to this exercise. First, once connected with your partner, have your partner make an initial offering to you. Once fully received, say "no," and add some comment of explanation. Then allow your partner to continue trying to convince you while you continue to deny the request with yet a different explanation. After the exercise, debrief and notice that this negation likely constrained and limited the conversation. Also notice if this negation was easy or familiar to you.

Secondly, have your partner make you an initial offering and you respond with "yes, but ..." Although you are beginning the sentence with "yes," the "but" negates the yes and this is essentially a more polite way to say no. Continue the scene for a few iterations with your partner continuing as in the first example. Again, notice the constraint of this conversation and notice if this response is familiar or easy.

Thirdly, have your partner make an initial offering to you where you would respond with the positive YES AND where you would agree with their offering and add to the scenario. Continue the scene with each utilizing the YES AND principle and watch where the scene goes. After the scene is over, notice that the scene was likely more expansive with possibilities than the previous scenes. Also notice how you feel and how often you generally respond in this manner.

You will likely find that the YES AND scenes will be more expansive, rich with ideas, move in a variety of directions, be more accepting and positive, more creative, and explore more avenues of possibilities.

I also suspect you may find that a negation, as in the first two scenes, is a common and familiar occurrence. Whether the reasoning be that we don't wish to engage, don't feel we have the time, don't wish to be interrupted, perceive we do not have the energy to move positively with the offer, or some other reasoning, saying "no" may be a habit for many of us. This exercise may bring you greater awareness of your default position and/or your comfort zone—and awareness is the first step in affecting a desired change.

Workplace

The concept of YES AND is useful in a business environment for a variety of reasons, including fostering creativity, positivity, openness, respect, and more. For example, in a typically busy organization, it is not uncommon for a manager to say "not now" when an employee asks for some time, or to say "no" to new ideas. In these cases, requests are interpreted as interruptions which, in turn, convey a message of unimportance to the employee. This negativity thwarts inspiration and creativity. Although saying no may be easy, as you (the executive/manager) may be dismissing yet another problem or situation being brought to your attention, it is harmful to the staff and the organization in the long term.

At a workshop in New York City, a manager told me, "I'm so used to saying no to my employees and shutting them down. I'm slowly changing to really listen to them, and I see that there's better teamwork that way."

Improvisational training helps us to acknowledge others' points of view more readily, to say yes more easily, and to then build upon it to explore what might be created. Saying yes is an opening statement inviting additional conversation, while saying no closes the conversation and tells our partners you are basically not interested in their thought or idea.

NO

Improv

A response of NO to a request was the first style of improv that I learned, and appears to be the opposite of the YES AND foundational principle of traditional improv. In fact, it is not. In this form, the actor is accepting and saying YES to the premise of the offer but NO to the actual request. For example, if one asks, "Can I move in with you?" the response could be, "I understand you need a place to live but I just don't have the room." In this case, the responder is saying YES to the premise (they want to move in) but NO to the request.

This style of improv generally consists of more acting vs. comedy, falls into the overall category of dramatic improv, and may also be considered conflict improv. In this improv style, one would ask for something from their partner, e.g., an item or favor, and their partner would refuse. Clearly, this creates tension between the actors and, as Pat Shay describes above, would dictate what the scene will be about, i.e., the actors will now be in conflict over this particular issue, with all related negotiations and arguments.

After the initial request is refused, the requesting actor would then attempt to use every emotion available to them—anger, vulnerability, sensuality, love, etc.—in their attempt to obtain the requested item. The receiving actor would in turn continually say no in one way or another. They could be harsh, understanding, gentle, loving, or however they authentically feel to respond to the request, but always ending with the negation of the request. The scene may last five to ten minutes, would focus on the drama of the specific conflict, and may include several tangents along the way.

There are generally compelling exchanges between the two actors, since they are listening deeply to each other, being self-aware of their emotional reactions, and replying authentically back to their partners. The initial request could be minor, e.g., "please lend me $100" or "may I please borrow your car for the evening" or it may be substantial, e.g., "I need $100,000 to pay off a gambling debt" or "I know this is a lot to ask, but I need a kidney from you." However strong the initial request, raising the stakes as your partner continually says no is an important dynamic of the scene, as it makes the scene more and more dramatic and compelling. You can certainly imagine the tension and drama between the actors if the negation of a request ultimately becomes a life-threatening decision.

Frequently, the audience has a personal vested interest in one of the two sides of this tension based on their own life experiences, and is generally quite curious as to the outcome of the scene. The actors themselves will not know how it ends as they will not know how their authentic self will respond. In most cases, the receiving partner will not be convinced and will continue to say no, while at other times they will be truly convinced and end up saying yes. (Generally, saying yes to the request would end the scene, and it would therefore only occur as a finale.)

The scene is quite authentic and may travel to various places— all within the universe of this particular conflict, argument, or negotiation. The compelling drama is generally very relatable to the actual lives of the audience members who are generally drawn into the negotiating exchange. Although the goal is not comedy specific and frequently dramatic, the lengthier scenes allow time for a variety of emotions, and there will likely be moments of comedy intermixed with the drama. However it evolves, this five-to-ten-minute scene is generally compelling and entertaining.

Uses

In the previous YES AND section, we included a caveat of when it would be important for an actor to say NO THANK YOU. This was aimed at situations where the actor took self-responsibility and declined their partner's offer for their own personal health, i.e., setting a safe boundary for themselves.

Setting a safe and healthy boundary for yourself generally requires a NO, and as such, would apply to any situation that necessitates the creation of a boundary. This would of course apply to both our personal and business life. An example of this occurred in an improv workshop I led in Morristown, New Jersey. In that situation, a scene was set up where two coworkers were discussing a joint project for which they were responsible. One of the employees was encouraging an unethical action regarding their joint report, while the other was resisting such an action. The resistant employee was successful in maintaining her position and later stated, "When I did that scene with John, he was asking me to do something inappropriate regarding a report we were doing together. I didn't want to do it and I repeatedly said no to all his pressure. It was very tough, and I wasn't sure I could do it. But

I did, and I was happy to learn that I can set a boundary when necessary, even though it was very difficult." Although this scene was a fictitious role-play, the participants acted with authentic feelings allowing for an effective simulation. As a result, the resistant employee discovered an important realization: that she could set a boundary that matched her inner values.

In these cases, saying NO is not only a boundary-setting action, but it is also our truth and, as truth, becomes our authentic response. In this vein, an authentic NO to a request (not the offered premise) is an appropriate component of any style of improv.

Exercise

After connecting to your partner, I suggest you start with a minor request that has some meaning to you. Allow your partner to hear your request and then hear their negative reply. Initially, set up the scene such that your partner's negative reply be emotionally neutral, allowing you to practice your set of emotions without being affected by any possible emotion of theirs. Once you hear their (neutral) negative response, reply with one of several emotions (anger, vulnerability, seduction, love, fear). After each of their neutral negative replies, repeat your request with a different emotion. Notice the differences of how you feel after each different emotion—an exercise in awareness.

Once you have discovered how you feel after each different emotion, repeat the exercise allowing your partner to provide their negative reply with whatever authentic emotion they may have. This will, of course, affect you in some way and, being authentic, you would naturally incorporate this into your response. For example, if their negation makes you angry then you may naturally repeat your request with anger. This would be your authentic emotional response. If their negation makes you sad, then offer your true vulnerability when repeating the request; if their negation is sweet or sarcastic, it may trigger your seduction response (not necessarily sexual); if their negation is kind and loving, it may trigger your loving reply. In this way, you are exploring your various emotions in your attempt to convince your partner to yield to your request.

You will not only explore yourself with these various emotions, and how you feel projecting these variety of emotions onto your partner, but you will also see how your partner responds to these various emotions from you. And their emotional and authentic responses will affect you, and vice/versa in this back-and-forth banter. As each of you listens deeply and receives the range of emotions from your partner, the key is to identify your reactions (self-awareness) and maintain authenticity throughout the process.

Workplace

It is important to learn how to say no in certain workplace circumstances. Severe cases may include your manager requesting you do something immoral, unethical, or illegal; strong cases may include situations that would cause you physical or emotional harm; moderate cases may include requests to overwork; and mild cases may include simple preferences.

In all cases, you want to listen deeply to accurately understand the request; be self-aware of your feelings and needs; reflect and understand the various consequences; use discretion; and finally offer your authentic response. Based on the situation, your response could be an immediate and clear reply, it could be a question for clarification, it could be a request for a later response, it could be a need for contemplation, etc. Whatever your choice, it should be a conscious decision, one based on self-need and self-respect, and aligned with your inner values.

Serve Your Partner, Serve the Scene

Improv

A basic tenet of improv is to serve your partner and serve the scene in the best way you can, i.e., the focus is not on you but instead on your partner and the scene. In that regard, you are always listening deeply to your partner, not interrupting them, offering them some piece of useful information, and being totally authentic with them. It is said that you cannot have a great improv scene unless both people contribute. Therefore, if you can make your partner great, you are also, although inadvertently, shining a light on yourself. When your partner wins, you win with them. This concept is confirmed in *Truth in Comedy* as they say, "The best way for an improviser to look good is by making his fellow players look good." This becomes a model of the power of cooperation versus competition. A participant in a New York City improv workshop put it succinctly saying, "Working together is much easier than competing with someone."

Exercise

Set up a scene with your partner that relates to a subject matter of their interest and/or expertise. During the scene, do your best to "set them up" with conversation about that subject, as they will generally have lots to say. Of course, you will respond with your YES AND extending and building the conversation on the subject matter. You will find that the conversation will be inspiring, meaningful, and easily conversant resulting in a successful improvisation. And although you might feel that they were the "star" of the scene, you will discover that your part was equally important and therefore the "star" performance was between you, that is, it included you—together you were the "stars."

Workplace

Such a cooperative arrangement may seem foreign in the workplace since competition is more prevalent as most wish to highlight their own achievements in order to attain a promotion or increased compensation. This competition or self-highlighting is prevalent between employees, between employees and their managers, between organizations and their clients, between organizations and their vendors, and more, as many believe that helping others reduces their own value. This is an unfortunate illusion of values.

Centering/Loading

Improv

Prior to beginning a scene, an actor will "load" to embody a proper mindset, i.e., place their body, emotions, and mind in an optimal setting or alignment for an effective performance. We see similar preparation in other forms of life—an Olympian visualizing their routine, an athlete listening to music, a singer vocalizing notes, a speaker quieting their mind, etc. For improvisers, this preparation or centering may consist of quieting the mind for relaxation, loosening their body with certain physical exercises, loosening their mind with music, or sparking their creativity through various improv warm-up exercises with their team improvisers.

| This, in effect, is a centering or alignment of the actor to balance their emotions and mind, to access a deeper level of connection, and to ignite their creativity. |

Although some level of nerves or anxiety is natural (and likely healthy) prior to a performance, excess anxiety could lead to fear which could lead to paralysis, and hence be counterproductive to the improvisational experience. Each actor will find their own particular preparation that is most effective for them.

Exercise

From the various practices of meditation and mindfulness reviewed earlier, I would suggest at least one of the following options:

- Still Meditations—Zen, Mantra, TM, Gazing, or Loving Kindness
- Moving Meditations—Sufi Walking Meditation or Yoga
- Guided Meditations—Body Scan, Singing Bowls or personal music, or Guided Imagery of your choice
- Intensity—If you are extremely wound up and unable to perform the above meditations, you may need to first perform a more intense exercise such as push-ups or running in place to relieve the excess tension and calm the body down prior to performing the above centering and alignment exercises.

Workplace

There are many moments when such a preparation would be helpful in the workplace. This may include attending a meeting, making a presentation to an internal or external group, having a one-on-one meeting with your manager, having a conference call with the client, and more. It is easy to state that we should always be prepared in every moment of our workplace. However, there are levels of importance of the various meetings with which we participate—and the higher the importance the more critical it becomes for us to be at our optimal performance level. It is also quite likely that we will be more nervous or anxious during these more significant meetings. Therefore, if we consider that there is a spectrum of importance levels in our various workplace activities, we should match our preparation level for each activity in relation to the activity's level of importance. You would therefore select the exercise options in relation to the time and energy you wish to designate for preparation of this workplace activity.

I suggest you take notice of how you perform with such preparation versus how you have performed in prior meetings without such preparation. I also suggest you note your state of being prior to, during, and post such meetings. All this added awareness will help maintain your mindfulness and will over time improve your general performance.

Deep Listening

Improv

From the very first line of an improv, listening is totally critical. Since there is no script, the actors will have nothing to work with if they do not listen to their partner. Their opening statement is basically the foundation upon which the scene will be built. If they do not listen, they will likely speak and reply in some discordant manner, not building upon the original offer and perhaps even invalidating their partner's statement. And this violates the fundamental YES AND rule of improvisation—ignoring your partner's words is effectively a NO rather than YES, and there is no AND to further build the scene. It is therefore essential to listen to your partner, to accept the validity of their statement, and to use that as the foundation upon which to build and offer your response.

As important as listening is, more important is deep listening. Deep listening involves more than listening to the words of your partner, for it involves sensing the feelings and intentions beneath their words. When one listens deeply, they are being attentive to the entire being, including body language, and therefore hearing their partner much more accurately. Words matter, but the sentiment and intention beneath the words—the subtext—are much more important. In our everyday lives, we commonly hear or say to people "I'm fine" or "okay, sure" or "I love you," and we can identify the variations of sentiments that are beneath each of these phrases, as they can be quite different from the stated words.

Truth in Comedy describes this concept by noting the difference between hearing and listening. They state, "Hearing and listening are two different things. When a player is given an initiation, he must let the words resonate inside his head for a moment, so that he can decipher the underlying meaning." They continue by saying, "An improviser must consider what is said, and what is left unsaid, as well. He must think, 'Why was that said? What does she mean by that? How does it make me feel?' If a player takes the time to consider what the other speaker means, then his response is more intelligent than the knee-jerk response .... A more carefully considered response takes a second or two longer, but the wait is well worthwhile."

The deep listening is mandatory in our improvisational scenes for at least two reasons. First, we want to fully embrace the intention of the comment made to us so that we can accurately react to it, and secondly, the audience will, consciously or unconsciously, feel the underlying sentiment of the words and would be confused if our reaction to our partner does not address or relate to their deeper intention. The audiences, like other people in our life, are quite savvy, and generally sense what is truly going on, i.e., what is truly being said—the true intention beneath the words. Therefore, if the actor does not speak the truth of their sentiments, they will be disconnected from the audience and their partner. And conversely, as we do listen deeply and respond to the truth beneath the words, we will connect with our partners, and the audience will be in sync with us and will continue to be engaged in the scene.

This deep listening, then, becomes an important prerequisite to connection, both to our partner and the audience. This concept is clearly also important in our relations to our friends, relatives, and coworkers. Only then can we truly connect with them in order to have an honest and productive dialogue. This deep listening fosters clear and effective communications.

The deep listening exercises at improv workshops are frequently eye-opening to the participants, as one from a Hackensack, New Jersey workshop stated, "I was amazed by the exercise where someone said one thing but meant something totally different. I experienced that exercise as the giver and receiver, and it impacted me. I now understand that I need to listen more deeply—to the true meaning under the words."

At a workshop in Madison, New Jersey, a participant said almost exactly the same thing, "I now understand that I must listen to the sentiment under the words, and not just believe the words as spoken."

Exercise

In improvisational acting training, there are exercises designed exactly to address this concept, and you can use them with a friend as an experiment. First, stand in front of your partner making good eye contact. Once you both feel connected, each will make a true statement to the other such as, "I like the shirt you're wearing." Each will likely sense the truth since the words support the true sentiment. Next, each would make a statement to the other that is untrue where the sentiment beneath the words is clearly different than the words, e.g., say "I love you" with anger and resentment, or say "I hate you" with joyous and loving sentiments. Such statements will likely confuse the brain but help us to experience the greater meaning of the sentiment versus the words. After these two initial exercises, each can make a statement to the other where the other would provide their assessment as to whether they believe them or not. Continue this process back-and-forth until you each feel a sense of completion. This exercise would not only sharpen your listening skills but would also give feedback to the speaker per chance they made a true statement that was not believable. In this case, that feedback is telling them that they are not projecting the true sentiments of their words.

This benefit to the speaker was exemplified by a participant in a Paramus, New Jersey workshop as they stated, "I frequently feel like I'm talking into the wind, and I'm very uncomfortable not knowing if my words landed. This happens at home and at work. I finally spoke up. Once I understood that I *was* truly being listened to, then I felt heard and more comfortable to speak again. Less stress ..."

These exercises help us to develop the skills of projecting certain emotions regardless of the words that are used and they also help us to be more authentic with our words, i.e., we strive to match our words and our emotions in order to present a single and clear message to the listener. I am sure we have all experienced words that were said to us that did not match the feeling behind them. We might have thought, "They said that to me, but I don't think they really meant it."

Workplace

Deep listening is useful in a business environment for a number of reasons. For employees, it can be critical that they understand what their managers are *really* saying; for coworkers and teammates, the project will be more efficient and successful with these listening skills; for managers, to truly hear the deeper sentiment of their employees, especially related to sensitive subjects, is critical to understand the employees' true issues. With the new awareness in these situations, if they sense a disconnect between the words and the sentiment, they now have the opportunity to either name it or ask questions for clarification purposes. Practicing this new awareness, with possible clarifications, will now provide you with clearer information and better understanding of the true situation.

A workshop participant in Philadelphia experienced this important insight and summarized it by saying, "Listening is key. I always want to talk and give my point of view, in business (sales) and at home. But when I do that, it's tough for me to focus and listen to the other person. I guess I have my agenda. But I see that when I do listen, I better understand what's going on with them and we have a better conversation. The talk may not go the way I planned it, but it goes better ..."

Communications

Improv

When we speak of communications, we are talking about a deeper truth and not superficial words, and the truth in communications can only follow the deep listening and understanding of the true sentiments of another. If there is any confusion about the meaning of the words, it is critically important to speak that truth. To make some assumption about what was said and carry on with a response may be totally off the mark, and therefore present a disconnect with your partner, coworker, and the audience. In a sense, it will invalidate the comment of your partner if you misunderstand them and respond in some disconnected manner. It is therefore imperative to honor your truth—in this moment and in all moments—and reply with your confusion or doubt in understanding your partner's statement. Your truth in that moment would be your confusion and your request to ask for clarification. Again, it will likely be apparent to your partner (and any audience) if you do not understand and if you ramble on with some unrelated comment. Your partner and the audience will generally see—consciously or unconsciously—your confusion and misunderstanding and will not be able to connect with you if you do not speak your truth. I find that this is one of the most common misconceptions of human behavior, i.e., that we believe we can fool people far more often than it actually occurs.

I would encourage each of us to think about times we were confused and pretended to understand as the conversation progressed. I propose that we cheated ourselves of an understanding and perhaps a worthy connection and conversation that would have followed.

Exercise

Notice the next time someone says something that you do not fully understand (I submit that you would be surprised at how quickly that next occurrence would be). At that time, or at the very next time, express your truth in a polite and appropriate manner, keeping the onus on yourself rather than the other. In other words, use "I" statements versus "you" statements. In this manner, you would always point to yourself and never to the other, e.g., say, "I'm sorry, *I* did not fully understand" rather than "I'm sorry but *you* were not clear."

Workplace

This exercise would also function in the workplace, remembering to keep the onus on yourself and to be respectful with your comments. In the workplace, it may be important to provide additional information to your listener (employee/manager/client) to ensure they felt heard and respected, e.g., "I understand and acknowledge ABC but I am unclear about XYZ." In this way, the listener would see that you have understood part of the conversation but need clarity in other parts.

Participant Insights

There are a variety of examples of participant insights that span different aspects of communications. Following are a few of these:

- In Darien Connecticut, a participant said, "There is constant change and sometimes chaos—clear communications and trust go a long way to a positive conclusion."
- In Stonybrook New York, a participant said, "I was amazed that conversations are much more effective when speaking in the client's language."
- Another New York participant stated, "In many conversations, people talk *at* each other without really connecting with each other, and the conversation is frequently flat. When we were guided to make eye contact, I actually 'felt' the other person and the communication was so much better. I see that a real connection is a critical part of a good communication.."

Self-Awareness

Improv

Once we have a clear understanding of our partner's comment, i.e., their deeper meaning, we must allow their sentiment to impact us and to honestly identify our emotional reaction to that sentiment. It may take a moment or two for their true sentiment to reach us, to be absorbed by us, and for us to react to it. It is likely only a second or two but may feel longer, especially when compared to the fast-paced conversation that frequently otherwise occurs, perhaps especially in the workplace.

Once we accurately identify how we are affected, we would then speak authentically from that place, i.e., we must speak words that match our true sentiment. This will then be a truthful response, and since it is truthful, it will maintain the connection and engagement to our partner and the audience.

Exercise

In our improvisational training, we may practice almost seeing the energy of our partner's sentiment travel from them into our bodies and spending five or ten seconds absorbing it to notice how we are affected by it. This can be practiced and explored with a partner or friend.

Stand in eye to eye connection with your partner and then allow your partner to speak a sentence and pause. During this pause, take your time (five to ten seconds) allowing your partner's sentiment to fully affect you in some way. After the ten seconds, define the effect their sentiment had on you and speak it aloud without concern of judgment or criticism. Note: You are not doing a scene or exchanging conversation based on their comment, but only identifying the effect or your emotional reaction to their comment—your self-awareness based on their comment. Exchange roles and continue to perform this exercise slowly and mindfully. With practice, this process becomes faster and faster. Although initially this ten-second self-awareness practice may not be practical in everyday life, your self-awareness skills will improve in accuracy and speed thereby allowing you to fully utilize them in everyday life.

Workplace

In business, there are many conversations that are necessarily fast-paced whereby such a practice would be difficult and perhaps impossible. In other cases, there are conversations that are necessarily slower and deeper, whereby this practice of receiving more deeply and accessing your deeper truths would be not only be relevant but important. Your discretion and judgment will make this determination. In all cases, practice will improve your self-awareness skills allowing you to utilize them more frequently.

The importance of an accurate identification of one's feelings is highlighted in Edgar H. Schein's book entitled, *Process Consultation*. Within his description of three modes of consultation (Expert Model, Doctor-Patient Model, Process Consultation Model), he discusses the ORJI Process where we observe (O), we react emotionally to what we have observed (R), we analyze, process, and make judgments based on observations and feelings (J), and we behave overtly in order to make something happen, we intervene (I).

Schein notes as background that the most important thing for managers or consultants to understand is what goes on inside their own heads and that we were taught that feelings should be controlled and in various ways denied. He continues stating that we also learned that feelings should not influence our judgments, that feelings are a source of distortion, and that acting on them would be defined as impulsive. But paradoxically, we often end up acting most on our feelings when we are least aware of them.

As such, Schein is recommending that we identify and become aware of our feelings *consciously* so that we may include them in our judgment and decision-making process rather than the feelings go underground whereby we may actually express them unconsciously thereby making poor decisions. Decisions based on unconscious feelings or thoughts are quite dangerous as we are not aware of the intentional source.

Therefore, improvisational practice whereby one practices to accurately identify their feelings and reactions is an important practice for managers and employees to create a more aware and conscious environment within which to operate.

Reflection

Improv

Schein's definition of ORJI describes an internal process whereby we observe (O), we react emotionally (R), we analyze, process, and judge (J), and we intervene (I). If we relate this to our improvisational process, we can compare his (O) to our deep listening, his (R) to our self-assessment, and his (I) to our acceptance and counter "offer" to our partner. The question that obviously remains is do improvisers analyze, process, and judge as he describes in (J).

We can argue that improvisers do not, as they do not analyze, but instead intuitively react without hesitation. On the other hand, we could argue that improvisers must maintain a very sharp focus in listening to all conversations, to think about how they can make connections with the other actors, and to devise scenarios with the situations presented to them. The question then remains: are they analyzing and processing? Perhaps part of the answer lies in the level of experience of the improviser.

For example, a novice is generally encouraged to not analyze or think but to just react, as their thinking process may be slow, and/or cause anxiety or even paralysis. They are frequently self-conscious and concerned if their response will be appropriate, humorous, clever, etc. As such, the recommendation for them to react and not think is an excellent exercise that will help them be freer, less limiting, more creative, and less concerned about consequences. They are encouraged to understand that there is no wrong answer, that creativity and uniqueness are sought, and that they are free of consequences in this safe environment.

As the improvisational experience is developed and self-consciousness disappears, several things would happen for the participant—anxiety will be minimized, self-assessment will be faster and more accurate, and inhibitions of responses will disappear. Once that basic level of improv is achieved, the participant/actor may find that some amount of processing may occur prior to the response to their partner. It may be misleading to call this process thinking, as it is a less cognitive process—and a more intuitive process—that is based more on their intention in the moment and their broad base of improvisational experience that may include seasoned filters. This intuitive process would not cause hesitation or paralysis but instead would grasp the scene dynamics as it is unfolding, allowing for a creative contribution to the scene. As such, the experienced improvisers are utilizing an intuitive process based on their intention and experience, perhaps at a lightning fast pace. In this sense, we can relate this intuitive process to Schein's "J" component of ORJI.

Whether we consider this reflection process to be intuitive, cognitive, or both, it may not always be lightning fast. There are applications that require detailed, and perhaps rigorous, levels of reflection, analysis, and judgment—situations at work or at home where your decisions may be highly consequential.

Therefore, the level of reflection will vary widely—from extremely low (improv comedy, think tank explorations), to moderate (daily decisions that have minor or moderate impacts), to extremely high (governmental decisions affecting global economies or strategic decisions that may change the direction of a corporation).

These levels of reflection (from extremely low to extremely high) may be related to the work of Daniel Kahneman in his book entitled, *Thinking, Fast and Slow*. In his book, Kahneman describes two systems of thinking: fast thinking, or System 1, and slow thinking, or System 2. He describes System 1 as our normal or automatic thinking process, one that works fast, does most of the mental work, impulsive with no control, useful for survival responses, is cognitively easy, and produces our "fight or flight" responses related to the sympathetic autonomic nervous system. System 2 thinking is described as deliberate, effortful, slower, more rational and logical, a cognitive strain, the ability to perform complicated computations, and more related to the parasympathetic autonomic nervous system.

If we relate this to improv, a curious question emerges: do improvisers use System 1 or System 2 thinking? Based on comments in the previous paragraph, we may conclude that novice improvisers would exclusively use System 1, while more experienced improvisers may use both.

Kahneman discusses the behavior of firefighters, noting that they may be using System 1 thinking or behavior during an actual fire. However, their actions are based on steep and rigorous training designed to account for the most likely of situations. In other words, their fast thinking actions are not random nor are they "flying by the seat-of-the-pants," but instead are acting on a strong body of knowledge and preparation. The same analogy would apply to emergency room doctors. Although they may be improvising in the moment, their actions are based on a strong body of knowledge and experience accumulated from medical school and throughout all their medical experiences to date. The same is true of experienced improvisers, i.e., they are not just "flying by the seat-of-the-pants" but instead improvising based on a body of knowledge and experience. Although it may be obvious that firefighters and medical doctors would undergo rigorous training, one may not realize that improvisers also go through training. I have often been asked the question, "How can you train to do improv?" Now that we have presented the various principles of improv, it is easier to see that these principles require practice to master and hence provide the answer to how to train for improv.

Regarding System 1 and System 2, we can see that the firefighter and emergency room doctor have exercised both—perhaps at different times, or perhaps simultaneously interlacing the two with exceptional speed, and therefore difficult to discern. And I believe this same dynamic applies to improvisational actors.

In general, it is difficult to declare an exclusive use of one side of any polarity and, hence, we have been given the symbol of yin/yang where the division of the two poles is not a straight line but instead a flow of one into each other, and where within each pole lies a small component of the other.

In the overall process, the goal is to help you develop greater awareness, authenticity, and consciousness. To that end, I am presenting related elements of the process for your consideration and understanding. Deep listening, identification of your feelings (self-assessment) and authentic responses are key ingredients to facilitate a positive connection to your partner. Reflection is a variable, and perhaps a complex component to define.

In addition to the various levels of reflection for consideration, I also acknowledge that the reflective process may present you with more than one possible authentic reply. In this case, my guidance to you is to ensure each of the possible replies is authentic and then to incorporate a level of discretion in your selection but to always ensure your response is authentic—this is paramount to the process of making a true connection.

Exercise

I encourage you to experiment with the different levels of reflection, from zero to extreme. With your partner, create three different scenes. In the first scene, practice zero reflection, i.e., respond to your partner's offers immediately, without hesitation, in total reaction. Continue the scene in this fashion. In the second scene, practice a moderate level of reflection in each of your responses, and in the third scene, experiment with a much greater level of reflection/analysis prior each of your responses.

After each scene, debrief your experiences with your partner. Then also allow your partner to debrief their experience of your performance as it may be different and surprising. Reverse roles and repeat.

Workplace

Once you have experienced the exercise above, you will likely have greater awareness of your personal process. This awareness should be coupled with the significance and setting of each of your workplace conversations. For example, there will be many conversations that are fast-paced and only moderately consequential, whereas there will be other conversations that will require deep and thorough analysis and/or will be extremely consequential based on your response. Clearly, you will naturally apply different levels of discretion in each of these cases.

Discretion

Improv

Once you have exercised deep listening of your partner's statement and have identified your feelings regarding their offer (self-assessment), and possibly reflected for a moment, you will verbalize your acceptance of their statement and expand it with your offering. During this process you may discover that you have more than one potential reply, each of which would be accepting and appropriate to the scene. Based on your level of improvisational experience, it may be clear as to which reply to offer, as your experiences may persuade you to select one over the other(s). For example, your experiences and foresight may tell you that reply A would have much more potential to expand the scene whereas reply B would likely be more limiting. In another example, your experiences may tell you that reply C may be too crude or unpleasant for this particular audience. Although this is all happening in a split second, it is your discretion that is coming into play in these situations.

In each of these options, it is important that each reply is authentic and that what you are determining, in that split second, are the consequences that each reply would likely cause. I also wish to note that authenticity is not defined as a confessional, but instead a genuinely truthful response of which there may be multiple; and from this place of truth, you will apply discretion to determine which reply will best serve your partner and the scene. Therefore, being authentic does not obviate discretion.

Exercise

After connecting with your scene partner, allow them to offer you a controversial initial statement that they have either prepared or created in the moment, the emphasis being controversial. After you receive their comment, quickly verbalize two or three different feelings or reactions that you have, i.e., do not play the scene out but just identify your two or three different reactions. Then have your partner repeat the initial statement with you choosing one of the feelings and play out the scene. Next, repeat that process a second and third time with the different reactions that you initially had. Although this is not totally ideal, in that the second and third scene would not be as fresh as it would have been initially, you will nevertheless see how the scenes play out with each of your initial possible responses. Again, this is not a perfect scenario, but is a method by which you can observe the potential consequences of each of your different reactions.

Workplace

With the practice of the exercise above, you should have a better awareness of consequences that could result from your feelings and reactions. This alone would be helpful to understand your interpersonal dynamics. Additionally, it is almost always prudent to apply discretion with your responses in the workplace, with various degrees of discretion for the variety of situations with which you engage. For example, in certain of your business situations, consequences may be extremely potent such that you may find that certain authentic statements might get you fired. And even in cases where leaving that job is best, you may wish to do that on your terms. In either case, it will be your discretion to make that determination.

Vulnerability

Improv

Embracing vulnerability—the willingness to put ourselves in positions of vulnerability—is a necessary ingredient to perform an improv. While some people are anxious to speak one-on-one with certain others, many are uncomfortable speaking to a group with a prepared speech, and very many would be uncomfortable giving an unscripted talk regarding even a subject of which they are expert. Imagine doing an improv in front of an audience where you have absolutely no idea what the subject matter will be—most, including many professional actors, are terrified of the thought. Improv is an extreme practice of vulnerability. Perhaps improv should be the definition of vulnerability.

With no script, improv actors must rely only on themselves and their partner. There is an understanding between the actors that together they will venture into unknown places, supporting each other throughout. They have essentially made an unwritten agreement to "jump off the cliff together," to be open and vulnerable, and to explore the journey together. They are mutually experimenting with various situations and accept that the scene may go to weird places and may totally fall flat on its face, which is also a learning and understanding, one that is inconsequential in our safe acting space. In this regard, they can use this forum to play-act various real-life situations to determine how they may feel or react and what consequences may ensue.

Exercise

To experience vulnerability, there are exercises of various degrees. The minimalist form would include being totally open with yourself, i.e., speak with yourself, perhaps in front of a mirror, and express your feelings about a particular challenging situation in your life. As you continue to speak, move deeper and deeper into the essence and deepest truth of the situation. Continue this process until you have reached your deepest point.

The next level of vulnerability would include performing this exercise with a partner with subject matter that could be about yourself or, more challenging, about your partner. Perform the exercise as above until you feel you have totally reached your deepest level.

The next level of vulnerability may be giving a prepared speech to a group of friends or employees. And if you wish to forgo all these preparatory vulnerability practices, take an improv class—you may be scared but you will likely have a blast!

Workplace

The exercise above will help you to understand your level of comfort or discomfort in each of the scenarios. You will then understand your abilities and the areas that need improvement. It is important to not attempt to hide vulnerabilities with statements that are untrue or inauthentic. Your coworkers will likely see through this creating likely difficulties for you. Instead, always be authentic and know the level of vulnerability that is within your comfort zone. As you stay in your comfort zone, it will be easy for you to be authentic, and as you practice vulnerability outside of the workplace, you will extend your vulnerability range and become more comfortable within the workplace in those former challenging situations.

Authenticity/Ambiguity

Improv

Throughout the improv dance process between you and your partner, you must continually be authentic in your words and reactions. This includes your action to openly receive your partner's offering, to accurately perform self-assessment, and to speak your truth based on your deepest feelings.

This process must continue throughout the entire scene. The scene may move into several different directions—there may be a mix of comedy, drama, sadness, sensuality, vulnerability, joy, or all of the above. Exercising authenticity throughout occurs without any prescribed agenda or written direction of the scene, and hence you have no idea what direction the scene may take. In this process, you would inherently accept the ambiguity of the situation since you have no idea how or where it will go. You are basically saying to yourself and your partner that as long as you are being open, vulnerable, and authentic, you accept the destination of the journey. Your pledge to each other is to embark upon a journey that is totally authentic and to trust the outcome without qualifications.

Exercise

To practice and develop authenticity, you may wish to try the following exercise. First, after connecting with your partner, you would share your honest feeling(s) in the following manner. Rather than simply state your feeling, you would share it, pause and focus on it, share again, pause and focus on it, share again, etc. In this manner, you would go more deeply into your feeling(s) in each subsequent iteration, perhaps even experiencing changes in your statement. The design of this exercise is to iteratively express deeper and deeper feelings, ultimately reaching your most authentic feelings. Once completed, you would reverse roles.

Secondly, you would make some statement, e.g., about your state of being or some belief you may have, and your partner would reflect if they believe you or not. Exchange roles and continue this process until both have made statements so authentic that their partner clearly believes them.

Thirdly, once you have both reached this level of authenticity, practice an improv scene with this same internal authenticity, i.e., speak only what is true for you in that moment. It may seem counterintuitive to be authentic in a made-up improvisational scene; however, we are not concerned with the fictional environment that you create but instead seeking the truth of your feelings in this fictitious scenario. Authenticity is about your true internal feelings not your outer circumstances. In the acting industry, it is said that acting is being real in fictional circumstances, and good acting occurs when the actor is authentic and truly feels/embodies the role they are playing.

Workplace

In business, we know that organizational structures are important in order to define the goals, purposes, and tasks for all the employees. Organizations also understand that innovation is important and is derived from their employees' abilities to think openly and freely. The issue of balance between these two apparent opposites is frequently critical for success of the organization and it is clearly understood that certain organizations require more structure while others more freedom.

For example, a factory that produces paint will have an assembly line that is highly automated and partially operated manually by their workers. In this example, precision and exactness are important for both the automated process and for the manual task. As such, this endeavor would be considered highly structural with minimal to no freedom or innovation. The formula for success of this task has been calculated precisely and dictated with the exact instructions for success. Innovation may occur if an assembly line worker may see a better way of performing the task but would not do so in the midst of the current operation. Instead, they may speak to their supervisor to discuss their innovative thought and this thought may eventually move through the system design experts who may ultimately incorporate the idea into the structured process. However, during the factory activity, the task remains precise and highly structured.

The counterpart to this highly structured activity would exist in a think tank, or other similar situation, where innovation and discovery are the main goal. In this case, the structure will be minimal—perhaps a simple definition of the overall goal—but the freedom within that structure will be maximized in order to allow the creative minds the best opportunity for innovative and new thinking.

While the think tank may be considered 95 percent innovative and 5 percent structural, the factory assembly line would be considered 95 percent structural and 5 percent innovative. Although this example shows the simplistic and obvious difference in balancing the two opposite characteristics, many professional organizations consist of tasks whose optimal balance may not be easy to determine. Involved in this determination is the attitude and belief system of the CEO. Although there is much written about the advantages of providing more freedom to employees, most organizations seem to continue to exercise more structure and control.

Accepting this ambiguity is counter to the goals of many organizations, as they frequently have clear goals and guidelines for success. However, even in the structured settings of these organizations, it would be wise to allow for ambiguity, for this process may in fact lead to surprise creativity, resulting in even a better outcome than originally planned. This would be an example of allowing the creative process within a structure.

Ambiguity, by its nature, allows for multiple reactions and responses, with each being equally authentic. In these cases, discretion is used to determine the best option. The best option will of course depend on the situation, e.g., in a short form improv show the actor would select the response they presume would be most entertaining for all, where in a work situation, one might select the response that would be more advantageous to them individually. This becomes an area that may involve a slippery slope, i.e., one may see an outcome that has a greater advantage but may be less authentic or perhaps even totally inauthentic. In this situation, we can refer to the work of James G. March, who discussed the decision-making process based on personal identity versus expected consequences. Simply stated, March describes that our decision-making process is generally a choice between identity, whereby we make decisions based on our internal values, or consequence, whereby we make decisions based on the anticipated consequences of those decisions. The latter decision is based on potential effects of our decision while the former is a much more authentic process of personal identification and values—much more authentic.

Therefore, the use of improvisational training would expose us to explore ambiguity, help to foster authenticity, and would expand our ability to be creative and innovative.

Timing/Comfort in Silence

Improv

Timing is an important element of any conversation. Once you complete the process of deep listening, self-assessment, the timing of your authentic response may be important to consider. It may be appropriate to speak immediately, or it may be appropriate to allow the most recent sentiments to "hang" for a moment or two to reach their fullest impact. This is clearly discretionary and requires judgment to perform precisely. You would develop the skill over time, based on trial and error. We can easily understand how timing is important for improv in a similar manner as it is for a standup comic.

Equally important in improv is the ability to be comfortable if there is no dialogue for several moments between the actors. Without developing this comfort, an actor would likely speak for the sake of speaking, i.e., to fill the uncomfortable silence. However, we have all seen the situation where an anxious person says something inappropriate to fill the void, and we all understand what just happened, as we have likely experienced this at some time for ourselves. Those statements are generally unimportant and clumsy and may or may not have consequences based on the situation. Improv actors learn how to develop comfort during these quiet moments trusting that something of significance will eventually emerge from one of the actors and, until then, they remain quiet, calm, and connected to their partner.

Halpern, Close, and Johnson in *Truth in Comedy* describe the importance of silence as follows, "Too many performers are terrified when the stage is quiet, but a few moments of silence doesn't mean nothing is happening. Just the opposite—it often leads into the most important moments in the scene."

We can make a connection between timing, anxiety, and comfort in silence. Our anxiety may make us uncomfortable with silence and cause us to speak too quickly and inappropriately. How often have we known we should wait to say something but could not because we were driven by our anxiety, and the results in those cases were generally awkward? Practicing the following exercise should help.

Exercise

Stand face to face with your partner, connect with them and wait a period of time (say thirty seconds) before someone starts a scene or conversation. During this time, it is important to observe the connection you have with your partner and notice what feelings or reactions emerge. Once the scene starts, speak from those emotions. During this exercise, it is important to stay mindful with your partner, i.e., become more and more connected versus distracting yourself somehow (counting time, tapping your foot, etc.). This exercise will not only help quell anxiety, but it will demonstrate the depth and changes that may occur during this mindfulness exercise with your partner. After some practice, you will feel much less anxious during any silence.

Workplace

Learning comfort with silence in the workplace is extremely beneficial. Conversations with your managers, clients, vendors, and coworkers will go much more smoothly, and silent moments will not be as awkward, preventing you from speaking inappropriately. In fact, your silence will allow others to speak and enable you to learn more from them—perhaps important information you would have never received. Your speaking will no longer be induced by your anxiety but instead will flow more naturally, resulting in more appropriate conversations and better communications. In all, your workplace demeanor will be calmer, professional, and more effective.

Relaxation

Improv

In an improvisational scene, unless there is one designated person to start the scene, the scene may be started by either actor. This can be a critical moment for the actors. A novice may be uncomfortable with this ambiguous moment and perhaps say something out of nervousness. Such words would usually be unhelpful to the scene. We all understand this situation. For example, when we meet someone new, especially if this person has some importance to us, our nervousness may kick in and we may say something that is not elegant—perhaps even quite clumsy. We are likely embarrassed and the person receiving those clumsy words may understand, as this same situation has likely happened to them on some occasion. Therefore, in a sense, that clumsy opening line does create a connection, but it is generally a very awkward one. If this would happen in an improvisational scene, the person receiving the nervous comment should actually be authentic and comment on it in some appropriate manner. The scene would then continue from that foundation. Such a response—acknowledging the nervousness rather than ignoring it—may also apply in our personal and business life, based on the particular situation. I suggest that you consider such an authentic response as possibly being appropriate the next time it may happen to you.

Experienced improvisational actors will generally avoid such nervousness that would cause them to speak clumsy or empty words. Instead, the actors aim to be relaxed, look into each other's eyes to make a connection that is meaningful, be comfortable in the discomfort, and be okay with the ambiguities that exist in that moment. Their goal during these empty moments is to continue to relax, to connect more deeply to each other, to wait for something meaningful to arise, and then to speak from that place of meaning. This may sound like a simple concept, but it is quite difficult and requires patience, relaxation, and much practice.

There will be times when relaxation is difficult and perhaps impossible. I did my first improv on stage in New York City only a few days after my first class. Not only was I not relaxed, but I was quite terrified! For two days prior to the performance,

I could not sleep or work at my desk. I kept wondering what I had gotten myself into—exactly how crazy was I? Standing backstage waiting to go on, I could not get centered or relaxed. I was panicking. In the few classes that I had taken, I learned that I must connect with my truth in order to have any reasonable dialogue with my partner. As I thought about that, I realized that my truth in that moment was total fear and panic, and I fortunately found a way to bring that into the scene. I ran out onto the stage with my nerves peaked and the first words out of my mouth to my partner were, "I'm sorry, I am so nervous to be meeting you. I haven't slept for two nights thinking about this meeting ...." I connected with my truth and brought it to the scene and that got our dialogue rolling. My partner was an experienced actor and picked up on my comment and we had a very honest dialogue based on my nervousness. From that point, it was easy to continue to follow her lead since I was already in connection with her. Amazingly, the scene was quite successful despite my fears and panic. The lesson here is about finding one's truth, being authentic with it, connecting with your partner via your truth, and continuing an honest dialogue. If I had not spoken my truth to her initially, but instead made some other unrelated statement, she would have been confused as my words would not have matched my emotions and would have made a connection between the two of us far more challenging.

Exercise

This exercise is similar to the one suggested for Centering/ Loading since they will both assist to bring you into a calm, relaxed, and more centering state of being. As such, the same exercises will be useful.

From the various practices of meditation and mindfulness reviewed earlier, I would suggest at least one of the following options:

- Still Meditations – Zen, Mantra, TM, Gazing, or Loving Kindness
- Moving Meditations – Sufi Walking Meditation or Yoga
- Guided Meditations – Body Scan, Singing Bowls or personal music, or Guided Imagery of your choice
- Intensity—If you are extremely wound up and unable to perform the above meditations, you may need to first perform a more intense exercise such as push-ups or running in place to relieve tension and calm the body down prior to performing the above meditations.

Workplace

It is easy to see how the related attributes of relaxation and centering are both qualities that will be helpful in the workplace. I have also spoken of anxiety which is the absence of relaxation, and have discussed the advantages and challenges that stem from these dynamic polarities. Practice of these exercises will help bring you into better balance, thereby allowing for your improved performance in the workplace.

Empathy/Caring

Merriam-Webster defines empathy as, "the action of understanding, being aware of, being sensitive to, and experiencing the feelings, thoughts, and experiences of another …." Others state it simply as "feeling tuned into the feelings of people around you."

Empathy would require deep listening, awareness, focus on your partner, and being open to their communication—all attributes important to improvisation.

At a conference in Stonybrook, New York, a business leader acknowledged its significance saying, "I didn't think empathy had a place in business, but I now see its value."

Caring is defined by *Merriam-Webster* as, "feeling or showing concern for or kindness to others." Clearly, this is directly related to the principle to Serve Your Partner. In both cases, the emphasis is on your partner, not on you.

In Pat Shay's book, *The Heart of the Scene*, he presents the fundamental improv principle of YES AND and then follows it with a humorous and clever statement, "The rest of this book can be summed up in three words: Show You Care." His message is to care as characters, care as players, care about the scene, and know how you feel toward your scene partner. In succinct fashion, these two main principles would go a very long way in producing a positive improvisational scene.

Communications Connection

A full and successful communications connection with your partner, whether a personal or business relationship, is critical for any productive communication, planning and/or decision-making session. (I distinguish this from the initial eye contact connection I suggest you make with your partner prior to any scene, as this communications connection represents a deeper experience of a successful cycle of eye-contact, deep listening, self-awareness, and authenticity.)

To obtain a true communications connection between two people, certain elements discussed in previous sections are required. If the elements have not been satisfied, it will be impossible to create a true and accurate connection.

The chart below summarizes the elements necessary for the connection. In almost all cases, if any element is missing, the connection will not be made.

Deep Listening—Deep listening to your partner is a critical element in the connecting process. If it does not occur, or occurs only partially, you will not have the accurate data upon which to respond, and there is no possibility for a successful connection.

Self-Awareness—As deep listening is being exercised, you must accurately perform self-awareness, i.e., identify your reactions and feelings to the initial statement. Without an accurate self-awareness, you cannot respond to your partner with your own truth, thereby preventing an authentic connection.

Reflection—Once you identify your reactive feelings, you may reflect upon your feelings and the situation prior to responding to your partner. (Reflection is not mandatory.) Reflection may cause you to identify multiple possible responses. Whichever choice is made, it must be authentic.

Authentic Response—An authentic response to your partner is the last element necessary to circle back to your partner who presented the original comment. Assuming your partner will exercise deep listening to your response, the connection will be completed, and the initial authentic communication loop will be satisfied. Your partner will then begin the process of deep listening, self-awareness, possible reflection, and authentic response on their end and continue the positive communication cycle with you.

Communications Connection—If all the prior elements are completed, you would have a successful communications connection to your partner. The chart below shows that in all cases, except one, it is mandatory for all elements to be successfully completed in order to obtain a successful connection. The exception is that reflection is not always required to create an authentic communication. In this case, you would simply respond authentically without reflection or contemplation. Although this connection will be authentic, indiscretion or undesirable consequences may result. There are cases where these consequences are insignificant or even valued for exploratory purposes, such as improvisational performances and work-related creative processes to foster creativity.

In many cases, it is common for people to over-reflect, perhaps thwarting improvisational creativity. In opposing cases, there are those who speak without thinking and without reflection. It is very likely that these people have experienced undesirable consequences at times and have naturally seen that some reflection is sometimes necessary.

Therefore, the practice of improvisation affords to be a positive tool to free limitations and to expand creativity. And in fact, one can argue that improvisation is also important for those who normally process without reflection, as they could playact various situations to observe the consequences of their actions, thereby allowing for adjustments should different consequences be sought.

Deep Listening (receive initial data)	Self-Awareness (identify reactive feelings)	Reflection (contemplation and discretion)	Authentic Response	Communications Connection	Reason/Notes
YES	YES	YES	YES	YES	Positive connection
NO	--	--	--	NO	Innacurate initial data
YES	NO	--	--	NO	Disconnected from self
YES	YES	NO	YES	YES	May be indiscrete or have undesireable consequences
YES	YES	YES	NO	NO	Inauthenticity will prevent connection

NOTE: With one exception, once a "NO" is experienced in this communications loop, the cycle is broken, and it is impossible to experience an authentic "YES" in the next phase of the cycle.

Chapter 10

Benefits of Improv

"The world is a slightly better place for having improvisation in it than it was before." Del Close

"The world of improv is a portal into mindfulness and magic." Patricia Madson

---

Chapter Highlights

1. The practice of improv provides a plethora of benefits.
2. Some benefits are popularly known while many others are not.
3. Improvisers accept that WE are smarter than ME.
4. Improv is based on love, not fear, seeks a win-win, and all ideas are valid.

There are many benefits to the practice of improvisation. In fact, when you review the following list you may have doubts as to whether these benefits are exaggerated and truly derived from the practice of improvisation. Although the answer is yes, i.e. that improvisation can provide these benefits, it is also true that the depths of each of these benefits would vary based on the individual and their level of practice. Having studied and performed improvisation since 2012, I can clearly see how improvisation can provide these benefits to those who practice this art form.

Although some of these benefits have been discussed or can be inferred from the exercises in the previous section, I have placed them here so they can be easily viewed as an assembled collection.

I have divided the benefits into two sections: the first section noting benefits that would be more popularly acknowledged and the second section noting benefits that may not be as obvious.

Popularly acknowledged benefits would include:

- Thinking on your feet
- Freedom of limitations
- Develop creativity
- Enhance public speaking skills

Other significant benefits, perhaps less known, would include the following:

- Improve listening skills
- Develop collaboration
- Keep an audience or partner engaged
- Develop trust
- Enhance flexibility and adaptability
- Foster positivity
- Discover hidden talents
- Develop comfort in discomfort
- Improved communications
- Improved social interactions
- Enhance confidence and self-esteem

- Quell anxiety
- Accept uncertainty
- Explore and practice intuition
- Laugh at oneself
- Awareness/Reading cues
- Concentration/Focus/Being in the moment
- Patience
- Tolerance
- Self-growth
- Final comments

Popularly acknowledged benefits:
Thinking on Your Feet

This is probably the most commonly acknowledged characteristic that people have made regarding the benefits of improvisation. In many conversations with friends discussing improvisation, their first comment or reaction is frequently, "Oh yes, thinking on your feet is really necessary in improv." Although there is a certain truth to this comment, I frequently respond to them by stating that improv is not really about thinking but more about feeling and reacting. If they seek more information, I explain to them that improv is about deep listening, feeling the sentiment of our partner's statement, then identifying our emotional reaction to that statement, and then responding authentically from that place. I explain that it is therefore more about feeling than thinking. The quickness that they experience in improv then comes from this process rather than from one's thinking. I then explain to them that if one merely responds from the mind, they may be able to have one or two responses but would not likely be able to maintain a longer scene with their partner. And that the only way to perform a scene of such length would be to identify the feelings and speak the truth of those feelings in a back-and-forth manner. I understand that the repartee is quick since we are taught to minimize or eliminate our filters, i.e., do not judge, but instead just respond from our feelings. This quick exchange of banter can easily appear to be one from the mind and hence the inaccurate conclusion that thinking on your feet is the element necessary for improv. I understand this distinction is subtle but it is critically important since thinking alone will not enable one to perform an improv successfully.

On stage and in life, the practice of improv will allow you to flow more easily as there will be less hesitation, or even paralysis, in a conversation. The result of this practice does allow you to dance or flow more easily with your partner, and this exchange will facilitate an improved social interaction with others. As such, in observing this by others, they may state that you are now thinking on your feet better than before, when actually you are more present, more feeling, and flowing more easily and naturally with your partner, resulting in a much better social interaction.

Freedom of Limitations

It is generally understood that improv requires or includes quick exchanges of conversation between people and, as such, it is easy for one to observe that one must be freer with few limitations in order to perform such an exchange. Also, for those who have seen improv, it is easy to see that the content and comments are sometimes odd, curious, imaginary, wild, and maybe outrageous, all characteristics of freedom of limitations. I have spoken to several people who have said, "I wish I could be that free and crazy," inferring that they are naturally limited and careful in their normal communications and would like to experience that level of freedom. In this regard, improv classes are extremely helpful, as most of us have been taught to be careful, discrete, courteous, accurate, respectful, and controlled. Although these sentiments are not negative in nature, together they cause us to contract and hesitate. As adults, we are taught to be serious and we have subsequently forgotten how to play. An improv class would give us total permission to play and be outrageous, thereby freeing some inner tensions that create limitations. Such freedom would uncover creativity, innovation, and more, as are described in other paragraphs in this section.

Develop Creativity

As discussed above, the release of limitations would allow the creative aspects of ourselves to emerge. These creative aspects may be hidden beneath the caution, the discretion, and the limits that we have placed on ourselves. Creativity is frequently discussed as emanating from our right, or intuitive, brain. Our daily life of work, family, and general responsibilities involve mainly the logical or left brain, and frequently avert significant use of our right brain. We have all seen classes and seminars whose main purpose is to open and expand the right brain, e.g., drawing from the right side of our brain, meditation, writing with the opposite hand, music of various forms, etc. Each of these activities are designed to access the intuitive parts of our brain to uncover and display our creative powers. Frequently the seminars are powerful, revealing, and life-changing, sometimes resulting in new life directions and new activities that create much more fulfillment in our lives. Therefore, to develop our creativity is not simply a superfluous exercise but instead a very important attribute to be discovered and expressed, and improv classes can be a source of this discovery.

Enhance Public Speaking Skills

This benefit can be easily understood since to perform improvisation requires you to stand and present in front of others, frequently an audience. Any such exercise over time will allow you to be more and more comfortable speaking in public and hence you can easily conclude that the improvisational exercises would help to enhance your public speaking skills.

There are other avenues for this specific skill, whereby one regularly stands up in front of a group to tell a story of some sort. These exercises have clearly worked as many people have successfully accredited these practices to their improved public speaking skills. The main difference between these techniques and improvisational training is that the generic trainings involve only a one-way communication (one speaking to an audience) and do not include any exchange of conversation, nor the identification of one's reaction to your partner's comments, nor the need to identify your feelings and reactions to your partner, nor the necessity of an authentic response. I applaud those who exercise the courage and practice of such activities.

However, I would say to you that the practice of improv is a much fuller practice that would develop much greater skill, much more personal understanding, and much more personal growth. As a New York improv participant said, "I am now less afraid to communicate directly and authentically."

Other significant benefits, perhaps less known:
Improve Listening Skills

Deep listening is a very critical component of improvisation. Although all understand the concept of listening, here we are discussing deep listening, which means listen for the sentiment and innuendo that are deeper than the words expressed. This is an absolute critical part of improvisation, for without deep listening, you would not understand the true sentiment that is being expressed and therefore cannot accurately feel your partner's true meaning, and therefore cannot respond to their true sentiment. Without deep listening, there is no connection between the partners and no successful improvisational scene. As you practice these skills, you will not only practice listening versus speaking, but you will learn to listen deeply. Clearly this skill is critical for any relationship—personal and business. There are professions that have been developed to teach people such skills, as without these skills, the lack of connection cannot result in a productive personal or business relationship. We all know of spouses who do not listen to each other nor communicate in any meaningful manner, and we all know of business relationships that are similar, and the subsequent negative results from such lack of connection. How many books have been written and how many therapists are there to help the population with this issue?

In business, poor listening skills between manager and employee is, in many cases, the cause of serious productivity issues. Also, in business, effective listening skills between coworkers would facilitate more successful projects, and a major teaching point for salespeople is to listen more intently to the client. How often do we see a salesperson focus solely on their "pitch" wanting only to give their pitch to convince the client of the benefits of their product or service? However, an integral part of sales training includes deep listening to fully understand what the client is requesting and/or needing. Listening is therefore such a fundamental activity in order for any communication to exist, which is necessary for any possible positive outcome, and the deep listening practices acquired during the study of improvisational training becomes a highly important tool for all phases of life.

Develop Collaboration

When I started the study of improvisation, I discovered one aspect of successful improvisation that I did not anticipate would be important, and that is the development of teamwork or collaboration. In all the classes I have taken, and especially in the performances for audiences, I can easily see its importance and benefits. In improv classes, the instructor is always developing a cohesive and cooperative group. This is done through various games and activities, all to promote a comfort level and a positive connection between the actors, i.e., to develop a cohesive group. This cohesion allows for an easier and deeper connection between the actors that does carryover to the scenes in a positive manner. The essence is that if there is no connection between the actors, there can be no meaningful improvisational communication and therefore no successful scene. When I first started taking improv classes, I was quite self-conscious and had no real desire to be an actor because of that self-consciousness. But being in class with others, all volunteering to be free, open, and outrageous, allowed me to feel that "we're all jumping off the cliff together." This bond and essential agreement allowed me to gradually be less self-conscious and more willing to be vulnerable and to expose my inner feelings and thoughts to my teammates without the filtering of a self-conscious mind. To perform improvisation requires us to have or develop a cohesive, cooperative, and collaborative exchange with others in order to create a connection necessary for an improvisational scene. Therefore, in a sense, it is not improv that creates the collaboration, but instead in the practice of improv one must first learn to develop collaboration in order to perform the improv. The result of course is that after the development of improv skills, we understand how to collaborate with others much more easily and this skill is easily transferable to other parts of our life.

In business, we can see how this practice would excel in the areas of teambuilding. I understand there are many team building practices in corporate America whereby teams are taken on day or weekend trips to forge such an alliance, and that these outings are generally quite successful. The practice of improvisation would easily be added to this list of teambuilding activities. And since the creation of various roles and role playing is quite vast, one can create a multitude of work related situations that would not only develop teamwork but also be directly applicable to certain work situations.

Keep an Audience or Partner Engaged

To perform an improv, you must stay in eye contact with your partner in order to create a connection and observe their feelings and sentiments. You must remain engaged with your partner to exercise deep listening and to then reply back to your partner from your deeper emotional state of being. Your partner, in turn, must do the same. This results in a positive connection and engagement between you, grasping true sentiments and replying authentically. This process involves full and total engagement from each of you, and such a practice will easily be transferred as it becomes part of your skill set.

I have observed, both as a student and teacher of improv, that it is not uncommon for the participants to have a difficult time to remain in eye contact with each other. At an improv workshop I lead in Philadelphia, this struggle was brought to light and expressed in a closing remark, "I was amazed at how difficult it was to look somebody in the eye when speaking to them."

Eye contact is the first step in developing such a connection and a successful improv requires a connection not only of the eyes but also of the heart and mind. Hence, this level of connection is new to many participants and this can be easily seen in the first classes of some new members. Improvisational practicing therefore teaches connection and engagement, perhaps the first time some have experienced such a practice.

Develop Trust

The trust that can be developed in improvisational practices relates both to trust between participants and trust within yourself. As discussed in a separate paragraph, connection and teamwork is developed in order to produce a successful improvisation and as such, trust is developed between the participants. This is the natural result of teambuilding. *Truth in Comedy* describes trust as follows, "When an improviser let's go and trusts his fellow performers, it's a wonderful, liberating experience that stems from group support." In addition to the trust between participants, you would develop trust within yourself as you experience your inner, perhaps hidden, sentiments that emerge in the improvisational format. These hidden sentiments may be newly uncovered and perhaps even feared prior to their emergence, and the observation of these newly expressed sentiments will create greater self-awareness and likely cause you to be more comfortable and trusting of yourself. How often have unexpressed emotions grown in fear to a point of exaggeration as they remained unexpressed? The unconscious mind is quite imaginary. Expressing these unconscious thoughts, these hidden sentiments, or perhaps even our wild imagination can be a healthy exercise of release. Once you see that your expression does not cause harm, as you may have imagined, to us or others, you will likely trust yourself much more.

Enhance Flexibility and Adaptability

The study and practice of improv will force you to move into areas unknown and likely uncomfortable. In these new areas, you will explore feelings, thoughts, and actions generally not expressed in daily life, especially as many have created a daily routine that, although comfortable, may actually be limiting in its full expression. Exploring these new areas will be revealing and opening in the sense that newly discovered characteristics of yourself will be uncovered. As you continue the practice of improvisation, you will encounter a wide variety of scenes and therefore would automatically be practicing expressions of various types and styles. This potpourri of your inner self being outwardly expressed would allow you to clearly see that there is much more to you than your comfortable daily routine. As such, you will see your adaptability to various situations and would have more confidence to engage in various conversations and situations with more flexibility.

Foster Positivity

The practice of "YES AND" improvisation would naturally cause you to be more accustomed to saying yes rather than no. This is an excellent practice for most of us, as I believe most are cautious and frequently begin our responses with "no" or "I don't know" or "let me think about it." I am not sure why this response in behavior is so prevalent—perhaps because we are faced with so many opportunities or suggestions and we have learned to be cautious and slow the process down; perhaps the overwhelm of data sent to us on a daily basis offering a myriad of products or offerings has conditioned us to begin a response with a "no"; or perhaps it reflects our fear of commitments. In any case, the practice of improv will allow us to become much more attuned to agreement and expansion by using the "YES AND" techniques.

This technique is especially useful in the business world when new ideas are presented, especially from employee to employer. Too frequently the employee is shut down because of an automatic "no" by their managers, while a more positive response, even one with no commitment, would be much more inspiring to the employee. In these cases, it is important to note that the manager is not simply accepting every suggestion but instead is responding in some positive manner, encouraging further discussion, thereby extending the conversation and inspiration of the employee.

After an improv practice of YES AND in a New York workshop, a manager said, "I was delighted to see how conversations go more smoothly when I am more accepting of the other person." Clearly, this was a successful improv exploration for this manager.

Discover Hidden Talents

During the practice of improvisation, you would go to places not normally explored in daily life. This may include humor, wild imagination, off-the-cuff thoughts, out-of-the-box ideas, sentiments of your personality that you consider surprising, speaking without thinking thereby accessing some undiscovered part of your brain, intuitive or reactive ideas. Throughout this process, you may discover ideas or talents previously unknown. When we are performing improv in its purest sense, it is almost as if we are listening to ourselves with wonder since our words are not predetermined; it is almost like we are listening to someone else speak. In this sense, we may likely discover parts of ourselves that were hidden or totally unknown. This exploration can be a very exciting process of discovery.

Develop Comfort in Discomfort

In certain personal or business conversations, there may be moments of silence, characteristically called "awkward pauses." This is generally quite an uncomfortable situation for both parties, hence the term awkward. Frequently, both parties are anxious and uncomfortable during these moments and someone, likely the most anxious one, will speak just to avoid the silence. The words subsequently spoken are generally meaningless and perhaps even negatively consequential. If you doubt this premise or have not experienced such awkwardness, I suggest in one of your next inconsequential conversations, you experiment by being silent while staying in eye contact with your partner. Explore what that feels like for you and notice how your partner will react to your silence.

In the practice of improv, we are taught, as artists, to be comfortable with the discomfort, i.e., the discomfort of silence or any other discomfort that does not rise to the level of personal harm. We are taught to remain calm or at least not speak gibberish during those moments but instead to be patient and wait for something meaningful to emerge from either you or your partner. This is a critical technique of an improvisational presentation, for an audience will be lost with statements that are nonsensical or not connecting to your partner or the subject at hand. In fact, the silence will generally be felt by the audience and draw them in to listen with anticipation for the next words. You may notice this dynamic in movies, i.e., that the silence between two partners can be a very dramatic moment and felt deeply by you, the audience. This silence then becomes very impactful. Teaching this discipline in improvisational training is an important one and one that is impactful not only to the scene but to our daily lives as the training quells anxiety during these moments of silence.

Improved Communications

Improv is clearly about communications between people, communications that must be created on the spot since there is no script. In order to have these communications meaningful, each partner must listen to the other in a meaningful way, in order to respond in a meaningful way, in order to present the audience with some entertainment value. I have stated prior that deep listening is a critical component of this communications dynamic for if you do not fully understand sentiments of your partner, you will not be able to respond in any connected manner. In the exercises of an introductory improvisational class, you would actually repeat what your partner has said in order to emphasize that focus, and understanding of your partner's comments are critical. This exercise moves back-and-forth between partners with each partner repeating what was said to them and then adding a comment extending that thought or at least based on that thought. Although this exercise may seem tedious, it is an excellent training for you to listen to your partner rather than to exclusively or primarily be thinking about what you wish to say.

The concept of focusing on what you wish to say rather than listening to your partner is a common one in all walks of life. Even in the field of acting where listening skills are part of the training, there are professional actors who are not truly listening to their partner but instead waiting for their "cue" so they may deliver their scripted line. In some of these cases, you can observe that the actors are not deeply connected to each other but instead just speaking "at" each other. This is also a frequent issue in personal relationships to the degree that professionals have written books and offer workshops on such communication skills. For example, Harville Hendrix and his wife Helen LaKelly Hunt are well-known authors of relationship self-help books and the creator of Imago Relationship Therapy. In this therapy, after one partner speaks, the other partner essentially repeats what they understood in order to confirm to the first partner that they have accurately heard what they have said. They then add their response to that and the communication exchange continues in this format. The essence of this technique is for each partner to affirm what they have heard in order for both partners to be comfortable with the accuracy of what was said. The introductory improv training I referred to provides similar affirmations and teaches each partner to listen carefully and to respond in a manner that connects to their partner thereby providing clear and accurate communications.

Improved Social Interactions

The practice of improv can unlock the tensions that prevent you from speaking with confidence. As you develop the skill to respond without heavy filtering, you will become more accustomed to conversation in general. There will be less tension, less hesitancy to speak, less filtering of words, less self-consciousness, and more openness. All of this will carry over into everyday conversation and you will find that you are more relaxed in conversation—both personally and business wise—and be more socially interactive, both with people you know and also, more strikingly, with people you do not know.

Enhance Confidence and Self-Esteem

Self-consciousness, lack of confidence, and self-esteem issues are interrelated. I believe that there are very few people with zero levels of these attributes. Instead, I believe that everyone has good levels of confidence in at least certain areas, i.e., most everyone excels at something and has confidence in that area. How often do we see an expert on some technological issue speak about their area of expertise with great confidence only to see the opposite in settings outside of their expertise? I experienced this myself as a child as I was confident in my schoolwork but socially awkward. As I began working in the area of mathematics and computer science, I saw many of my colleagues with similar issues—they were brilliant and genius and confident when discussing mathematics and physics but quite uncomfortable in certain other settings, perhaps especially social. The practice of improvisation forces us to stand up in front of a partner and possibly an audience, extremely vulnerable, i.e., we have no lines but yet we must speak with some level of meaning and connection. Clearly, this is a process whereby we can gradually and slowly gain confidence in performing in such a manner. During this process, confidence and self-esteem will naturally grow, especially in areas where we are not expert. This is an amazing training for such confidence and self-esteem building.

Quell Anxiety

For those afflicted with various levels of anxiety, the practice of improvisation will be helpful, although perhaps challenging. However, if you begin at an appropriate introductory level, you will gradually become comfortable with the exchange of unscripted sentiments, of being comfortable understanding that you will not know what you will say next, with relaxing into the discomfort of an unscripted scene, with embracing the awkward silence that may occur in a scene, and with the total surprises that generally occur when performing improvisation. The confidence that is gained in these uncomfortable situations will naturally quell any baseline anxiety and this comfort level will gradually carry over into your everyday life. The use of mindfulness exercises previously discussed will be extremely helpful during this process, one that will be a gradual but effective process.

Accept Uncertainty

Uncertainty seems to be a concept that many in society attempt to overcome. Consider how many professions exist to predict certainty of situations that are clearly uncertain. For example, how many weather forecasters exist and how frequently are they broadcast? Their forecasts change from day to day and from hour to hour and yet we continually look to them for some level of certainty. If any other professional were incorrect that frequently, they would lose their job in a moment. Although they do provide probabilities upon which we make our plans, we still look to them for certainty for such plans and are clearly disappointed when they are incorrect. In fact, we joke about how incorrect they are with great frequency, yet we continue to listen for certainty. Other similar professions include economists and other financial forecasters. We also seek certainty from our medical professionals, asking for prognoses and duration of remaining life. Although we inherently understand that all these professionals are giving us their best estimates, we seek certainty and we base our life plans on such predictions—however illusory they may be—and our reactions to inaccurate predictions may be intensely disappointing.

There is an expression, used mostly in the business world, called FUD. Standing for fear, uncertainty, and doubt, this concept is used in the marketing world to sway potential clients away from competitors. As an example, larger more established organizations would instill concerns to potential clients when they were looking at newer, upstart organizations. These organizations would promote certainty over uncertainty and perceived risk. This too is an illusion as there is no certainty that the established organization would maintain its position. In addition, a decision to avoid fear and uncertainty of a newer organization would preclude the opportunity for a better product or solution, the lack of perceived risk diminishing the possibility of a greater success.

Improv is all about uncertainty as we have no plan nor any expectation of where the scene may go or how we would react within the scene. The practice of improv therefore allows us to experience this uncertainty and see that we not only survive it but frequently enjoy it. The uncertainty becomes an adventure, sometimes leading to great joy while other times leading to less joy. In either case, we learn to work through the uncertainty and to even enjoy the anticipation of the unknown. We see that any disappointment is less consequential than we had forethought and, experiencing this, we develop a comfort in, or at least acceptance of, the uncertainty.

Accepting uncertainty also aligns us with truth and the truth of life. We are not in denial about the reality of uncertainty, while also not being stressed over its existence. We are in alignment and in harmony with its reality and existence.

Explore and Practice Intuition

In our everyday life and perhaps especially in our work life, many of us are generally utilizing our logical mind much more than our intuitive mind. Daily life demands that we carry out tasks for ourselves, for our families, for our coworkers, all with the goal of successful completion. These tasks are generally goal oriented and require more of our logical mind than our intuitive mind. Our intuitive mind may be exercised more frequently with our avocations, whether it be music, art, dance, or other similar activities. In our current society, we are more driven by the tasks and goals that utilize and require the logical mind. I do not believe this is ideal as I believe that the use of the entire mind—logical and intuitive—should be employed in unison much more frequently to achieve optimal results. However, our education system focuses clearly on the logical and prepares us for the workplace that usually continues in the same vein. I personally have been a proponent of enhancing our decisions by incorporating both the logical and intuitive mind in many of our decisions.

In our culture, there are several practices outside of work that foster and support the intuitive mind, e.g., meditation, yoga, tai chi, artwork, music, and more. Our medical professionals have even recommended such practices in order to foster better levels of health. It is therefore well known that we are out of balance regarding the exercise and utilization of our intuitive versus logical mind. The practice of improvisation is an excellent tool to enhance our intuitive skills as it teaches us to relax and "let go" of the logical mind. During this practice, we are given many exercises to gradually bring us to that place of a quiet mind allowing us to access our intuitive and non-task oriented parts of ourselves. Over time, this practice will become more and more comfortable within our beings and we will naturally utilize it more frequently.

Laugh at Yourself

In our serious and task oriented lives, we are frequently measuring ourselves against the goals we have set. This review frequently leads to self-criticism and sometimes self-congratulations, but rarely to self-laughter. Self-congratulations results from tasks well done and self-criticism results from our judgments of tasks performed poorly or incompletely. There is little room for self-laughter, for self-laughter tells us that we made a mistake and that we are okay with it, even finding humor within that error. In our highly pressured society, we devote little space for self-laughter. In the practice of improvisation, self-laughter emerges as a natural result of certain scenes and there is an understanding and agreement that this is more than okay. In improv, we say there are no mistakes, just happy accidents. We laugh at ourselves from being in a silly circumstance and possibly forgetting a character's name on stage, but understand they are not really mistakes and there are no serious consequences.

Therefore, in order to be free enough to perform improvisation, we must accept the fact that there will be happy accidents made and that that is part of the process. To work hard at not making mistakes would be a contraction of our energies preventing us from being fully open to explore what creativity might emerge. In this way, we accept mistakes as part of the process for we would otherwise not be able to delve into those deeper intuitive and creative parts of ourselves that provide a richness of color and hidden talents that were previously unknown. There are of course certain areas in the business world where mistakes are totally accepted, such as in think tanks and research centers where successful breakthroughs occur in very low probabilities. However, most business sectors do not share this type of environment.

Awareness/Reading Cues

Being aware, or reading cues, of our surroundings is a survival attribute in the animal kingdom for they may otherwise find themselves at the fatal prey of their antagonist. As humans, we may not have that same sense of urgency. However, to be lacking in awareness or of reading cues, may cause us to miss critically important information—whether its format be in words, actions, or otherwise. In the process of awareness, there are communications—communications that could be critically important or at least information useful to the comfort and/or health of our lives. Awareness would facilitate better communications with our partners, would allow us to take action that might otherwise have not been taken, and provide understanding of life dynamics enabling us to facilitate a more fulfilling situation and/or life.

At a workshop in Madison, New Jersey, a young man had an important awareness emerge during an improv scene. He summarized it by saying, "I realized that I have trouble sticking up for myself. I just want to be a nice guy and have people like me. The next time I have a potential confrontational situation, I will get some support." In this case, his new awareness will help him to get the support he needs for his personal comfort and health.

Concentration/Focus/Being in the Moment

Clearly focus and concentration are important aspects for any task at hand—personal or business. In our fast-paced society and in our fast-paced business world, it seems that quick movements and quick decisions are applauded and time spent concentrating or focusing is sometimes considered to be time wasting. During improvisational training, you must focus and concentrate on what is being said and on what is being portrayed in all moments. The action within the scene is sometimes slow and deliberate and sometimes fast-paced. In either case, we must exercise total concentration and total focus on what is happening, for if we miss a cue, we will be lost in the context of what is happening and will have no appropriate response. This concept also relates to being in the moment, as that necessitates a focus on the present moment and on avoidance of distractions by outside interferences. The inability to be in the moment and the inability to focus has become more prevalent in our society in general as the pace of life and business continues to increase in speed. How many people are diagnosed with ADHD? How many people have physical ailments such as anxiety, headaches, and hypertension? How many prescription drugs have been formulated to address these issues? Many activities and programs have been created to help slow our systems down, to help us focus on the present moment, to help us quiet the chatter, and to help us relax and focus on our internal systems. Although some of these programs, e.g., meditation, may have originated in the consciousness community, the medical profession has acknowledged their value in terms of the physical, emotional, and mental health of patients and are utilizing them in the medical profession as well. Improvisational training and practice can assist in allowing us to focus, concentrate, and be in the moment, thereby shedding the anxieties and disturbances that stress the various levels of our being.

Patience

Patience is a characteristic necessary to perform a successful improvisation. It is necessary to develop deep listening that is an absolute requirement for improvisation, and it is a characteristic necessary to be able to be comfortable in the moments of awkward silence. The development of the skills of deep listening and being comfortable during silent moments will automatically develop a quality of patience. It is easy to understand that developing this quality would have a positive impact in our personal life as well as in our business relationships and activities.

Tolerance

Listening and accepting what our partner offers us in an improvisational scene will naturally develop tolerance, for tolerance is essentially saying yes to a situation, person, or idea rather than saying no. The essence of intolerance is to say no because something is different than who we are or what we would like. We easily see this dynamic in our society today as various factions cling to their ideologies and philosophies. Although education and understanding are keys to bridging the polarities, we must first exercise tolerance to acknowledge the difference rather than demonize the opposing viewpoint. In improvisational training, the rules are to say yes to whatever is put before you, no matter how crazy, wild, or different it may be, excepting situations that may cause us personal harm. (In fact, we may play characters we ideologically oppose in an effort to artistically explore them). And in fact, when we say, "YES AND," we are not only accepting what is before us but are expanding our partner's viewpoint in some meaningful way. Acceptance and expansion of what is presented to us is, by definition, a tolerant attitude and quite opposite from any level of intolerance or demonization.

Self-Growth

It is obvious that the attainment of even some of the above benefits will provide personal self-growth. The level of growth will be dependent on our level of commitment and exploration. "Follow the fear (or discomfort)" is an improv phrase used to identify places to explore for personal understanding and growth, both as an artist and in our personal life. In *Truth in Comedy*, Chris Farley speaks of his respected teacher Del Close stating, "From Del, I learned to face my fear. He taught me to follow that fear and trust that something will come to me, to step off the cliff and take a risk." In these cases, it is totally up to the improviser—us—to determine our personal safe boundaries as we explore in this safe and accepting setting. Improvisers are taught to operate with acceptance, tolerance, sincerity, and empathy. In that vein, this becomes a very safe environment to explore our fears and discomforts.

Final Comments

Improvisers accept that WE are smarter than ME, and that together we will explore and discover at a higher intelligence.

- Improv is based on love, not fear; in business, many organizations are based on fear.
- In improv, all ideas are valid; in business, ideas are frequently invalidated.
- In improv, we seek win/win, knowing that we totally depend on each other; in business, there is too frequently a win/lose attitude.

The practice of improvisational principles will provide (self) growth for both the individual and the business.

Chapter 11

Business Unpredictability and Improvisation

"The greatest danger in times of turbulence is not the turbulence—it is to act with yesterday's logic." Peter Drucker

"People don't resist change. They resist being changed!" Peter Senge

"The growth and development of people is the highest calling of leadership." Harvey S. Firestone

---

Chapter Highlights

1. Although the idea of constant change and need for preparedness in organizational life is not new, today's business uncertainties, ambiguities, complexities, and the pace of change are unprecedented.

2. There is a need to shift from short-term financial tendencies to decision making that is values driven.

3. Many thought leaders are advocating alternative approaches. Many require high standards and values and can be accomplished with wise and responsible leadership.

4. Improvisation is inevitable and necessary, but must be based on awareness and values.

Imagine jumping on a large trampoline alone. You find it fun and perhaps exhilarating—somewhat. The bounce you get is predictable and proportional to how high you jump. Now imagine just walking on the trampoline. It is less predictable and you have to adjust your body weight and balance as you walk. However, all your energies are directed to maintaining your balance and not falling—not much fun. Now let us invite a friend over and both of you jump on the trampoline together. You get the thrill of the jump, the bounce, and its unpredictability. The level of fun and exhilaration rises. As you add more people (within reason, there is a limit) to the trampoline it becomes even less predictable and in addition to being more fun, you will need to adjust your jumping and body weight on the fly; you may fall and you have to find a way to recover from the fall. Soon, with practice, you will have developed a repertoire of skills that help you respond to the uncertainty and unpredictability; falling and recovering could become part of your set of trampoline capabilities. However, there will be surprises that you will still need to respond to on the fly. Now, there are constraints you will need to work with. It is very important that no one gets hurt and each jumper's individual actions has to work within this important constraint. In this chapter, we will use trampoline jumping as a metaphor for managing, leading, and working in organizations.

Unpredictable Organizational Life

Even though the trampoline will serve as a metaphor, we must recognize that it is an oversimplification of organizational life. At the risk of articulating a cliché, the uncertainties, ambiguities, complexities, and the pace of change are unprecedented. The year 2020 made that clear that there is a premium on being prepared for the unexpected. Every institution on the planet had to find a way to cope with the COVID 19 virus. While the scale and scope of the impact of COVID 19 was beyond anything we have experienced in a very long time, we should note that the frequency of unexpected and unprecedented events have been increasing. We have faced severe storms that have put lives, property, and infrastructure at risk. The effect and frequency of climate change driven events are only projected to rise in the future and we will experience frequent disruptions of the routine. The lack of predictability is multidimensional. In addition to the plethora of environmental issues, we have technology changing at a rapid pace, close to a billion people on the planet living in extreme poverty and suffering from hunger, migrations of people driven by poverty and war, a depletion of planetary resources, gender and racial inequality, and increasing concentrations of wealth in the hands of a few. In addition, the United Nations projects that the world's population will rise to around ten billion by the middle of the century placing the future humanity and the planet in further jeopardy. In addition, these issues are interrelated in ways that we know and ways that we do not know. Addressing one of the issues often has unintended consequences for others. Not only are there more people jumping on this trampoline—some of them are invisible. Essentially, to state the obvious, organizational life is complex, dynamic, and very difficult to predict. How do organizations, their leaders and members prepare?

The idea of constant change and need for preparedness in organizational life is not new. Management scholars have for long discussed tensions between mechanistic and organic types of organization (e.g. Burns and Stalker, 1961). In stable and predictable organizational environments, the drive towards efficiency makes logical sense. Gareth Morgan (1998) used the metaphor of a machine to describe such an organization. A machine is designed to produce a predictable and reliable output every time. They are however limited by their own configurations and can only adapt to small variations in their environments, if at all. On the other hand, dynamic and less predictable environments call for the need to adapt to the unexpected. Such environments call for adaptive capabilities to respond to the unexpected. Most organizations however need both; some mechanical routines that ensure resource efficiency and some adaptive capabilities that enable them to respond to changing environmental conditions. Management scholars (e.g. O'Reilly & Tushman, 2011) have for long discussed the need for ambidextrous organizations— those that are designed to deal with routine and change at the same time. The emergence of increasing competition, globalization, and technological development has generated a complex dynamic forcing the leadership of organizations to develop ways to respond by higher levels of empowerment and delegation and developing strategies that are less restrictive and more responsive to this environment. For instance, the notion of "Strategy as Simple Rules" (Eisenhardt & Sull) was proposed as a necessity in the face of growing environmental complexity. Companies empowered their managers to improvise and act with speed when they recognized the need to defend a company position or take advantage of an opportunity they recognized. Indeed many technology companies would attribute their innovations and growth to such policies. The number of jumpers on our metaphoric trampoline has grown and all the trampoline jumpers now have to adapt to this changed environment.

However, these organizational innovations must be approached with caution. For instance, Eisenhardt and Sull used Enron as an exemplar manifestation of Strategy as Simple Rules. We know the epilogue to that story. While the company broke new ground in the energy markets, its employees took extremely risky decisions on behalf of the company and when these risks did not payoff, they indulged in unethical behavior that eventually led to the downfall of Enron as well as its audit firm, Arthur Anderson. Many Enron employees lost their life's savings and thousands in both companies lost their jobs.

> **Each person attempting to maximize their own positions, ignoring the well-being of others led to the downfall of everyone.**

Metaphorically, each person attempted to maximize his or her own enjoyment from trampoline jumping leading to devastating injuries.

Principles, Values, Integrity

The top leadership at Enron was directly responsible for both, creating the conditions that encouraged and incentivized people in the company to take undue risks. They were the key protagonists and the story drives home an important lesson. Leadership has a key role to play not only in focusing on business performance and growth, but also to ensure that this performance and growth is governed by principles, values, and integrity.

Principles, values, and integrity prescribe mere threshold of responsibility for leaders of organizations. As noted earlier there are several "grand challenges" like climate change, poverty, and inequality that fall well within the scope of an organizational leader's responsibilities. At the minimum, leaders need to make sure that they and their organizations do not contribute to making these problems worse. At best, leaders need to focus their own and organization's attention to addressing the pressing problems facing humanity today. It calls for a deep appreciation of the interconnectedness of life and nature on the planet. Responsible and wise leaders understand and appreciate that their decisions have consequences beyond the boundaries of the organizations they lead and that it is their obligation to make sure that they not only eliminate harm, but also enhance wellbeing for current and future generations (Maak & Pless, 2006; Nonaka & Takeuchi, 2011).

Academicians and practitioners have used a multitude of adjectives to qualify leadership over the years. Transactional, transformational, values-driven, narcissistic, destructive, liberating, positive, wise—these are just a few examples. Our focus is on values-driven leadership—a reflection of our own beliefs. We believe organizational leaders must be committed to the development of their people and the creation of conditions that enable employees to find meaning and fulfillment in their work. Similarly, they need ensure that they have a net positive impact on society and the planet; they must eliminate or mitigate *any* harms caused all along their supply chains.

We are aware of very few leaders that meet this high standard. Unfortunately, the prevailing business environment does little to encourage business leaders to move towards these higher standards because of the pre-occupation with maximizing shareholder wealth. In an era of rapid change, uncertainty and equivocality, the natural tendencies are to maximize financial outcomes, often at the expense of other stakeholders. There is a need to shift those natural tendencies to decision making that is values driven. Mary Gentile (2012) shows the importance of this perspective. She points to the importance of enlivening a purely intellectual perspective of ethics with action by empowering actors to give voice to their values. Leadership that empowers in this manner is values driven.

Seeking Moments of Greatness

Robert Quinn (2005) notes that all of us, at times experience "moments of greatness." Referring to these moments as a "fundamental state" he draws distinctions between leadership at these moments in contrast to those in a normal mode, he makes the case that leaders are at their best when they act from their deepest values and instincts. In the Normal state, leaders tend to focus on their own interests and needs, operate within their own realm of knowledge, and comply with others to maintain the peace. In contrast, in the Fundamental state, leaders are driven by their values, take the risk to explore the unknown, put the interests of others over self; they observe their external environment in the interest of learning and recognizing the need for change. While Quinn notes that this fundamental state is a shift away from the routine, he also points out the potential of making it more common place. Imagine working in an environment where every member of the organization feels comfortable to be authentic without fear and finds fulfillment and meaning in their work. Indeed, as the pace of change, uncertainty, and equivocality increase, developing authentic values driven responses are even more important to avoid the pitfalls that cause the downfall of businesses like Enron.

In Search of Happiness

Emily Esfahani Smith (2017) offers a very interesting and perhaps counter-intuitive take on human happiness. She suggests that we intuitively seek happiness by seeking quick gratification, often by pursuing material possessions—money and the trappings of wealth. Based on her research, Smith asserts that true and sustainable happiness is built on a foundation of meaning. She has identified four essential pillars necessary to find meaning in our lives.

The first pillar provides a clear direction especially for organizational leaders. It calls for an experience of Belonging.

There is a rise of loneliness in the world. The increasing use of communication technology and social media has led to an increase in the volumes of superficial communication and a decrease in real connection. Creating opportunities for greater and meaningful connection is an important task for organizational leaders and leads to a sense of community.

Second, finding Purpose that is focused on matters beyond self. True purpose varies by individual. For some it may involve taking on large global problems like climate change or poverty. Others may find meaning in things closer to home, like taking care of children. Note the parallel here with Quinn's Fundamental state where the collective good has more importance than self-interest.

As we navigate the joys and challenges of life, we develop an identity for ourselves. This identity is reflected in Storytelling—the stories we tell about ourselves. When those stories are tied to purpose and belonging, they become a powerful source of reinforcement and fulfillment. They bring clarity to our lives. Organizational leaders can create the space for people to develop their own stories through engagement and empowerment.

Finally, Smith advocates Transcendence as a pillar where we connect with a higher reality. We are able to rise above the busyness that preoccupies us to give time and space for reflection. Through transcendence, we see ourselves in context of the vast world and universe around us. Paradoxically, it both affirms our sense of self even while recognizing that that self is a small part of a much bigger reality.

Positive Defiance

Kim Cameron (2012), in discussions on Positive Leadership appeals to our sense of possibility. He places the notion of deviance on a continuum—from negative to positive. While we typically think of deviance in a negative sense, he points to those leaders that channel the energies of people towards doing good in massive ways. They take on challenges, set "Everest" goals that border on the impossible, and find ways to deliver on those goals. These challenges and goals would be way out of reach in a "normal" or routine organization. However, they are the norm in positively deviant organizations and would be impossible to achieve without the passion and commitment of organizational members. Cameron invokes the Heliotropic Effect as a means to engender this passion and commitment. The Heliotropic effect is a manifestation of the tendency of entities to gravitate towards sources of energy. Plants demonstrate this effect in the most obvious fashion as they lean towards the sun and other sources of light. Positive leaders highlight those things that energize people to take on immense challenges. The late Ray Anderson, the founding CEO of Interface Carpets provides a great example of this effect (Anderson and Lanier, 2019). Due to a personal epiphany, Anderson decided to transform his company and eliminate all negative environmental impacts in twenty-five years—Mission Zero. For a petroleum driven company, Mission Zero is an Everest Goal. It called for transformational change at all levels and functions throughout the company. Nothing was too small or too large in the journey to Mission Zero. Anderson states that in all his years of experience he had never seen anything ignite the passion and commitment of Interface employees to the level that Mission Zero did. In effect, Mission Zero was the source of light and energy that truly inspired and motivated the members of the Interface organization. In 2020, the target year, Interface declared Mission Zero accomplished!

Tying It All Together

All organizations and their leaders are responsible for a variety of stakeholders both within and outside the organization. For business organizations, values based leadership calls for a break from the tradition of shareholder primacy to addressing the rights of multiple stakeholders. In 2019, the Business Roundtable endorsed this shift with a new declaration on the purpose of business. Over 200 CEOs of major companies signed this declaration, which named customers, suppliers, employees, and communities in which they work as stakeholders in addition to shareholders as stakeholders of the firm. This is a step in the right direction.

Responsible and wise leadership calls for deeper examination of the negative impacts of the firm all along the value chain. This involves paying attention to typically unseen and/or unheard stakeholders impacted along the value chain. For instance, extraction of materials through mining often impacts local indigenous populations negatively—their health and their lifestyles.

We also live in a deeply interconnected world. Our planet is an extremely complex ecosystem. As noted by Peter Senge (2006), in complex systems, the relationships between cause and effect are subtle and separated in time and space. These complexities are therefore often invisible and lead to unintended consequences. While we might not be able to fully comprehend and predict the unintended consequences of our decisions, we must appreciate that the potential for them exists. Preserving the planet so that current and future generations may live reasonably good lives heightens the importance of taking values based decisions today. Considering these broader issues calls for leaders to go well beyond the Business Roundtable 2019 statement of purpose to include the Earth and all species that are integrated part of our complex ecosystem. Not only are there many jumpers on that trampoline, but there are also many invisible jumpers!

We have established the complexity of the environment for all organizations and their leaders. Leadership needs to match this complexity with matching capabilities and capacities within the organizations. While the shareholder perspective sought to simplify and narrow the focus of leadership's attention, the stakeholder perspective is a recognition that the reality is much more complex. Because this complex environment is emergent, uncertain, and less predictable, leaders need to ensure that organizational members are committed to a purpose, actively engaged in the purpose of the organization, and empowered to act in response to the unexpected. In other words, they need to be ready and empowered to *improvise*.

As noted earlier, improvisation without guardrails can result in disaster. It raised Enron to new heights, but resulted in self-destruction. One of the key principles of improvisation is an understanding of and caring for the mutual interests of all actors. However, a theatrical improvisation event is time bound, has few actors, and is spatially constrained. In contrast, in organizational life, time has no limits, the number of actors (stakeholders) is huge and it is spatially unconstrained. In terms of time, the impact of decisions could be felt decades and centuries later. Climate change is a clear example. Similarly, an organization typically impacts a large number of stakeholders who, as we have noted, could often be unseen and unheard. Spatially, with due apologies to Shakespeare, All the World's THE stage. Upholding the principle of caring for all actors is indeed much more complex. In this context, an unshakable set of values and principles are clearly necessary.

As discussed earlier, both Quinn and Smith affirmed that having a purpose beyond oneself is a key factor in experiencing "moments of greatness" and happiness that is sustaining. For leaders and organizations, this means focusing on a purpose that enhances the well-being of people and the planet without causing harm. As noted by Cameron, such a purpose can be a source of energy that produces the helioptropic effect and has the potential to fire up the energy of organizational members to step out of their familiar comfort zones and develop and commit themselves to Everest Goals.

Such commitment would not have much meaning if it were not tied to a sense of self and acting in ways that are consistent with it. According to Smith, Storytelling provides a channel for articulating this sense of self. Naturally, actions need to be in alignment with the stories and self-identity. Without this authenticity, the stories would be hollow and self-fulfillment would be elusive.

Most traditional views of leadership are linked to the exercise of power over organizational members. Values-based leadership in the context of improvisation involves liberating organizational members to make the choices appropriate to the dynamic situations that emerge in the course of their work. Naturally, trust is a critical factor in enabling such empowerment. Leaders who empower depend on articulating purpose, creating a sense of belonging, building a culture of excellence and most importantly articulate the values that guide organizational behavior. They demonstrate the authenticity of these values by ensuring that all actions and decisions are consistent with them. Leadership in this context calls for a delicate balance of guidance without control.

We started this chapter using the metaphor of the trampoline. We showed that there are numerous jumpers on this trampoline, all sharing the common purpose of fun with jumping. However, it is impossible to have fun without making sure that others on the trampoline are safe from injury. More jumpers raise the likelihood of injury call for more care. However, metaphors are limited and the trampoline surely does not capture the complexity of a real world organization.

Conclusion

The title of this book is *Improvisational Leaders*. At face value, the title may lead you to think that the book's message is to lead "by the seat-of-your-pants" and without much planning, strategy, consciousness, or awareness. Nothing could be further from the truth.

You may have years of higher education, advanced degrees, corporate training, strategic planning experience, regular staff meetings, a daily TODO list, frequent meetings with management, and more, and yet you will still need to improvise daily. However, this improvisation should be based on a strong foundation of business knowledge, of self-awareness, of awareness of the environment within which you operate, of cause and effect (consequences), and of a level of consciousness that includes care for yourself, others, and all stakeholders involved.

Awareness and consciousness are key foundational attributes for the successful improvisation. Hence, I have attempted to present the building blocks to achieve the goal of awareness and consciousness for the improvisational leader.

The first step is to ensure both your linear and nonlinear minds are accessible and cooperative in order to have a clearer awareness of yourself, your feelings, and your values. Once that awareness is acknowledged, it is important that the nonlinear brain be integrated with the linear brain. I offer many options and exercises for this endeavor, including the practice of improvisation.

Once this awareness of self and others is developed, you will then be more conscious and can more easily apply these attributes and realizations to your business environment. The goal, of course, is to develop leaders who are not only skilled in the linear aspects of their chosen careers but who are also adept in the nonlinear aspects of their leadership skills.

The term leadership does not only apply to those in a position of authority and power, but applies to the leadership qualities within each one of us. Our individual leadership skills may be either stifled or inspired based on our individual managers and the style of management they employ. Micromanaging may identify specific steps the manager wishes the employee to utilize, but will limit the employee's creativity. On the other hand, conveying to the employee the higher level goal, with fewer detailed instructions, will generally allow the employee's ingenuity to emerge. Based on the particular task, this may be advantageous to both the manager and the organization. Once again, awareness is a key element for the manager to make this decision.

I also believe that to exercise awareness is a sign of respect for ourselves and others, with self-awareness being a sign of self-respect and awareness of others being a sign of respect for them. Exercising awareness and respect of others says that you care about them, that you value their input, and that you value their ability and their creativity to contribute to the task. It's a shared responsibility attitude; it incorporates the brainpower of more than yourself; and it recognizes a strong and positive collaboration effort.

All the messages in this book are aimed to provide you with greater awareness of yourself and others; the self-awareness exercises are aimed to give you more groundedness, a greater clarity of your inner self, and a greater peace of mind; the improv exercises are suggested for you to explore your tendencies, fears, courage, creativity, joy, and more; and finally, your understandings and explorations from these exercises are aimed to expand your creativity and leadership skills in the workplace, as well as in your personal life, resulting in greater self-fulfillment.

There are many books written about leadership, fulfillment, business, consciousness, and creativity. And in recent decades, there has been much discussion and writing about the intersection of these attributes. Each book will have a different entry point or a different slant on how to reach what most are discussing—a greater consciousness, fulfillment, and flourishing for the individual and their organization. A partial list of these books is noted in the reference section of this chapter.

How you achieve your internal awareness and fulfillment is unique to you. Do you need to read another book on how to get there, including this one? Will you read these books and understand the concepts—on an intellectual level or on a deeper visceral level? Will these books help you to open your nonlinear mind and align with your linear skills? Or will these books incrementally help to expand your awareness and consciousness? Of course, only you have these answers. I, and others, offer these books to serve you however we can.

I am happy to see many people having these discussions as it means that these messages are increasingly in the collective consciousness, and will hopefully soon reach the "hundredth monkey" level.

I wish you joy, fulfillment, and success on this amazing journey!

Appendix A

The Kybalion Principles

Below are selected principles from *The Kybalion*, a study of hermetic philosophy of ancient Egypt and Greece (1912).

The Principle of Polarity

"Everything is Dual; everything has poles; everything has its pair of opposites; like and unlike are the same; opposites are identical in nature, but different in degree; extremes meet; all truths are but half-truths; all paradoxes may be reconciled."

The Principle of Correspondence

"As above, so below; as below, so above."

The Principle of Vibration

"Nothing rests; everything moves; everything vibrates."

The Principle of Rhythm

"Everything flows, out and in; everything has its tide; all things rise and fall; the pendulum-swing manifests in everything; the measure of the swing to the right is the measure of the swing to the left; rhythm compensates."

The Principle of Cause and Effect

"Every Cause has its Effect; every Effect has its Cause; everything happens according to the Law; Chance is but a name for Law not recognized; there are many planes of causation, but nothing escapes the Law."

Appendix B

Meditation Styles

Hindu/Yogic Meditations

Hinduism is a religion, or way of life, founded in India thousands of years ago. Yoga and meditation are spiritual practices that have emerged from this tradition and have become quite popular in the Western world. There are many forms aimed specifically to achieve certain goals. I will review several of them below.

Transcendental Meditation (TM)

One of the earliest and most popular forms of meditation in the United States is Transcendental Meditation, commonly known as TM. It was introduced to the Western world in the 1950s by Maharishi Mahesh Yogi and was popularized through its use by The Beatles and other U.S. celebrities.

As part of TM, you would create a personal mantra, which is a word or sound that has some positive connotation for you. You would then sit with your eyes closed for twenty minutes, twice a day, repeating the mantra that you have selected.

This meditation style is simple and easy to learn. The challenge consists of the ability to sit quietly for a period of twenty minutes and to maintain focus on your specific mantra.

Mantra Meditation (OM)

Similar to TM above, this practice entails repeating a certain specific mantra, e.g., the word "OM," while seated in a comfortable position. There are a variety of such mantras offered by the Hindu and Buddhist traditions, with each mantra having a specific meaning.

This meditation style is equally straightforward as TM, with the exception that the various mantras used would have specific meanings and intentions.

Gazing Meditation (Trataka)

Trataka is a meditation technique that involves focusing the eyes on a specific object such as a candle or symbol. It is typically practiced in a comfortable seated position with the eyes open. Alternatives involve sequencing the eyes open, to capture the image, and then closed to practice maintaining the image. The development of focus, concentration, and inner calm can be realized with this practice.

This style of meditation is one of the easiest to learn especially since we have likely found ourselves staring at a flame, sunset, or other attractive object in such a gazing manner at various times in our life. The only challenge might be the ability to sit still for a longer period of time than what we may have experienced in a previous gazing moment.

Chakra and Third Eye Meditations

These two meditation styles are similar in that, once seated comfortably, one would focus their attention on specific parts of their body. With the Chakra meditation, one would focus sequentially on the seven chakras (energy centers spanning from the base of the spine to the top of the head) repeating a specific and different mantra for each chakra.

In the Third Eye meditation, you would focus your attention on the third eye—the space on your forehead between your eyebrows, with the goal of energizing your intuitive sight.

Each of these meditations would activate the areas of specific focus while also facilitating relaxation and inner calm.

Kundalini Meditation

Kundalini meditation is related to the practice of yoga and is intended to move energy from the root chakra (at the base of the spine) upward through each of the other six major chakras, with the intention of purification and enlightenment.

This is considered a more advanced form of meditation to be explored after basic meditation techniques have been experienced.

Tantra Meditation

The original true essence of tantra meditation has little to do with the sexual nature with which it is currently associated.

Tantra meditation involves the movement of energy within the body through the use of meditation, sound, movement, and breath. In this regard, it is closely related to Kundalini meditation and is a comprehensive approach aimed to enhance spiritual growth and physical well-being.

This is considered a more advanced form of meditation.

Pranayama and Kriya Meditation

Pranayama meditation involves a controlled movement of your prana (life force energy) through a rhythmic control of the breath.

Kriya meditation utilizes pranayama as well as other meditative practices as a comprehensive spiritual growth path. This technique was brought into international awareness by Paramhansa Yogananda's book entitled, *Autobiography of a Yogi*.

Most consider these styles of meditation to be more appropriate for the advanced meditator.

Buddhist Meditations

Buddhist meditations emanate from traditions passed down through the generations by The Buddha who sat in meditation to achieve his enlightenment. It is believed that this practice originated in India and spread to China, Japan, other parts of Asia, and eventually to the West. Below are descriptions of the various Buddhist meditations.

Zen (Zazen) Meditation

Although some consider Zen and Zazen to have subtle differences, most consider these to be similar and to be the primary practice in the Zen Buddhist tradition. Meaning "seated meditation," the essence and goal of this meditation is to simply sit quietly, suspending judgments and allowing mental thoughts and images to simply pass by without further consideration.

This is a simple form of meditation requiring only a comfortable seated position and a quieting of the mind. Some consider this form of meditation easier than focusing on a specific mantra, while others find the mantra focusing to be more helpful.

Vipassana Meditation

Vipassana is a meditation of insight and self-observation. Its focus is to be aware of exactly what is happening in the moment, to be mindful of what is occurring in your body and around you, and to be aware of your senses (smell, touch, etc.) in every moment.

Some believe that this is the oldest of meditations taught by the Buddha himself and the basis of many other meditation styles.

This is a straightforward form of meditation that requires you to be in a seated and quiet position. Different than Zen meditation, Vipassana meditation focuses directly on sensations as they are happening rather than allowing thoughts and sensations to pass through to achieve an emptiness. Although these two (and several other) types of meditation may appear similar to the outside observer, they are internally quite different.

As Zen and Vipassana meditations are internally different, you may wish to explore them each to determine your preference.

Mindful Meditation

The term Mindful Meditation has come to mean different things as it has become popularized. Some feel that the term Mindful Meditation has become a generalized terminology for many forms of meditation, as they are all mindful in some way. While experts may note the subtle differences between Vipassana and Mindful Meditation, they also note similarities and perhaps even consider them siblings.

Many consider the term Mindful Meditation to be a high-level title, with Vipassana Meditation being a form of Mindful Meditation.

Loving Kindness Meditation (Metta Meditation)

The practice of Metta meditation involves sitting in a comfortable and relaxed position, breathing deeply and slowly to release anxieties, focusing on the heart, and offering loving, kind, and benevolent feelings toward oneself and then to others.

This meditation technique is a concentration practice and more akin to prayers offered by Western religions. As such, it may be most familiar and therefore one of the easiest to develop.

Walking Meditation

Thich Nhat Hanh is a Vietnamese Buddhist monk who promotes peace, meditation, mindfulness, and "engaged Buddhism," and communicated his messages in over 100 books. In *The Miracle of Mindfulness,* he encourages mindful and meditative walking. He states, "When you are walking along a path to a village, you can practice mindfulness ... if you practice mindfulness you will experience that path ... whether it's sunny or rainy, whether the path is dry or wet ... then we will consider the act of each step we take as an infinite wonder, and a joy will open our hearts like a flower ..."

Chinese Meditations

Taoist Meditations

Taoist meditations are associated with the Chinese philosophy and religion of Taoism dating back to Lao Tzu. The meditations are frequently presented as three basic types: concentrative, insight, and visualization.

There is also a focus on moving energy through the body. Certain meditations focus on emptiness, i.e., emptying the mind and observing the inner calm, while other types of Taoist meditations focus on breathing techniques to move energy through the system, and yet others focus on visualization.

There is quite a variety of techniques and styles emanating from the various teachers of these practices. Hence it may be difficult to precisely define an individual technique as a standard. This characteristic makes it quite different than TM, for example, which is precise and clear in its instruction and hence likely easier as an introduction to meditation. As such, the Taoist meditations would be more appropriate for the experienced meditator.

Qigong (Chi Kung) and Tai Chi

Designed as a healing art, Qigong is an ancient Chinese exercise and healing technique that involves meditation, control breathing and movement exercises. It is considered a moving meditation that coordinates a movement flow, rhythmic breathing, and a calm meditative demeanor. There are many forms and styles of Qigong, as each teacher has created their own forms and movements, frequently very different from each other.

Tai Chi is a derivation of Qigong, sometimes considered the martial arts form of Qigong. Tai Chi is more standardized in its form and therefore more portable from one location to another, whereas Qigong is generally unique to the individual teacher or style.

As moving meditations, Qigong and Tai Chi require time and dedication to learn the forms and the movements. As such, it would be more attractive to those wishing a moving meditation and who have the time and dedication to learn the movements.

Sufi Meditations

Sufism is the esoteric or mystical component of Islam. Similar to other esoteric traditions, their meditative practices are aimed to achieve purification and enlightenment. Sufism is noted for its heart centered practices of love, song, poetry, and dance. Its origins dating back to the prophet Mohammed, there have been several notable personalities including Rumi with his loving writings and Hafeez with his loving humor.

Although many of the Sufi practices have been influenced by the traditions of yoga and India, the Sufi meditative practices are always based on the connection to God, whereas some practices from India are more secular.

Meditation of the Heart

In this meditation, the student will focus on their heart, their consciousness, their soul, and their connection to God.

This is a straightforward meditation that allows one to expand their heart and their connection to their creator, generally expanding their loving feelings towards themselves and others.

Muraqabah (Watch Over)

This is a Sufi meditation whereby one watches over their spiritual heart and focuses on their relationship to the creator.

This is also a straightforward meditation but has a specific goal that may provide you with a helpful focus.

Sufi Mantra Meditation

In this meditation, the meditator will hold a set of beads and move from one bead to the next while saying a specific mantra, generally the name of God, Allah.

The style of meditation is very similar to the Christian meditations/prayers recited with the use of rosary beads, moving from one bead to the next.

Sufi Gazing Meditation

As recommended by Rumi, one would sit in silence gazing at a photo of the beloved creator.

Clearly analogous to the Hindu gazing meditation (Trataka), the only difference being the object of the gaze.

Sufi Walking Meditation (Nazar bar Kadam)

The Sufi practice of walking meditation is called Nazar bar Kadam, which literally means Watch Your Step. In this practice, one would walk consciously and mindfully, focusing on their spiritual path. Their practice of focusing on the feet is intended to avoid distraction and to maintain the intended focus.

This is a moving meditation that is straightforward and allows the meditator to quiet their mind and focus with deep intention each step that is taken. Each of us may have experienced such a meditation when, for example, we were taking a slow, solitary walk on the beach.

Sufi Whirling

Sufi music and dancing are core activities in their expression of love. Sufi Whirling is a deep meditative practice whereby each of several whirlers would gracefully and slowly spin repeatedly with the goal of dropping the ego and moving into deeper states of meditation and higher levels of consciousness. There may be a dozen or more engaging in this activity with a facilitator guiding them, as necessary. (I have personally observed this practice in Istanbul, Turkey, and was struck by their depth, beauty, and flowing movements directed by their inner guidance and an occasional loving hand-touch by the facilitator.)

This is clearly a moving meditation versus a still meditation and considered an advanced form that should be attempted only with a facilitator.

Sufi Zikr

A Sufi Zikr, also spelled Dhikr, is a treasured practice and ceremony honoring the Remembrance of God, Allah. It is generally filled with dance, music, and chanting in joy and celebration. It is a ritualized, sacred, and joyous ceremony.

In addition to a sacred celebration, a Sufi Zikr is an active meditation performed in an organized setting by the leaders of the Sufi community. One can easily "drop" into meditation via the rhythmic patterns of the drumming, singing, and dancing.

Christian Meditations

Although there are some commonalities between Christian meditations and the ancient Eastern meditations, the biggest difference is that many of the Eastern meditations are focused on emptying the mind whereas many of the Christian meditations are aimed to fill or focus the mind on spiritual Christian passages and devotions. Some describe this difference as meditation is listening to God whereas prayer is speaking to God. However, there is at least one Christian meditation, Centering Prayer, that is more akin to Eastern meditations.

These Christian meditations are quite familiar to the Western Christian world and are therefore likely more easily practiced.

Christian Prayer

This practice would generally involve the repetition of Christian beliefs and sacred words, as one would do, for example, by reciting the rosary.

In the United States, most were brought up in this tradition of speaking to God in such a sacred and devote manner.

Christian Reading

In this practice, one would read sacred scriptures and teachings in a contemplative and thoughtful manner, exploring the deeper meanings and intentions of these writings.

A common example of this would be Bible reading done in a mindful and conscious manner.

Centering Prayer

Centering Prayer is a method of meditation used by Christians placing a strong emphasis on interior silence. This movement can be traced to several books published by three Trappist monks in the 1970s: Abbott Thomas Keating, Fr. Meninger, and Fr. Pennington.

In this practice, one would sit comfortably and choose a sacred word that best supports their sincere intention to be in the Lord's presence and to then open to His divine action within you. If interruptions occur, simply return to the chosen sacred word as the anchor.

Sitting Meditation

Unlike many of the Eastern traditions of a sitting meditation, this practice would generally involve the activation of one's heart and soul as they are thinking of God and related teachings.

Similar to certain Eastern traditions of mindfulness, it is important to remain focused on the subject at hand to prevent the mind from becoming distracted with other non-related thoughts.

Guided Meditations

Although not common, several of the meditations described above may incorporate a facilitator guiding the meditator through the process. This is frequently helpful for beginners and for those who easily lose focus. The meditator would simply follow the instruction of the facilitator to keep them on track and to help them move more deeply into the intended state of meditation. Although an experienced meditator may find this distracting, beginners and certain advanced meditators find this guided facilitation helpful to promote the intended results.

Below are specific forms of meditation where a facilitator is generally guiding the meditation. This format of guided meditation is quite relaxing, very helpful for beginners, and also a joy for the experienced meditator.

Relaxation and Body Scans

In this style of meditation, a facilitator will guide the meditator with the intent of creating a deeper level of relaxation. One of the most common forms of such a meditation is called a body scan. In this technique, the facilitator would guide the meditator to sequentially focus on different parts of the body, suggesting they either simply observe that part of the body or perhaps visualize it moving into a more relaxed state of being. The goal is to ultimately relax the entire physical body, producing all of the related health benefits of such a relaxation, and allowing the meditator to reach a deeper level of relaxation and a higher level of consciousness.

This style of meditation is generally quite easy to follow for even the newest of beginners. There are also videos and audio recordings of such facilitations making it quite easy for anyone to access.

Guided Imagery

In this form of guided meditation, the facilitator is guiding the meditator to not focus on their body but instead to focus on some peaceful or inspiring imagery, based on the purpose of the meditation. For example, if the purpose of the meditation is relaxation, the facilitator may guide the meditator to a favorite place of theirs that is peaceful and calm allowing them to virtually be in that environment and feel the relaxation and joy of their personal experience. Although the facilitator may select a specific scene, e.g., a spectacular sunset on a beautiful beach, many facilitators will allow the meditator to select the particular environment that brings them the joy and relaxation particular to them.

Another common example of a guided imagery would include the facilitator guiding the meditator to receive a personal message. In this type of meditation, the facilitator would generally guide the meditator to walk on a particular path (perhaps up a mountain, through a forest, down the cave, etc.) to eventually meet a teacher or guide who will provide them with a message or answer to a specific question. This meditation can be fascinating to the first timer.

Sound Bath (Singing Bowls)

In this guided meditation, the meditators would either sit or lie comfortably, preparing to receive the frequency and vibrations of beautiful sounds. Typical sounds used in this practice include singing bowls (crystal bowls tuned to various frequencies), gongs (gongs and symbols of various frequencies), and perhaps other subtle musical instruments such as flutes. The meditators would deeply relax while the facilitators orchestrate and coordinate the sounds of the instruments. Deep relaxation would occur with some participants possibly falling asleep, facilitating the health benefits associated with such a relaxation.

Yoga

Yoga is a group of physical, mental, and spiritual practices or disciplines that originated thousands of years ago in ancient India. The poses, or asanas, are designed to open various parts of the physical body to enhance its health, to relieve emotional stresses, and to activate spiritual centers in the body.

In the United States, yoga has become quite popular and is offered in many different styles ranging from the physically quiet (restorative or yin) to the physically powerful (Vinyasa), and from the deep meditator style offered in yoga centers, to the physical exercise format offered in your local gym.

The words yoga and meditation go hand-in-hand as they are so deeply interconnected. Most yoga centers would carry a meditative atmosphere in all its classes allowing the student to drop into a level of meditation during the practice. An advanced form of yoga that combines the deepest parts of meditation and yoga is performed in a practice called "meditation in motion." In this form, the practitioner would flow through various yoga movements in a deeply meditative state, without thought or structure, creating a beautiful flow of meditative movements. It is a totally creative and spiritual experience. In this regard, this practice would be akin to Sufi Whirling, Qigong, or other meditation in motion techniques.

Although yoga can be performed on your own once you learn the asanas, it is more frequently practiced with the aid of a facilitator—live or on video. As there are classes for many levels of experience, and as its popularity is strong, it is generally convenient to find a class at your level in near proximity to you. The movements are generally performed at the student's pace in order for the student to easily follow.

Below are some traditional styles of yoga that are commonly offered.

Classical Hatha

Hatha yoga is considered the classical and more traditional style of yoga, providing a basic practice of asanas (poses) and breath work in a softer and less dynamic format designed for the beginner and general public. Yoga offered at your local gym will most likely be a form of classical hatha yoga while your local yoga center will provide hatha yoga plus many additional styles as noted below.

Ashtanga/Vinyasa

Ashtanga and Vinyasa are dynamic and rigorous forms of yoga that are closely related. However, their uniqueness stems from the fact that Ashtanga yoga incorporates a set formulation whereas Vinyasa is a more creative flow based on the discretion of the instructor. They are considered athletic, vigorous, and physically demanding.

Iyengar

Iyengar yoga is characterized by the words precise and meticulous. Props (blocks, bolsters, straps, etc.) are used to facilitate and ensure proper body alignment. It is a slower and less dynamic form as compared to Ashtanga/Vinyasa yoga.

Bikram

Bikram yoga is a proprietary system of hot yoga devised by Bikram Choudhury and popularized in the early 1970s. Classes consist of a fixed sequence of twenty-six postures, practiced in a heated room, perhaps 100°F, aimed to help remove toxins from the body.

Kundalini

Kundalini yoga is an energy-based style of yoga that combines movement, chanting, and breath work with the goal of moving energy through the various energy channels (chakras) of the body. It is intended to provide inner vitality as well as spiritual awakening.

Yin/Restorative

Yin yoga and Restorative yoga are similar yet quite different. Their similarity includes a slower pace with poses held for a longer period of time as compared to other forms of yoga. However, Restorative yoga is by definition completely relaxing and supported by necessary props, while Yin yoga is about performing passive deep stretches. Props are used in both forms in order to align the body properly enabling the student to maintain the position for longer periods of time.

Integral Yoga

One of the early introductions of yoga to Americans occurred in the 1960s by Sri Swami Satchidananda. He taught what he termed "Integral Yoga," a combination of physical and spiritual practices, and a psychological and philosophical approach to life.

The physical practices of Integral Yoga are based in six different branches of classical Yoga, including Hatha yoga, and are taught using an integrative, or "integral," approach to address all aspects of the individual.

Mind Body Medicine

I am using the term Mind Body Medicine as a generic title to describe the many holistic practices that incorporate various meditative techniques with traditional medical modalities to aid in the healing process. Although the specific and various meditative techniques have been described in this text, several institutions have coined phrases that may imply a unique style of meditation. I wish to clarify that their uniqueness is not the specific meditative technique they utilize, but instead the integration of the meditative technique with the more traditional medical protocols. I totally applaud this integration and approach, as it embraces our whole being in the healing process.

I list one such approach below as an example of this practice and to support these efforts.

Relaxation Response

Herbert Benson, MD, has been a pioneer in Mind Body Medicine, and one of the first Western physicians to bring spirituality and healing into medicine. He found that meditation reduced metabolism, rate of breathing, heart rate, and brain activity. Dr. Benson labeled these changes the "relaxation response."

Through further study, Dr. Benson found that the necessary two basic steps to elicit the relaxation response are: the repetition of a sound, word, phrase prayer, or movement, and the passive setting aside of intruding thoughts and returning to the repetition. He states that this can be done using any number of meditative techniques, such as diaphragmatic breathing, repetitive prayer, qi gong, tai chi, yoga, progressive muscle relaxation, jogging, even knitting.

As you can see, Dr. Benson utilizes a variety of existing meditation techniques in this approach. I totally applaud his pioneering efforts and this holistic approach to healing.

References

Chapter 1: Today's Business Climate

Estés, C. P. (1996). *Women Who Run with the Wolves: Myths and Stories of the Wild Woman Archetype*. Ballantine Books. https://www.therandomvibez.com/

Chapter 2: Duality

Orzel, C. (2010). *How to Teach Quantum Physics to Your Dog*. Scriber.

Orzel, C. (2014). *Particles and waves: The central mystery of quantum mechanics*. YouTube.

Ransom, S. (2016). *The Left Brain Speaks, The Right Brain Laughs*. Cleis Press.

Sherman, C. and Sukel, K. (2019). *Right Brain, Left Brain: A Misnomer*. Dana Foundation.

Siegel, E. (2020). *In Quantum Physics, Even Humans Act As Waves*. Forbes.

Three Initiates. (1912). *The Kybalion*. Yogi Publication Society.

Tsao, F.C. and Laszlo, C. (2019). *Quantum Leadership*. Stanford University Press.

Zdenek, M. (1983). *The Right-Brain Experience*. McGraw-Hill Book Company.

Chapter 3: Success

Heider, J. (1985). *The Tao of Leadership*. Humanics Publishing Group. (Adapted from Lao Tzu's *Tao Te Ching*.) https://www.apassion4jazz.net/quotations.html https://libquotes.com/billie-holiday/quote/lbu2h3q
Yogananda, P. (1944). *The Law of Success*. Self-Realization Fellowship.

Chapter 4: Concepts of Self

Gentile M. (2010). *Giving Voice to Values*. Yale University Press.
HearthMath https://www.heartmath.com/science/
Kidder R. (2005). *Moral Courage: Taking Action When Your Values Are Put to the Test*. William Morrow, HarperCollins Publishers.
Koppett K. (2013). *Training to Imagine*. Stylus Publishing, LLC.
Liew, M. (2017). "Top 10 Most Popular Personality Tests." Learning Mind.
Medical News Today https://www.medicalnewstoday.com/articles/321037#what-does-the-research-say
Merritt, B. & Hines, W. (2019). *Pirate Robot Ninja, An Improv Fable*. Pretty Great Publishing.
Pappas, S. (2017). "Personality Traits & Personality Types: What is Personality?." Live Science.
Plos One Journals https://journals.plos.org/plosone/article?id=10.1371/journal.pone.0071275
Seligman, M. (2002). *Authentic Happiness: Using the New Positive Psychology to Realize Your Potential for Lasting Fulfillment*. Simon and Schuster.

Chapter 5: Meditation

Mayo Clinic https://www.mayoclinic.org/tests-procedures/meditation/in-depth/meditation/art-20045858

Merriam-Webster https://www.merriam-webster.com/dictionary/meditate

NCCIH https://www.nccih.nih.gov/health/meditation-in-depth

Positive Psychology https://positivepsychology.com/meditation-therapy/ (Mosby's Medical Dictionary, 2009)

Psychology Today https://www.psychologytoday.com/us/basics/meditation

Psychology Today https://www.psychologytoday.com/us/blog/feeling-it/201309/20-scientific-reasons-start-meditating-today

Wikipedia https://en.wikipedia.org/wiki/Meditation

Tsao, F.C. and Laszlo, C. (2019). *Quantum Leadership*. Stanford University Press.

Chapter 6: Mindfulness in Daily Activities

https://www.apassion4jazz.net/quotations2.html

https://www.azquotes.com/author/3731-Miles_Davis

Barrett, F. (1998). *"Creativity and Improvisation in Jazz and Organizations: Implications for Organizational Learning."* Organization Science.

Baumgartner, J. (2011). *"Visualize It."* Psychology Today.

Buddhist Door Global https://www.buddhistdoor.net/news/research-confirms-the-health-benefits-of-drum-meditation

Business Insider https://www.businessinsider.com/what-is-a-runners-high-and-what-causes-it-2017-6

Carrane, J. (2017). *"6 Reasons Actors Should Take an Improv Class."* https://jimmycarrane.com/6-reasons-actors-should-take-improv-class/

https://cen.acs.org/articles/93/web/2015/10/Exploring-Molecular-Basis-Runners-High.html

Cohn, P. (2020). *"Sports Visualization: The Secret Weapon of Athletes."* https://www.peaksports.com/sports-psychology-blog/sports-visualization-athletes/

Csikszentmijalyi, M. (1990). *"FLOW: The Psychology of Optimal Experience."* Harper and Row.

Dancing Mindfulness https://www.dancingmindfulness.com/

Daniel, D. (2007). *"Creative Visualization: A Tool for Business Success."* https://www.cio.com/article/2438170/creative-visualization--a-tool-for-business-success.html

http://www.ellafitzgerald.com/about/quotes

Exact Sports https://exactsports.com/blog/how-great-athletes-find-the-zone-part-i/2011/05/04/

Gawain, S. (1978). *Creative Visualization.* Bantam Book.

Gelles, D. (2017). *"How to Be Mindful When You Are Dancing."* New York Times. https://www.nytimes.com/2017/08/30/well/mind/how-to-be-mindful-when-you-are-dancing.html

Goldstein, T. (2015). *"Mindfulness and Acting."* Psychology Today.

Inrhythm https://inrhythm.com.au/blog/what-is-mindfulness-what-does-it-have-to-do-with-drumming

Jackson, S.A., & Csíkszentmihályi, M. (1999). *Flow in Sports.* Human Kinetics.

Jacobson, S. (2020). *"Harley Therapy Counselling Blog."* https://www.harleytherapy.co.uk/counselling/about-us

Kraus, S. (2003). *Psychological Foundations of Success.* Next Level Science.

Lehigh University https://www.lehigh.edu/~dmd1/sarah.html

Mackey, J. and Sisodia, R. (2014). *Conscious Capitalism.* Harvard Business School Publishing Corporation.

Melody https://melodyful.com/types-of-drums-around-world

Neason, M. (2012). *The Power of Visualization.* http://www.sportpsychologytoday.com/sport-psychology-for-coaches/the-power-of-visualization/

Psychology Today https://www.psychologytoday.com/intl/blog/talking-about-trauma/201501/the-heart-is-drum-machine-drumming-therapy

https://www.psychologytoday.com/us/blog/the-mind-stage/201502/mindfulness-and-acting

https://www.psychologytoday.com/us/blog/the-psychology-dress/201111/visualize-it

Quinn, R. (2005). *"Moments of Greatness."* Harvard Business Review.

Road Runner Sports https://www.roadrunnersports.com/blog/achieve-ultimate-runners-high/

Runners Connect https://runnersconnect.net/why-runners-high/

Runners World https://www.runnersworld.com/training/a20851505/how-to-achieve-a-runners-high/

Scientific American https://www.scientificamerican.com/article/new-brain-effects-behind-runner-s-high/

Sporting News https://www.sportingnews.com/us/other-sports/news/what-does-in-the-zone-mean-athletes-peak-performances/1kugz4tuad8j513rgnpophp65q   ???

Stay In The Zone https://stayinthezone.com/

Study.com https://study.com/academy/lesson/types-of-drums-around-the-world-names-music.html

Suster, M. (2011). *"How I Use Visualization to Drive Creativity."* https://www.businessinsider.com/how-i-use-visualization-to-drive-creativity-2011-2

WedMD   https://www.webmd.com/fitness-exercise/features/runners-high-is-it-for-real#1

Wikipedia https://en.wikipedia.org/wiki/Creative_visualization

YouTube https://www.youtube.com/watch?v=ZZon_4dfwtg

Chapter 7: Psychological Exploration

AcademyofBioenergetics.(2020).http://academyofbioenergetics.com.

American Psychological Association (APA) https://www.apa.org/ptsd-guideline/patients-and-families/cognitive-behavioral

Baum, Will. https://www.psychologytoday.com/us/blog/crisis-knocks/201003/mindfulness-based-stress-reduction-what-it-is-how-it-helps

CoreEnergetics.org https://www.coreenergetics.org/

http://www.ellafitzgerald.com/about/quotes

GoodTherapy® https://www.goodtherapy.org/learn-about-therapy/types/neuro-linguistic-programming https://en.wikipedia.org/wiki/Transpersonal_psychology

Hellinger.com https://www.hellinger.com

HellingerInstitute.com https://www.hellingerinstitute.com

"*Introduction to Gestalt Therapy*" by Gary Yontef and Lynne Jacobs is a chapter in *Current Psychotherapies*. Corsini, R. and Wedding, D. (2014). *Current Psychotherapies*. Cengage Learning Inc.

Peter Levine, PhD. https://www.thetraumatherapistproject.com/podcast/peter-levine-phd/

Massachusetts Society for Bioenergetic Analysis. (2020). https://www.massbioenergetics.org.

Max McDowell. https://jungny.com/carl-jungs-approach-to-therapy-and-dream-analysis/

New York Society for Bioenergetics Analysis. (2020). http://bioenergetics-nyc.org/bioenergetics

Norem, J. (2008). *The Positive Power of Negative Thinking*. Basic Books.

Neukrug, E. Editor. (2015). *The SAGE Encyclopedia of Theory in Counseling and Psychotherapy*. SAGE Publications, Inc.

Pacific Gestalt Institute http://www.gestalttherapy.org/publications-resources/

Psychology Today https://www.psychologytoday.com/us/basics/positive-psychology

Psychology Today https://www.psychologytoday.com/us/basics/cognitive-behavioral-therapy

Psychology Today https://www.psychologytoday.com/us/therapy-types/mindfulness-based-cognitive-therapy

Ramachandran, V. Editor-in-Chief. (2012). *Encyclopedia of Human Behavior* (Second Edition). Academic Press.

Reichian Institute. https://reichianinstitute.org/about/

Reichian.com. http://reichian.com/brochure.htm

Dr. Ida Rolf Institute. https://rolf.org

Rolfing® by Anne https://rolfingbyanne.abmp.com

Salters-Pedneault, K. (2020). *"Dialectical vs. Cognitive Behavioral Therapy for BPD."* https://www.verywellmind.com/cbt-dbt-treating-borderline-personality-disorder-425195

Stone, H. & S. https://www.voicedialogue.org/

Stone, T. https://www.voicedialogueconnection.com/

Stone, H. & S. (1989). *Embracing Ourselves*. Nataraj Publishing, division of New World Library.

Taylor, S. (2015). *"Transpersonal Psychology."* Psychology Today. https://www.psychologytoday.com/us/blog/out-the-darkness/201509/transpersonal-psychology

Tsao, F.C. and Laszlo, C. (2019). *Quantum Leadership*. Stanford University Press.

WebMD.   https://www.webmd.com/mental-health/mental-health-hypnotherapy#1

Wedding, D. & Corsini, R. (2014). *Current Psychotherapies.* Cengage Learning, Inc.

Wikipedia   https://en.wikipedia.org/wiki/Mindfulness-based_stress_reduction

Woldt, A. & Toman, S. editors. (2005). *Gestalt Therapy: History, Theory, and Practice.* SAGE Publications, Inc. "*Gestalt Therapy Theory of Change*" *by Gary Yontef, Ph.D. is Chapter 5.*

Yontef, G. (1993). *Awareness, Dialogue, and Process.* The Gestalt Journal Press, Inc.

Chapter 8: The Improv Environment

Barrett, F. (1998). *"Managing and improvising: lessons from jazz."* MCB UP Ltd.

Bastien, D. and Hostager, T. (1988). *"Jazz as a Process of Organizational Innovation."* Communication Research.

Cunha, M., Cunha, J., Kamoche, K. (1999). *"Organizational Improvisation: What, When, How and Why."* International Journal of Management Reviews.

Fisher, C. and Barrett, F. (2019). *"The Experience of Improvising in Organizations: A Creative Process Perspective."* Academy of Management.

Madson, P. (2005). *Improv Wisdom.* Bell Tower.

Schein, E. (2013). *Humble Inquiry.* Berrett-Koehler Publishers, Inc.

Chapter 9: Improv Principles

Gesell, I. (1997). *Playing Along.* Whole Person Associates.

Halpern, C., Close, D., Johnson, K. (1994). *Truth in Comedy.* Meriwether Publishing.

Kahneman, D. (2011). *Thinking, Fast and Slow*. Farrar, Straus and Giroux.

Koppett K. (2013). *Training to Imagine*. Stylus Publishing, LLC.

Madson, P. (2005). *Improv Wisdom*. Bell Tower.

March, J. and Simon, H. (1993). *Organizations*. Blackwell Business.

Schein, E. (1987). *Process Consultation*. Addison-Wesley Publishing Company.

Chapter 10: Benefits of Improv

Halpern, C., Close, D., Johnson, K. (1994). *Truth in Comedy*. Meriwether Publishing.

Hendrix, H. and Hunt, H. (1988). *Getting the Love You Want*. St. Martin's Press.

Chapter 11: Business Unpredictability and Improvisation

Anderson, R., & Lanier, J. A. (2019). *Mid-course Correction Revisited: The Story and Legacy of a Radical Industrialist and His Quest for Authentic Change*. Chelsea Green Publishing.

Burns, T. & Stalker, G. M. (1961). *The Management of Innovation*, Tavistock, London.

Cameron, K. (2012). *Positive leadership: Strategies for extraordinary performance*. Berrett-Koehler Publishers.

Eisenhardt, K. M., & Sull, D. N. (2001). Strategy as simple rules. *Harvard business review*, *79*(1), 106-119.

Gentile, M. C. (2012). Values-driven leadership development: Where we have been and where we could go. *Organization Management Journal*, *9*(3), 188-196.

Maak, T., & Pless, N. M. (2006). Responsible leadership in a stakeholder society–a relational perspective. *Journal of business ethics, 66*(1), 99-115.

Morgan, G. (1998). *Images of organization: The executive edition.* Berrett-Koehler Publishers, Inc. and Sage Publications, Inc.

Nonaka, I., & Takeuchi, H. (2011). The wise leader. *Harvard business review, 89*(5), 58-67.

O'Reilly III, C. A., & Tushman, M. L. (2011). Organizational ambidexterity in action: How managers explore and exploit. *California management review, 53*(4), 5-22.

Quinn, R. E. (2005). Moments of greatness. *Harvard business review, 83*(7/8), 74-83.

Senge, P. M. (2006). *The fifth discipline: The art and practice of the learning organization.* Currency.

Smith, E. E. (2017). *The power of meaning: Finding fulfillment in a world obsessed with happiness.* Broadway Books.

Conclusion

Carroll, M. (2007). *The Mindful Leader.* Shambhala Publications, Inc.

Ehrenfeld, J. and Hoffman, A. (2013). *Flourishing.* Stanford University Press.

Hines, W. (2016). *How To Be The Greatest Improviser on Earth.* Pretty Great Publishing.

Kofman, F. (2006). *Conscious Business.* Sounds True, Inc.

Laszlo, C. and Brown, J. (2014). *Flourishing Enterprise.* Stanford University Press.

Mackey, J. and McIntosh, S. and Phipps, C. (2020). *Conscious Leadership.* Penguin Random House.

Mott, R. (2012). *Holistic Business Living in 3D.* Holistic Books.

Poonamallee, L. (2021). *Expansive Leadership.* Rutledge.

Sanford, C. (2017). *The Regenerative Business*. Nicholas Brealey Publishing.

Schneider, B. (2008). *Energy Leadership*. John Wiley & Sons Inc.

Tsao, F.C. and Laszlo, C. (2019). *Quantum Leadership*. Stanford University Press.

Waddock, S. (2015). *Intellectual Shamans*. University Printing House.

Appendix B

Benson-Henry Institute https://bensonhenryinstitute.org/about-us-dr-herbert-benson/

Farrell, M. (2009). *Bikram Yoga's New Twists*. Forbes.

Integral Yoga Institute https://iyiny.org/about-us/founder-and-lineage/

Live & Dare https://liveanddare.com/types-of-meditation/

LIVESCIENCE https://www.livescience.com/38192-qigong.html

Nhat Hanh, T. (1975). *The Miracle of Mindfulness*. Beacon Press.

Wikipedia https://en.wikipedia.org/wiki/Centering_prayer

Wikipedia https://en.wikipedia.org/wiki/Taoist_meditation

Yoga Synthesis https://www.yogasynthesis.com/an-integrative-approach

Yoga Journal https://www.yogajournal.com/practice/not-all-yoga-is-created-equal

Yogananda, P. (1946). *Autobiography of a Yogi*. The Philosophical Library, Inc.

Review Requested:

We'd like to know if you enjoyed the book.
Please consider leaving a review on the platform
from which you purchased the book.

CPSIA information can be obtained
at www.ICGtesting.com
Printed in the USA
BVHW031024170422
634535BV00004B/95